W9-BGP-728

Billion-Dollar Kiss

Billion-Dollar Kiss

THE KISS THAT SAVED *DAWSON'S CREEK* AND OTHER ADVENTURES IN TV WRITING

Jeffrey Stepakoff

GOTHAM BOOKS

GOTHAM BOOKS
Published by Penguin Group (USA) Inc.
375 Hudson Street, New York, New York 10014, U.S.A.
Penguin Group (Canada), 90 Eglinton Avenue East, Suite 700, Toronto, Ontario
M4P 2Y3, Canada (a division of Pearson Penguin Canada Inc.); Penguin Books Ltd,
80 Strand, London WC2R 0RL, England; Penguin Ireland, 25 St Stephen's Green,
Dublin 2, Ireland (a division of Penguin Books Ltd); Penguin Group (Australia),
250 Camberwell Road, Camberwell, Victoria 3124, Australia (a division of Pearson
Australia Group Pty Ltd); Penguin Books India Pvt Ltd, 11 Community Centre,
Panchsheel Park, New Delhi – 110 017, India; Penguin Group (NZ), 67 Apollo
Drive, Mairangi Bay, Auckland 1311, New Zealand (a division of Pearson New
Zealand Ltd); Penguin Books (South Africa) (Pty) Ltd, 24 Sturdee Avenue,
Rosebank, Johannesburg 2196, South Africa

Penguin Books Ltd, Registered Offices: 80 Strand, London WC2R 0RL, England

Published by Gotham Books, a division of Penguin Group (USA) Inc.

First printing, June 2007
10 9 8 7 6 5 4 3 2 1

Copyright © 2007 by Jeffrey Stepakoff
All rights reserved

Gotham Books and the skyscraper logo are trademarks of Penguin Group (USA) Inc.

LIBRARY OF CONGRESS CATALOGING-IN-PUBLICATION DATA

Stepakoff, Jeffrey.
    Billion-dollar kiss : the kiss that saved Dawson's Creek and other adventures in
TV writing / by Jeffrey Stepakoff.
        p. cm.
    ISBN 978-1-592-40295-3 (hbk.)
    1. Stepakoff, Jeffrey. 2. Television writers—United States—Biography. I. Title.
    PN1992.4.S785A3 2007
    808.2'25—dc22
    [B]   2006102541

Printed in the United States of America
Set in Sabon • Designed by Elke Sigal

Without limiting the rights under copyright reserved above, no part of this publication may be reproduced, stored in or introduced into a retrieval system, or transmit-
ted, in any form, or by any means (electronic, mechanical, photocopying, recording,
or otherwise), without the prior written permission of both the copyright owner and
the above publisher of this book.

The scanning, uploading, and distribution of this book via the Internet or via any
other means without the permission of the publisher is illegal and punishable by law.
Please purchase only authorized electronic editions, and do not participate in or
encourage electronic piracy of copyrighted materials. Your support of the author's
rights is appreciated.

While the author has made every effort to provide accurate telephone numbers and
Internet addresses at the time of publication, neither the publisher nor the author
assumes any responsibility for errors, or for changes that occur after publication.
Further, the publisher does not have any control over and does not assume any
responsibility for author or third-party Web sites or their content.

FOR ELIZABETH, OF COURSE

CONTENTS

Author's Note .... *ix*

1 Billion-Dollar Kiss *1*

2 Bochco's Blood *8*

3 How'd You Like to Make Ten Grand? *27*

4 Green Envelopes *52*

5 Written By *74*

6 Breakfast at the Polo Lounge *90*

7 The Funny Business *107*

8 Life and Times of a Story Editor *123*

9 The Hollywood Gold Rush *144*

10 The Seasons of L.A. *170*

11 Vertical Integration and Segregation *196*

12 Kissing Katie Holmes *224*

13 Adventures in Hair & Makeup *254*

14 The New Reality *275*

Epilogue *300*

Acknowledgments *307*

Index *309*

L ook, nobody writes a book like this without a little trepidation. I'll explain in greater detail later about exactly why I wrote this. But for now, I want you to understand that this is something I felt I had to do. Believe me, I enjoy watching The Donald fire wannabe execs just as much as most. I see the entertainment value in *American Idol*. But when these shows, and the likes of *The Bachelor* and *Wife Swap* and *Are You Hot?* consistently became the principal offerings from the handful of international conglomerates that control nearly everything we see on TV, I realized it was time to say something.

I came to Hollywood and started writing for television in 1988. That was right about where and when an explosion started, what can really only be described as a modern-day gold rush. The deregulation and consolidation of the media industry, along with record-breaking syndication revenues, fueled a virtual mania for scripted entertainment that quite literally made the TV writer one of the hottest commodities of our generation. The studios fought with one another for the opportunity to throw money at us. It was wild.

But every mania has a dark side. In 2001, the television business hit the skids, reality TV replaced scripted programming as the predominant form of television, and Sony, one of the world's biggest studios and my employer at the time, fired many of its TV executives and folded its network television production division. My position as a coexecutive producer on *Dawson's Creek* and working for Sony during this revolutionary time gave me a front-row seat to the upheaval in Hollywood.

Now, in order to fully appreciate this unreported chapter in the Hollywood story, you have to understand TV writers, our lives, and what it is precisely that we do. So along with a frank, ringside account of the rise and fall—and, I think, rebirth—of TV, I have set out to take you into our world. I have written in great detail about our craft, not what I learned in school, but what I learned on the set and in the story room. I'll take you to those places, as well as pitch meetings and casting sessions and backstage on shows you know and love. I'll share with you what it feels like to see your name on the screen, to see stories taken from your life—your personal *Wonder Years*—performed for tens of millions of people all around the globe. I'll take you behind the scenes and into a world where high-powered careers, entire networks—billions of dollars— ride on the fleeting whim of a twentysomething writer.

This is a tale few know, fewer talk about, and no one writes about. I do not claim to present an entirely objective or exhaustive history of Hollywood. My account is a personal one. This is the story of television, the story of the television writer, and this is also my story.

—Jeffrey Stepakoff
April 2007

"Mr. Sarnoff next gave a little talk, in which he cheerfully, and with enormous self-effacement, admitted that the real problem of television was not its mechanical vagaries but finding programs for it when it finally gets ironed out."

—E. B. WHITE, *The New Yorker*, 1936

CNN Reporter: *"A cliché in Hollywood is 'She was so dumb she slept with the screenwriter'—they're at the bottom of the totem pole. Do you think that's still true?"*

Robert McKee: *"If I were an aspiring actress trying to get ahead today, I'd sleep with a TV writer."*

—CNN, 2004

ONE

Billion-Dollar Kiss

"Content is king."

—Sumner Redstone

In 1999, at the end of a summer that was hot even by L.A. standards, I sat in the story room with the other *Dawson's Creek* writers and tried to keep my panic in check. When you write one-hour TV—feeding the massive apparatus that produces a $2.5 million mini-movie every six days, day in and day out—you are certainly accustomed to round-the-clock doses of heart-thumping, stomach-churning, no-way-in-hell-will-we-make-the-deadline anxiety. But the panic that gripped the writing staff on *Dawson's Creek* this particular day was a special kind—an unforgettable kind.

To say that the show was starting to sink would be polite; at this point at the beginning of Season Three, we were already deep, deep, underwater. When I was hired onto the writing staff a few weeks earlier, *Dawson's Creek* was the hottest show on television. Oh, word was out around town that *"The*

Creek was a crazy place to work" and "*Dawson's* was a nightmare, beware!" But every writer heard those decrees about every show in town. I mean, unless you were lucky enough to work for Phil Rosenthal on *Everybody Loves Raymond*, nicknamed by writers as "Everybody Loves Everybody," you knew you'd inevitably put up with a certain amount of insanity if you took a staff gig. That was a given. But the truth is, I had no idea what I was signing up for. I don't think any of the writers really did.

We had been called into the Room to break story, as was our habit; but on this particular day, we had been called much earlier than was our habit. The mind-numbing sound of smashing metal at the body shop on Olympic and Barrington, which our story room overlooked, hadn't even started yet. Like small animals able to sense an oncoming natural disaster, we knew from the position of the sun, the ubiquitous Venti-sized cups, and the alarming quiet, we were officially entering Crisis Mode. One of our bosses, executive producer Paul Stupin, paced the cagelike conference room, a nervous mother hen encouraging every idea that hatched from the writing staff. "I love it! I love it!" was shouted at even the most inane story ideas. You had to feel for the guy. A former suit who'd made his name developing *90210*, Paul openly displayed that special breed of nurturing enthusiasm endemic to nonwriting producers—he had authority and responsibility, but ultimately his fortunes would be determined by the skills of the other eight people in the room, the writers.

Two of these other eight people were also both our bosses—and they were completely at odds with each other. Part of this was simply a difference in sensibility. Coming off

Party of Five, coexecutive producer Tammy Ader wanted us to do touching stories where Dawson saved the creek from industrial pollution. Coming off *The X Files*, executive producer Alex Gansa wanted us to do dark stories about a promiscuous girl named Eve. The more the new writing showrunners would disagree, the more anxiously enthusiastic the nonwriting showrunner would become. In the center of this mad triangle sat the new writing staff, aimlessly pitching anything and everything, looking for direction, and wondering what the hell Sony, our studio, was thinking when they created this scenario.

Kevin Williamson, the creator, had just "left" the series because, in his own words to *Entertainment Weekly,* he was "starting to crash and burn." The rest of his writing staff (with one exception) had also "left." The ratings were falling. The viewers were disgusted with the campy and arbitrary story lines. As one critic put it, fans felt that the zeitgeist-hip *Dawson's Creek* was fast becoming "a stagnant pond." And the actors— James Van Der Beek, Katie Holmes, Josh Jackson, Michelle Williams—were miserable. Some of them weren't speaking to each other, which made writing scenes where they had to work together quite challenging. Some of them just flat-out refused to do the material we were giving them. I'd never even heard of anything like this before. Oh, and when they soon got wind of our "edgy" new story arch—Pacey and Jen (Josh and Michelle) becoming "bump buddies," having a purely sexual romp in a bathroom stall at school—the actors literally threatened mutiny, what one writer would later call "the Coup." Urgent calls went in to agents. Emergency visits were made to executive offices.

On this particular morning in the *Dawson's Creek* story room, we knew that if we didn't come up with a smart, respectable story line that had some drive, the WB, our network, was going to shut down production. What *was* Sony thinking? How did such a promising new show go south so fast? And was there even a chance that the forces gathered in the Room could save *Dawson's Creek* . . . not to mention ourselves?

⚡

It's impossible to explain what it was like to be a television writer in Hollywood in 1999, or why *Dawson's Creek* was in grave trouble, without explaining the money. Even in its most prudent days, it's hard to imagine a more speculative business than television. The traditional model has always been that the studios deficit-finance their shows, eating substantial losses on the pilots that never air and the series that get canceled, because the occasional hit more than pays for all those failures when it's sold into syndication. But in the nineties, hit TV shows became so wildly valuable—more than a billion dollars in revenue for shows like *ER* and *Friends*, by some accounts more than *$3 billion* for *Seinfeld*—that the studios essentially disregarded costs and started doing just about anything to make sure their shows got and stayed on the air.

Combined with all the new networks and channels in need of programming, this created a wild seller's market for TV writers, making us the focus of a feeding frenzy that rivaled even the irrational exuberance for dot-com stocks simultaneously underway in the equity markets. Never before in the history of Hollywood—arguably, in the history of American industry—had so many twenty- and thirtysomethings made so much money so fast. Assessing a writer's level of skill is always a matter of subjectivity on some level. But due to the unique market forces at play during this time, the time-honored fundamentals used to determine our value were thrown out the window. The entire negotiation process started to ignore what a writer had done and focus on what a writer might do. Cool suddenly had tremendous cachet. Hip became currency. Kids right out of school were given a quarter million dollars a year to write TV. And any writer with a track record of any kind, like Alex Gansa, was suddenly an extremely valuable commodity, particularly in the hands of the Creative Artists Agency (CAA), who got Alex a mid-seven-figure deal to work on *Dawson's*—a show that he openly loathed.

The anxiety was escalating in the *Dawson's Creek* story room. Tammy Ader stood at one of the five large dry-erase boards mounted on the walls and wrote all sorts of words in a wide variety of cheerful colors. "Pretty in Pink Story!" "Risky Business Part 2!" "Pacey Gets Motorcycle, à la Rebel w/o a Cause." Whenever the story process hits a speed bump, TV writers will often pitch classic paradigms—also known as movies we might be able to rip off. Paul's cheerleading efforts for the possible story lines just made Alex even more disheartened. It's not that he was above stealing from movies. TV writers on deadline will shamelessly pilfer just about anything for inspiration. Current events, bible stories, the sex lives of interns are all fair game for next week's show. Alex hated the *tone* of Tammy's stories. He championed mysteries, crime stories, and characters that weren't quite like what you'd find on the network that aired *Felicity* and *7th Heaven*. "I sold out," was the explanation Alex oft offered the writing staff as to why he took the *Dawson's* job. "Sony backed the Brink's truck up to my front door and started dumping money until I just couldn't say no anymore."

As the day progressed and the story process did not, moving from constructive dialectic into something less collegial, twenty-seven-year-old Greg Berlanti, a former movie producer's assistant who had just started writing TV the year before, said something that changed all our lives: "Pacey kisses Joey."

What? I remember thinking. "You can't do that. Joey is Dawson's girl. Remember, they are *soul mates,* and that is the closest thing we have to a franchise around here."

But Greg was so impassioned, as was his usual state, that he jumped up, grabbed a cheerful color marker from Tammy, and drew a triangle on one of the boards, writing "Pacey" at one point, "Joey" at another, "Dawson" at another. "No, I'm serious," he said. "Pacey kisses Joey. Think about it!"

And that's when it hit me. Of course! *A love triangle.* Heresy is exactly what the show needed. Not only did we have a story, we had a *story engine,* a dramatic problem that would create many other stories. There had been a love triangle on the show before, between Dawson, Jen, and Joey. There had once even been a kiss between Joey and Pacey. But these stories never went anywhere. As one person closely affiliated with the series put it, "Those ideas were floating around in the ether; Greg pulled them out and focused on them." For the first time, we had a series. The Katie Holmes–Josh Jackson

Kiss, the love triangle it created, and the stories that it bore drove the show to 128 episodes, six seasons, and international acclaim.

The Kiss also seemed to justify this new formula for valuing writers on their future potential. For its speculative investment of a few hundred grand in Greg, Sony now had the potential to realize a billion-dollar return. The bigger issue, though, was how many other Gregs were not providing a comparable return? What the studios were about to discover was that even with the occasional billion-dollar kiss, by the time you figured in the costs of all the other Gregs on all the other struggling shows that did not pay off, and added all that to all the enormous unproductive deals like Alex's, and added all that to the costs of producing all these failed series and failed pilots, the business model had become flawed. In fact, it was so flawed that our studio, Sony, would soon settle or just pay off much of their $75 million in TV writer deals, fire seventy of their prime-time TV executives and employees, and drop out of the broadcast television business.

At the beginning of the new millennium, studios and production companies all across Hollywood, in their hunger for hit shows, flirted with disaster. They would soon learn that the formula for creating a hit—some combination of talent, passion, and luck—was as elusive and ephemeral as true love's kiss. It was something that money alone, even in great quantities, could not buy. On the day *Dawson's Creek* was saved, the entire television industry was teetering on the verge of insolvency, and we didn't yet know it. But we were about to find out. Our careers, our lives, and the nature of entertainment would never be the same.

TWO

Bochco's Blood

"Television! Teacher, mother, secret lover."
—HOMER SIMPSON

I was living in Pittsburgh in January 1988, finishing my graduate work in playwriting at Carnegie Mellon University, when I met my first real television writer, John Wells. Until that point, my carefully constructed life plan had been the same as all good playwriting students: get my degree, move to New York, find a roach-infested apartment, and start writing black-box theater. But after meeting Wells, I began to realize that writing and starvation did not necessarily have to go hand in hand. This meeting began a sequence of events that led to my first television writing assignment.

Wells graduated from Carnegie in 1979. He worked in motion picture marketing and production, produced some plays, and had just recently started to focus on television. After writing a few scripts for *Shell Game* in 1987, Wells was working as an executive story editor on a half-hour film show called

Just in Time. He came back to CMU to lecture the graduate students in the drama department about working in the entertainment industry.

In a telling sign of the times, however, Wells's arrival was not met with a stampede of résumé-shoving, wide-eyed young students. Sure, some curiosities were piqued, mainly those of the diligent, the unwavering note-takers determined to absorb every ounce of the education for which we were soon assuming decades of debt. But as far as I can remember, no one was running around saying "I have to meet this guy. I have to hear how I can get started in Hollywood." This was partially a function of the murkiness surrounding television writing, and partially due to the fact that in 1988, especially for drama students, it was uncool even to watch TV, let alone consider working for it. You see, we were artists! We were studying Shepard and Mamet and Brecht. Those of us who watched the occasional *Cosby* episode kept it to ourselves.

Nonetheless, we were all required to attend Wells's lecture. With a sort of big-brother charisma that at once exudes authority and camaraderie, John described a world in which sets were built, just like in the theater, but not taken down after a handful of performances. He discussed how a new kind of quality television—like a powerful drama that would air on ABC in a few weeks called *China Beach*—was becoming more and more popular. And he hinted at a coming conflict between Hollywood writers and the studios that were growing increasingly frustrated with the writers' demands for a bigger piece of what they created. When someone asked Wells about the kind of money writers earned, he didn't miss a beat: "Look, there are three hundred people making a product for three hundred

9

million. Writers are paid accordingly." That this sounded very much like a negotiating position was lost on most of us present at the time.

By the end of the lecture, even the most committed theater students were intrigued, both with Wells and the place he described—a place where he said writers were not only respected, but needed. After that lecture, I couldn't get this place out of my mind.

Over the next few weeks, I stayed in touch with Wells, elevating myself, I believe, from annoying student to obsessive wannabe. During this time I also began searching for others who might actually be able to help me find a way to pay the rent by writing. I went to the dean's office and found a newsletter put out by the drama department's West Coast alumni. I riffled through the recent accomplishments of the school's luminaries, recognizing pretty quickly that most of them, such as Holly Hunter, Ted Danson, or Jack Klugman, would have very little use for me. Then I came across the name of a former playwriting student who, in my wildest dreams, I hoped might at least talk to me. My professor wrote a recommendation that I mailed along with my earnest letter of introduction, and a few days later Steven Bochco's assistant called, saying he'd be happy to meet me.

On Monday, February 22, 1988, I arrived in Los Angeles. No one ever forgets his or her first time flying into the L.A. basin. The implausible sight of ten thousand square miles of concrete—what was not so long ago an entire desert—paved and plumbed, lit up like some great endless movie premiere, with little regard for fault lines, geographic constraints, or limitations of any kind, imparts a devil-may-care sense of possibility. The effect is heightened by the first action taken by most who land at LAX: turning back watches. This gives the distinct impression that coming to Los Angeles has somehow cheated time. Indeed, one arrives in L.A. feeling younger.

On Wednesday, February 24, I drove up to the 20th Century Fox main gate on Pico in my subcompact rental, my mullet perfectly blown dry, as was the fashion (business in the front, creative in the back). I found my allotted parking place and stepped out of the car. Carrying the slim leather briefcase that my mom gave me when I started a job in advertising three years earlier, and wearing the blue suit I had worn to a Macy's buyer training program interview three and a half years earlier, I looked suspiciously like Michael J. Fox in *The Secret of My Success*. (Okay, I looked like someone *trying* to look like that.) Walking across the lot, gaping at the palms and fake sets, the soundstages and celebrities, my rep tie flapping in the Santa Ana breeze might as well have been a banner that read, FRESH OFF THE BOAT. Nevertheless, everyone I passed smiled at me. Not just because they knew I would soon find out that no one wears suits like that on the lot except agents—and I was certainly no agent—but because L.A. loves, or more precisely, respects, the neophyte. For that overdressed kid with the silly haircut can literally be your boss by the next fall television season, and an industry titan the next. But I'm getting ahead of myself . . .

Steven's office was in a legendary bungalow deep in the backlot dubbed "the Old Writers Building," which I soon learned was a reference not to the forty-four-year-old Bochco, but to the indentured contract writers who toiled for the studio during the thirties and forties. I sat in Steven's outer office, my legs crossed, perspiring like a bar mitzvah boy on the big day. Steven's assistant, Marilyn, offered me some water, or rather, a choice of many different kinds of water. (Who knew there were so many different kinds of water!?) This made me perspire even more. As I opened a sparkling Crystal Geyser, I was instructed that, "He's ready for you." I stood, adjusted my tie, wiped the sweat from my brow, and entered his office.

And there in front of me, talking on the telephone, was the writer whose new series, *L.A. Law,* had just swept the Emmys, arguably the most important person in the entire television business—wearing Keds, jeans, and a T-shirt that read ENTERTAINMENT PROFESSIONAL.

Bochco put the phone down, turned to me, and said something that I would come back to again and again: "Hey, kid, what do you think a pint of my blood is worth?"

Steven explained to me that he had just accepted a new series development deal with ABC, but before it could be finalized the network wanted to take out an insurance policy on his life. Evidently, after the nurse took Steven's blood, it was somehow lost. And now ABC wanted more. He told me that he felt like he had given enough blood to networks over the years, and that this time he was gonna make 'em pay. He was joking, of course. Well, mostly.

This was not the first time I'd heard about Steven's deal. It had gotten a tremendous amount of media coverage. The landmark deal called for Bochco to develop ten shows over eight years. The trades and other press reported the widely rumored terms of the deal: It would pay him $10 million and he would retain *ownership* of the shows, so that whatever profit they earned after their initial broadcast would be his. The town was abuzz. The *Los Angeles Times* ran a story entitled STEVEN BOCHCO, THE $10-MILLION MAN. Eyebrows were raised. This was an unprecedented deal. But, in fact, it was more unprecedented than most knew.

The entire deal had a veil of secrecy around it. The American Broadcasting Company was so concerned that the precise terms of the Bochco deal would get out that it even refused to send the contract to the State Mutual Life Assurance Company, which needed to see it in order to write a disability policy for Steven. ABC and the insurance company went back and forth on this for weeks. Finally, when State Mutual flatly refused to write a policy on a contract that it wasn't allowed to see, insurance executive Ralph Diller flew out from Boston, drove onto the 20th Century lot, was escorted by a guard to a secure room, searched, and left alone with the contract for three hours. Afterward, his handwritten notes were examined and he was allowed off the lot.

State Mutual ended up writing a $20 million policy for five years to insure ABC's investment. Clearly, this was no $10 million over eight years deal. (Years later, *Time* would put it closer to $50 million.) Throughout his years of providing special risk and unusual coverage policies for entertainment professionals and athletes, Ralph Diller had never encountered this kind of "extraordinary secrecy" before. What was ABC so concerned about? What was in that contract that was so sensitive? "Trade secrets," was the explanation given to the insurance company. Perhaps ABC was concerned about the precedent they were setting. Perhaps they were concerned that other writers might start demanding more money and, even worse, greater profit participation. Just a couple of years earlier, the Writers Guild of America had gone on strike for more participation in the revenue streams of what they were creating. That strike ended terribly for them, but another one was shaping up, and this one looked like it could be epic. Perhaps the contract was so sensitive because the times were so sensitive. It wouldn't be long before a $10 million deal would barely be headlines, but in 1988 it was a shitload of money to give a TV writer. Perhaps ABC was trying to keep the floodgates closed.

Steven and I had a great meeting. We talked about Carnegie and writing and shows we liked. He agreed with me that *thirtysomething*, his Emmy competition, was good but said he couldn't do something like that because "the brushstrokes were too small." By the end he offered me a PA (production assistant) position when I graduated. As relieved as I was to have a respectable offer of employment, I couldn't stop thinking about his question and what it really meant to be a TV writer. *What is the value of a TV writer's blood?* Here was this affable man, dressed like a playwright, who wrote what he wanted, controlled what he wrote—hell, who *owned* what he created—a man so vital, so essential to the creative process that his very being had to be insured. What little I knew about Hollywood suggested that the contract writers who once occupied Steven's office in the Old Writer's Building, no matter how talented, were not this irreplaceable. Pretty much everything I (and everyone else) knew about TV writers was based on *The Dick Van Dyke Show*, and I sure couldn't imagine Rob Petrie owning his own series, not to mention running his own production company. Even a clueless fresh-off-the-boat kid could see that things were changing for the Hollywood writer.

After that meeting, I knew with certainty what I wanted to do with my life. Perhaps it was this ultimate control over the creative process that I found so appealing. Or perhaps it was the fact that a writer of television could dare merely to entertain thoughts about valuating his heart. What is the worth of a man's blood when that man is directly responsible for some of popular culture's greatest works, as well as more than a billion dollars in revenue? (And is a pound of his flesh any less valuable when this man is responsible for the likes of *Cop Rock*?) How do you place a price on what runs through the veins of a TV writer?

Bochco's question could not have been more prescient; for this would soon become the central issue in Hollywood.

Later that afternoon, I drove over the hill and met with Wells on the Warners lot. It was raining outside that day, and I was drenched as I entered his small office. It may have been my aggressively eager manner, or my dripping blue suit and rep tie, or the fact that I was simply wearing a suit and tie, but Wells spent most of the meeting kind of laughing at me. I fired off question after question until John finally told me to relax and explained that the best way to break into television writing was to find a show that I liked and write a sample episode, a "spec" script. When I was finished with it, he said, I could send it to him.

I don't know if Wells was trying to get me off his back or if he really thought I'd do it, but when I got back to Pittsburgh I put most of my theater work on the back burner, tolerated the teasing from my classmates, and started watching television.

Okay, I confess. This was not the first time I had watched television. This was not the first time I had watched a lot of television. The truth is, I knew the names of all the Sweathogs. I continued to watch *Happy Days* even after Fonzie jumped the shark. I could hum the complete theme songs to *The Streets of San Francisco*, *The Rockford Files,* and *S.W.A.T.* I proudly carried my *Starsky & Hutch* lunchbox to school. "Kiss my grits," "Dynomite," "Da Plane, Da Plane," "Book 'em, Danno," and "Good night, John Boy" were all part of the lexicon of my youth. And while Daisy Duke, Jaime Sommers, and Julie the Cruise Director certainly inspired much of the "must-see TV" of their day, I thought Valerie Bertinelli, with her winged and feathered locks, was the most definite evidence of a divine force in the universe I had ever seen. The truth is, I was raised on television. From *The Courtship of Eddie's Father* to *Maude,* from *Mary Tyler Moore* to *M*A*S*H*, TV entertained me and taught me. For better or worse, television was my first, and I'm sure my most influential, window on the world.

Now of course, my intimate relationship with television was not an oddity. Kids all over my neighborhood watched with a similar zeal. Although in the late seventies about 75 million American households had television, the most loyal and fastest-growing audience was young people. When I grew up, kids all across this country embraced their small screens with an ardency that made social critics wary, laid the seeds for sweeping conservative advocacy, and generally scared the bejesus out of parents. The only three possible contenders for our attention—sports, comics, and the opposite sex—could never ultimately usurp the supreme place that television had in our lives. TV in the seventies was as dependable and accessible as a best friend. One late-show comedian ruminating on his own obsession with television remembered the day his frustrated father asked him which he liked better, TV or his dad. The kid's response: "Which channel?"

However, even though we were committed to *watching* television with an unrivaled passion, it never occurred to the vast majority of us that *making* television was a viable career option. I certainly didn't know any TV writers. I didn't even know anyone who knew anyone who was writing in Hollywood. When I grew up, kids didn't tell their parents, "I want to be the next Norman Lear." An expressed interest in being an astronaut was met with much less skepticism than a desire to write for show business. In fact, kids would dream of being Steve Austin, a former astronaut who became the Six Million Dollar Man, before they'd consider being a Hollywood writer. We'd sooner dream of being Oscar Goldman than William Goldman.

In 1979, I wrote my first play for extra credit in tenth-grade drama class, a suspicious act, I suppose, not so much for the play's odd amalgamation of Tom Robbins–esque dialogue and Cat Stevens music, but rather because this was the one class in which I actually maintained a regular A. That was the same year my anxious parents took me to a private guidance counselor who administered the Motivational Appraisal of Personal Potential (MAPP) Assessment. This test, given to a lot of wayward youth in the seventies, determined what my parents and teachers had suspected: I was best suited for a "creative" profession. The test then matched me with several creative careers for which I would be best suited, such as iron fabricator, brick mason, mechanical illustrator, and advertising copywriter.

I imagine the main reasons the tests and the counselors who administered them overlooked TV writer as an option for kids like me was mainly because it was such an obscure profession. Most of the young people who really knew anything about it in the seventies already had family members in show business or grew up around it in Los Angeles. I'm sure Bochco's father, who was a concert violinist, wasn't too surprised to discover his son's interest in an artistic career. Consider David Kohan and Max Mutchnick, future creators of *Will & Grace*, who learned about television as they literally grew up on Hollywood soundstages. David's father, Buz, was a well-known TV writer who wrote for shows like *Happy Days*, *The Odd Couple,* and *The Carol Burnett Show*. Max's mom was a marketing exec on the Paramount lot. *Lost* creator J. J. Abrams's parents produced TV movies. *Buffy* creator Joss Whedon's dad was actually a TV writer. He wrote for many series while Joss was growing up, including *Benson*, *Alice,* and *The Golden Girls*. Even Joss's grandfather wrote TV, including *The Dick Van Dyke Show*, *The Donna Reed Show,* and *Leave It to Beaver*. TV writers lived and worked in a close-knit esoteric community, in many ways figurative and literal, as a tight family.

The primary way the few outsiders found out about the field and gained access to it was through a handful of select collegiate organizations that maintained strong ties to alumni in Hollywood. The Harvard Lampoon, an undergraduate humor organization that produced a satirical magazine, was the most notable. After brave Harvard students like Andy Borowitz, a former president of The Lampoon, laid a beachhead in Hollywood in the early eighties, before creating *The*

Fresh Prince of Bel-Air, many other "Lampoonys" followed, like Paul Simms, who would create *NewsRadio*, and Bill Oakley and Josh Weinstein, who would executive produce *The Simpsons*.

Meanwhile, the rest of us kind of stumbled toward Hollywood. Our arms out, reaching through the fog, we followed an inner compass that, despite being overlooked by aptitude tests and our caregivers' attempts to recalibrate it, always, instinctively, pointed to magnetic west.

Before stumbling into Wells, Bochco, and others who I would learn were key members of the growing "West Coast Drama Clan," Carnegie Mellon's answer to the Harvard Lampoon, I focused my attention on playwriting. After gaining admission to the University of North Carolina at Chapel Hill with help from its drama department, I spent much of my college years writing plays. You see, in the absence of film and TV writing classes, playwriting filled a void. Drama departments in the eighties were fertile little islands for writers. Plays were regularly produced. Clubs quietly flourished. Drama departments offered a training ground where students could take chances, make mistakes, and safely find their voices as writers.

UNC had a radio, television, and motion-picture department, but with its roots in radio and public broadcasting, the department seemed, well, dusty. And television studies as a proper course of study just didn't exist in any meaningful way at this time, mainly because the medium was not deemed worthy of study. Learning about television as a vehicle to deliver news and information was one thing. But studying TV shows in a critical and scholarly context was viewed as only slightly less ridiculous than studying the crafts that enabled one to create them. Aside from the fact that no one in mainstream academia had the pedagogical or professional skill set to teach such courses, it would have been career suicide for a tenure-track professor to try to convince a dean that Sitcom Writing 101 had merit. This was the scenario at colleges all across the country. With the exception of a handful of specialty schools in L.A. and New York—Cal Arts, AFI, the film schools at NYU, Columbia, USC, and UCLA—the few film and television departments that existed at universities were out of their element when it came to nurturing and training young writers.

Writing programs in general were not high on the agenda of academic administrators in the eighties. For that matter, virtually all the liberal arts were avoided like a plague by student bodies across this country. Another reason so few people were thinking about a career writing in Hollywood is because, in the eighties, it appeared that there was only one career worth having—and it was not in Hollywood, it was on Wall Street. In fact, 20 percent of all enrolled college students in 1980 were business or management majors, nearly double the amount just ten years earlier. In 1962, English was the most popular major at the University of Michigan. In 1982, economics was number one.

There was a fever going around campuses, and it was hard not to catch it. Ronald Reagan—the former head of the Screen Actors Guild who turned in suspected communists in Hollywood—had just been elected president. The Young Republicans were easily the most popular group on campus. Whatever angry protest was coming from the Sandinista card table in front of the student union was inevitably drowned out by legions of preppy, *National Review*–wielding econ majors. There was no Jack Kerouac or Ken Kesey. The voices of my generation were Jay McInerney and Bret Easton Ellis, with their tales of fantastic wealth and excess. From Joel Goodsen in *Risky Business* to Alex Keaton in *Family Ties* to Bud Fox in *Wall Street*, the message was crystal clear: "Greed is good."

As my own senior year approached, it didn't take long for me to realize that dramatic writing was not a critical part of the skill set most desired by campus recruiters. Not that I wanted to work on Wall Street. I didn't. What I really wanted to do was simply feed myself by writing. If that eccentric endeavor didn't work out, I figured a living doing *something* creative would suit me just fine. As much as I appreciated the drama department for helping me attain access to an excellent education, it was clear that a major from the department was not going to go very far to help pay for that education. Journalism, with a concentration in advertising, seemed a responsible and palatable compromise. Advertising was the de rigueur occupation of the day for creative types. It did not conflict with the findings of the high school MAPP test. My parents were relieved. And I figured I'd be like Tad Allagash, the partying ad man in *Bright Lights, Big City*.

But six months into my purportedly enviable job at Ogilvy & Mather advertising, I took off my Vuarnets and realized— this is work. Though the yuppie trappings were shameless fun, I could not get past the sense that this was not just a transitory adventure. This was My Life, and for the first time since birth I could now see the rest of it. There were suits and ties and eating cereal out of a coffee mug on the way to an office with sealed windows and work that was fine and respectable but that, *I'm sorry*, I did not want to be doing. Something was absent from this life. I realized I missed my beret-wearing, clove cigarette–smoking drama colleagues. I longed to be in a class that started with the phrase, "Let's close the door and pull our seats into a circle." But mainly, I missed the writing. I missed it so much that I was willing to trade knowing with a high degree of certainty what tomorrow was going to be like for a shot at more time to write. So somewhere between standing on the racetrack at Talladega passing out Hardee's hats and composing copy about the safety of an insecticide whose active ingredient was made in Bhopal, I decided to apply to grad schools. I was accepted at AFI, Columbia, and Carnegie. I chose the last because of the focus on playwriting that seemed, at the time, familiar. In the summer of 1986, bucking the almost universally accepted wisdom of the time, and with my mother standing on the front lawn crying, I left my $17,000-a-year hard-won job in the Real World and drove off to be a writer.

A good argument can be made that modern television was invented while I was in college—at least that's how I felt as I followed Wells's advice and looked for a show to write in the spring of 1988.

The programming from the 1987–88 television season that came over the nineteen-inch glass tube in my little apartment in Pittsburgh was better than anything being written for the American theater. This is not hyperbole. *The Slap Maxwell Story*, *thirtysomething*, *The Days and Nights of Molly Dodd*, *The Wonder Years*, *Frank's Place*, *Hooperman*, *A Year in the Life*, *Crime Story*, *China Beach*, the shows that aired the season I finished graduate school, led a widespread renaissance that redefined mass entertainment. The term "boob tube" suddenly wasn't so accurate. These new, so-called quality shows were thought-provoking, revolutionary, and culturally and socially resonant; they shared many of the qualities one might apply to a critical and common definition of (dare I use the *A* word?) art. And although these shows focused on different subjects and had broadly disparate points of view, they all had something fundamental in common: They were all created and led by writers, writers who had been given uncommon amounts of creative leeway.

Perhaps an even better argument can be made that modern television actually reached a popular critical mass around 1988 but, in fact, was invented on January 15, 1981, the night *Hill Street Blues* premiered. This is a show that Bochco and Michael Kozoll would only agree to develop and run *if* they were given complete creative freedom, something fairly rare for a TV writer at that time. Fred Silverman, NBC's president, acquiesced. With its hard-hitting cinema verité realism, fast pacing, and interwoven story lines, *Hill Street* literally broke all the rules and established a new model for the television show, a model that influences nearly all quality episodic dramas today.

Until this time, TV writers made their two-dimensional characters move around like chess pieces. Characters were forced to service a story with its predicable car chases and fourth-act resolutions. The good guys always won. Wrongs were always righted. But in *Hill Street*, *character* motivated story, as opposed to the other way around. Bochco and his writing staff created stories by asking "What would Renko do? What would Furillo do? How would these characters *really* behave in this kind of situation?" The results created honest storytelling that was rough around the edges and often unresolved. Just like in real life, *anything* could happen.

While *Hill Street* (which was based on life in Pittsburgh's Hill District, a place I can assure you most Carnegie Mellon students spent as little time in as possible) was a critical darling, it was never really a popular success. Most people I knew could easily hum the hit theme song but rarely watched the actual series. Nevertheless, the show laid the groundwork for a new kind of television. Syracuse professor Robert J. Thompson refers to this new form of TV as "writer-based" drama. Although I didn't know it at the time, the year I began to focus on a career in television was right at the dawn of what Thompson calls "the second golden age of television." *Cagney & Lacey, St. Elsewhere, L.A. Law, Moonlighting*—some of TV's greatest shows were created during this era, laying the groundwork for many more to come. And it wasn't just dramas. In the spring of 1987 a fourth television network, the Fox Broadcasting Company, launched several irreverent comedies, including *Married . . . With Children* and *The Simpsons*, that not only broke the molds but were wildly popular, too—the former ran for eleven seasons and the latter is still in production. Before long, it wouldn't be so "uncool" to watch—or aspire to write—television.

This new kind of television not only changed the product, it changed the way the product was made. Shows began to be developed not just around the performing talent, but around the writer. Network executives stopped thinking strictly about what kind of show they needed in a particular slot, and focused more on writers with whom they wanted to be in business. Studio executives began to concern themselves first and foremost with the *showrunner*—the writing executive producer—and later with what show would actually be run. About the time I wrote my first TV spec script, "*What is the price of a writer's blood?*" was being pondered with increasing urgency in executive suites all across Hollywood. The question became a sort of theme for the approaching train wreck between the writers and the studios.

I chose *Molly Dodd* as the show I wanted to spec. A darker half-hour version of *Ally McBeal*, I loved the writing on the show and thought its tone was similar to the kind of work I was doing in my playwriting classes. And I saw playwright Eric Overmyer's name in the credits. I wrote a script in about a week and mailed it to Wells. He mailed it back with encouraging notes a few days later. I addressed the notes, sent it back to Wells and soon received word that he wanted to send it around to some agents. A few days later I learned that two of the agencies wanted to meet with me, one of which was the William Morris Agency. I was ecstatic. After quickly riffling through my cassettes to find the appropriate music—I think I settled on a Grateful Dead bootleg—I jumped up and down in my bedroom for quite some time. On May 15, 1988, I graduated. On May 16, I left for Los Angeles.

Several of my friends pointed out that what had happened to me was quite extraordinary. They were right. Even in 1988, before TV writing was big, it was pretty amazing to get such a break in such a short time. Getting a break in television is about all the expected things. You demonstrate you can do the work by writing good spec scripts. You work your ass off networking and making relationships with people who can help you. Sometimes writers get started faster than others because of talent. Sometimes because of force of personality, an obsessive determination to break in and do the job. In my case, as in most, I suppose all these things had some part. But the other (and some would say most important) reason all writers get started is because of fortuitousness. I had the good fortune of meeting someone who was selfless, confident, and kind enough to go to bat for me. Not all writers are so lucky as to meet someone like Wells, and certainly not as quickly as I did. Indeed, what I would soon learn is that simple luck had something to do with not only why some writers got started quickly and why some didn't; it had to do with *a lot* in television.

Although things were going swimmingly for me, this was about to change. For as I headed west, I had completely overlooked the well-publicized fact that Hollywood was virtually shut down. One of this country's longest, most expensive and divisive labor stoppages was under way, the Writers Guild of America's strike of 1988. Yes, I had caught a break—in a business that was in explosive and unprecedented upheaval, whose entire future was in jeopardy.

THREE

How'd You Like to Make Ten Grand?

"When television is good, nothing is better.
But when television is bad, nothing is worse."
—Newton N. Minow, Former Chairman of the FCC

t's quite a thing to put absolutely everything you own in the world into a small car. If that doesn't make you take stock of your life, joining those possessions and driving across the country by yourself will. The transcontinental drive to Hollywood has acquired a status of somewhat mythical proportion. Most people who work in the entertainment industry have made this literal rite of passage.

Here's the reality: America is big. Very big. Although it seems like a romantic idea for the first five hundred miles or so, let me assure you, by the time you're parked at a rest stop at three A.M., making dinner out of Combos, beef jerky, and the Stuckey's pecan logs you bought back in Terre Haute—the last town you passed with motel rooms—the romance wanes. There's a stretch of I-70 in Kansas that runs through so many miles of corn you'll promise yourself you'll never touch another Frito for the rest of your life. There's a stretch of I-10 in West Texas, between San Antonio and El Paso, that is so long and straight and utterly mind-numbing that AM radio preachers start to make good sense.

An amazing thing happens to freeways as soon as you enter L.A. County. Suddenly, they are referred to with the definite article "the." You get stuck in traffic not on Interstate 10, but on "the 10." Construction frequently takes place on "the 101." A favorite locale for a slow-speed chase is "the 5." Although I can find no sociological study on the topic, I believe that this way of referencing freeways can be attributed to the significance they play in the lives of Angelenos. Europeans don't just have a run-of-the-mill mountain range, but "the Alps." The religious don't just have a good book, but "the Good Book." When so much of your life is spent on a particular road, when the lives of so many are so broadly affected by the vicissitudes of that road, it becomes "the 405." One of the very first things you learn upon arrival is that to live in L.A. is to drive in L.A.

The automobile is the first of several building blocks an aspiring writer needs to survive in Los Angeles. Just like in Maslow's Hierarchy of Needs, certain primitive requirements must be met before new arrivals can focus on higher pursuits. After adequate transportation has been attained, one must next find shelter, food, and a good answering machine.

Shelter, albeit temporary shelter, had already been arranged for me when I arrived in L.A. My father gave me a coupon he had received as a business perk for a three-day stay at a new hotel that had just opened in Beverly Hills, the Four Seasons. Suffice to say, the doormen did not rush with their usual flair to open the dirt-covered doors of my filled-to-the-roof Honda hatchback. Permanent shelter soon took the form of a room I found for rent on a bulletin board at UCLA. The room (and I use the word loosely) was actually a portion of a garage that had been hastily drywalled, and that had a bathtub set up under a rigged spigot and a broken-down mattress tossed on the concrete floor. Despite the questionable living conditions, the "room" was located in Brentwood Hills, one of the most beautiful and expensive parts of the city. I paid $100 a week to the elderly widow who owned the house, *and* I had to perform chores. I mowed her lawn, trimmed her hedges, lugged in five-gallon water-cooler bottles. Anything that needed to be done, she'd call the boy in the garage. Okay, it wasn't the Four Seasons, but truth be told, I couldn't have been happier. There was no daily housekeeping service, no palm-shaded swimming pool, but I was in L.A., and I was surviving.

Because of the strike, Bochco didn't have any work to offer me. But my father had a colleague in the furniture business who was married to someone that worked in movie marketing. The marketing exec sent my résumé to human resources at Universal, and the HR department there sent me to meet the studio's head of motion-picture research, who needed some cheap and willing help. Because feature films have such a long lead time and, once written, no longer have any use for writers during the production process, there were many movies still in the pipeline. I was offered an internship, for which I was paid $265 a week before taxes. If you've ever been to a mall in L.A. you've surely been accosted by out-of-work actors offering you free tickets to a screening of a new movie. If you go to the movie, you'll be asked afterward to fill out a questionnaire. Well, I was the schmuck who stayed up all night and tabulated the responses on the hundreds and hundreds of questionnaires.

It's been said that television is a writer's medium and film is a director's. This is mostly true. One of the first things I learned in Hollywood is that film, in reality, is a researcher's medium. And the result of all of the research that goes into creating the Hollywood film produces a unique American art form: story by vote.

But it was great. I got to drive onto a major studio lot every day. I squatted in an unoccupied office, and it wasn't long before maintenance put my name on the door. I had access to a copy machine, a computer, and all the film and TV scripts I could find the time to read. I ate lunch in the commissary next to Steven Spielberg. I rode the elevator with Lew Wasserman. I urinated next to Telly Savalas. I quickly learned that if I looked like I knew what I was doing, people figured I did. When I had a free minute, I would slip out of the 1320 Building overlooking Lankershim and walk the backlot. A few weeks prior I was walking around a college campus; now here I was, strolling around the *Back to the Future* town square. And at night, if I didn't have a screening to attend, I would hole up in my stolen office and write.

In television, network executives can control when or if to air a show. Studio executives can make comments and attempt to influence certain creative choices, like casting or long-term story arcs. Yes, executives control the green light, but at the end of the day, once a scripted television series is up and running, it is primarily controlled by writers. Woe betide those who try to alter this natural condition; story by vote and story by force have ill effect on the medium. For better or worse, a TV show sails or sinks with the writer in charge of the ship. The smartest and most respected TV executives I have met understand this.

What television studio executives began to realize in the late eighties—a realization that set them apart from their motion-picture counterparts—is that the most influential decision a studio can make on a TV show is simply deciding which writer to place in charge. It is probably this distinction more than any other that is responsible for the rise of television as a quality artistic medium and the simultaneous descent of the motion picture into, first and foremost, a corporate product.

This is why after a studio releases a film it is frequently followed by a "director's cut." In television, pretty much everything you see is the vision of the original storyteller.

⌒✐⌒

Purely by coincidence, my meetings with the two agents who responded to Wells were set up on the same day, May 26, 1988. I distinctly remember telling someone that, strike or no strike, it would be the most important day of my life. (I also remember that this self-seriousness would be quickly remedied when I started working on the staff of a sitcom.)

William Morris. The William Morris Talent and Literary Agency—just saying the name made me feel like I was in show biz. As far I was concerned, in the late eighties, there were three agencies that controlled the known universe: Creative Artists Agency (CAA), International Creative Management (ICM), and the William Morris Agency (WMA). And the last one seemed to me to be the best of the triad. It was the largest, oldest, and most diversified of the major agencies—even people who didn't know what a TV writer did knew about William Morris. I mean, my grandmother knew about William Morris. The other meeting I had was with a woman I'd never heard of named Beth Uffner. Evidently, she worked alone and had a little roster of clients. I figured I'd meet with her in case things didn't work out with Morris—you know, as a backup.

My first meeting was with this Beth Uffner, which was fine with me. It would give me a chance to warm up before my meeting with Morris later in the afternoon. As I pulled out of the Universal lot in my hatchback, I passed the ever-present sign at the front gate announcing that a smog alert had been issued.

As though some divine art director had taken it upon himself to create a fitting backdrop for the ruinous war that the strike was becoming, the summer of 1988 was one of the worst smog seasons on record. (There were 187 days over the EPA standard that summer, including fifty-four Stage 1 alerts. The summer of '88 was the last time a Stage 2 smog alert was ever issued.) During that summer, Angelenos realized that something had to be done. Changes had to be made. The summer of '88 was a crossroads, a turning point for Los Angeles, and you could feel it everywhere. It was literally in the air.

The crimson hues of the particulate-filled sky made the San Fernando Valley floor look like the set of *Dune*. As I drove along Ventura, the main artery of the red planet, taking in the errant palms that lined the boulevard, signs of the strike were everywhere. Much of the $6.5 billion a year the film and TV industry directly contributed to the California economy had dried up. And the aggregate economic impact of the strike, the cessation of indirect revenues, such as the demand for gas, food, and services by the 230,000 people who worked in the industry, was even more devastating. DuPars, an industry coffee shop, was deserted. Hampton's and Art's Deli, other storied haunts, were empty. Many local businesses had to lay off employees. Others closed entirely. Dry cleaners and bakeries, auto dealers and banks, nearly all businesses in Los Angeles felt the pain.

I drove through Studio City, past Laurel Canyon and Whitsett, and pulled into a crappy little mini-mall next to Jerry's Deli. Could this address be right? I parked my car in front of a cheap nail salon and got out. Unsettled by the stench of corned beef and acetone, I marched up the steaming concrete steps to the second floor of the strip mall, found a door marked BETH UFFNER & ASSOCIATES, and entered.

The office was small, cluttered; imagine "old Hollywood" with a female twist. I introduced myself to the harried assistant who was juggling the ringing telephone and the directions that were being shouted at her by a gruff voice in one of the back rooms. As I sat, I noticed that the walls were covered with framed tear sheets from *Variety* and *The Hollywood Reporter*, ads that congratulated various clients of Beth Uffner & Associates for their nominations and wins of Emmys, Humanitas Awards, Writers Guild Awards, every kind of prize given to a television writer. A lot of the names I recognized from the excellent TV shows that I had been watching: Bob Brush, Roger Director, Michael Weithorn, Lydia Woodward, Russ Woody. *You're telling me these writers are represented here?* I thought.

"Send Jeffrey in!" the back-room voice called out. Phone to her ear, the assistant pointed me toward the back. I rose and, feeling oddly like a boy who was being sent to the principal, sheepishly entered the back office. A fifty-year-old woman with wavy brown hair and large plastic-rim glasses sitting behind a desk looked me right in the eyes and said, "You better make this deal happen or there will be hell to pay."

"Excuse me?" I gulped.

"You're not getting off the hook this easy."

"Excuse me?"

"Stop messing with my client!"

I just stared at her, speechless. And she just stared right back at me. Who *was* this woman? Then she held up her index finger. It was right about then that I realized she was wearing a telephone headset.

Except for the Time-Life operator on the commercials, I don't think I'd ever seen anyone actually wear one of those things before. She indicated she wanted me to sit. I did. She continued her conversation, chewing out some poor executive while staring directly at me, sizing me up. Although I can't be sure, I think she was trying to keep a studio from using the strike as an excuse to cancel one of her client's deals.

Finally, she finished her call, ripped the headset out of her thick hair, introduced herself, and immediately launched into a critique of my spec script. She liked it. She thought the "market would respond" to it. But she had some very specific directions for my next spec. I asked her a few questions. She asked even more. Finally, she broke into a smile, satisfied, even tickled. Then she told me to bring in fifty copies of my *Molly Dodd*. "I don't photocopy," she said. "That's my client's responsibility."

She got annoyed when she found out I had a meeting with another agency. "You want to drive over the hill, fine. But make them wait. It's good for them to wait. You'll meet with them, they'll love you, but you'll see. You'll end up signing with me."

She was the most unapologetically aggressive person I had ever met. Having been raised in the polite South, I had no reference point for someone like this, especially a woman. This single-minded forcefulness, characteristic of agents, when combined with the maternal instinct, made her scary, downright ferocious. But at the same time, there was something comforting about her. In a world where a mattress on a garage floor was home and whether to buy gas or dinner was a frequent decision that had to be made, the idea of being taken care of by her suddenly seemed very appealing.

"All you care about now is getting a job, but trust me, in three years you'll be calling because you're not being paid enough. The only time I'll hear from you then is when there's a problem." If there was such a thing as the mother of all agents, this must be her.

As I was trying to leave, she said to her overwhelmed assistant (who I began to understand was the "Associates" in "Uffner & Associates"), "Doesn't he look nice?" But before the assistant could answer, she turned to me and added, "When you go to your meetings, don't you dare dress like that. You don't need to be the best-dressed person in the room. Remember, you're a *writer*."

As I drove up Coldwater and down into Beverly Hills, I felt disoriented. But as I pulled up to the William Morris offices, whatever bewilderment I felt was immediately superseded by something greater: awe.

William Morris was everything Uffner & Associates was not. Furthermore, it was everything I expected—and more. The WMA agency occupied the entire building, most of a city block, really (in fact, in 1998, the *entire street* was renamed William Morris Place). The palms that lined the front of William Morris Plaza in perfectly planted symmetry seemed to breathe easier than the ones in the Valley. As I left my vehicle with a white-suited valet in front of the Plaza and entered the commodious well-appointed lobby, everything began to feel surreal, dreamlike. The effect was certainly compounded by the massive, circular reception desk where I was greeted and offered bottled spring water by a stunning long-haired finalist in the genetic lottery—I'd never seen a human being this beautiful in person before. And behind her were not one, but *two* more supermodel-hot receptionists, their overlapping voices blending and harmonizing to create a melodious mantra as they worked the phones: "William Morris, may I help you? William Morris, may I help you? William Morris, may I help you?" The sound of harps playing at the gates of heaven came to mind.

Historically speaking, talent agents haven't exactly been the most beloved people in show business. At the end of the nineteenth century, as vaudeville became the predominant form of American entertainment, agents sought out performers and then sold their services to the vaudeville theaters for a cut of the pay. Aware of how popular and *well-represented* performers affected costs on vaudeville, early Hollywood producers made sure their actors remained anonymous. Actors' names were not listed in credits. Close-up shots were avoided. Performers were not featured in advertising. But despite their efforts, the studios were unable to keep the genie in the bottle. Movies created an intimacy between audience and actor. And unlike Broadway theater, motion pictures were a purely populist medium. Common folks felt a kinship with the personalities they saw on screen, and they wanted to know more. So whether the studios liked it or not, Hollywood had given birth to the "star system."

In the twenties and thirties, actors, or rather, stars, became the central product in Hollywood, more important than any other aspect of a movie. Audiences were sold a Mary Pickford film, a Charlie Chaplin flick. Young actors were found, molded, and promoted, rapidly becoming household names. Publicity departments flourished at the major studios, churning out all manner of carefully constructed behind-the-scenes information about their stars. Fan magazines appeared. A culture of celebrity was created and it was a very good time to be a representative of those celebrities.

There's an old Hollywood legend that an agent would not drink tomato juice during this time because people might think that the agent was drinking his client's blood. Whether or not agents were indeed bloodsuckers, no one disputes the phenomenal rise in the price of blood during the twentieth century. According to the *St. James Encyclopedia*, billings at the William Morris Agency went from $500,000 in 1930 to $15 million in 1938, a thirtyfold increase in just eight years. It's fair to say that the vast majority of this money was not coming from writers. The studios during this era were factories, quite literally. The immigrants turned moguls who ran them churned out products with the same kind of assembly-line mentality that Henry Ford applied to automobiles. Stars were created by publicity departments while writers typed away in story buildings. The difference between the two crafts was that stars were designed and marketed as unique talents, whereas writers were simply replaceable hired labor. Sure, there were certain types that could be cast in certain roles, but each actor had his or her own style, personality, and box-office draw. A studio often assigned numerous writers, who might not even be aware of each other, to work on the same project at the same time, but actors were perceived as generally inimitable. The Pandora's box for the studios was that while it was in their interest to create stars, the power of the stars ultimately began to threaten the iron grasp that the studios had on the business.

In the 1950s, after the tightening of labor laws and a series of antitrust suits, the studios lost their ability to keep talent in long-term contracts. Actors now began to form their own independent production companies, competing with the very studios that created them. Agents also began to get "back-end" deals for their actor clients. This guaranteed not just a salary, but a share of the box-office revenues. In 1950, Lew Wasserman, an agent with Morris's biggest rival, the Music Corporation of America (MCA), got Jimmy Stewart a historic profit-sharing deal that amounted to half the profits of his western *Winchester '73*. The era of indentured labor and the so-called studio system was ultimately usurped by what could rightly be called the "agent system." Agents began to leverage their management of talent, most notably by creating "packages" around their stars. Agents put together projects staffed exclusively with clients from their rosters and offered the package to studios as a whole. If a studio wanted to be in business with a particular star, they now had to accept an entire package of costars, directors, writers, and supporting talent from one agency.

William Morris, who had experience with the concept from the days of the vaudeville circuits, mastered packaging in the new rapidly developing medium that was challenging the movie business—television. Shows like *The Andy Griffith Show*, *Gomer Pyle U.S.M.C.*, and *Make Room for Daddy* (from which it still purportedly draws packaging fees) brought great wealth to the agency. When an agency packaged a show, rather than draw a 10 percent commission from its talent the agency received a packaging fee—5 percent of a show's license fee (the money a network pays a studio for the right to air a show), *plus* a 15 percent stake (today it is 10 percent) in the show's ultimate adjusted gross, typically syndication revenues less any costs not covered by the network. As this practice became increasingly standard in the emerging medium, agencies were no longer mere representatives, they were equity partners, just like their clients who got back-end deals. The business was changing.

The promise of acquiring an ownership position in a series' syndication potential—which could be worth tens, perhaps even hundreds of millions of dollars—redefined the nature of talent representation. Other agencies followed Morris, and the TV package soon became the bread and butter of the agency business. But rather than strictly building their businesses around actors, talent agencies began to shift the spotlight to writers—the force that was starting to drive the TV package.

While marquee actors still had their place, the nature of the business, the way television was made, soon created a demand for talent that could manage stars, oversee production, and, simultaneously, write. As quality writer-driven television became more and more popular, having a capable and talented writer-showrunner attached to a project became just as important as the actor. Eventually, it would become more important.

By the late 1980s, when I came to Hollywood, agents began to seek and market television writing talent with the same vigor that studios in the thirties and forties applied to finding and selling stars. Writers were discovered, guided, and then promoted by agents to studios as unique talents with distinctive "voices." Like star actors, writers—especially TV writers—were represented as inimitable. Agents created an aura, a buzz, around their writing clients. New TV writers, like I was about to be, were referred to as "baby writers" and were strategically positioned, marketed to fill a specific niche or perceived need. Agents often instructed us to focus exclusively on a certain genre—say, family sitcoms or one-hour police dramas. Sometimes we were even positioned as masters of a subspecialty. Agents called network and studio executives all over town to talk about their hot new clients who could write "half-hour with heart," "procedurals with edge," "strong female protagonists," and "killer punch-up." Many young writers became near instant sensations before they ever had their first job.

Superagent Mike Ovitz applied the concepts of TV packaging, which he learned at William Morris, to motion pictures, making CAA what most viewed as *the* premiere Hollywood talent agency. With clients like Tom Cruise, Dustin Hoffman,

Kevin Costner, Sydney Pollack, and Steven Spielberg, CAA basked above all in the glamour and prestige of the movie business. According to *The New York Times*, in 1988, the same year the Ovitz-packaged hit *Rain Man* was released, CAA pulled in revenues of about $65 million. However, around that same time, William Morris received about $60 million from a *single* deal—its share in the syndication revenues of *The Cosby Show*. Movies may have been a glamorous business, but television was a far more lucrative one. By the late eighties, TV packaging had become more than the bread and butter of Hollywood. It was the main course. Perhaps not as fancy as movies, but far more sustaining.

Years later, a very well-known television director told me that he was going to encourage his sons to become writers. "Why?" I asked.

"Because in television," the director replied, "he who writes holds the keys to the kingdom."

This was true. However, writers may have held the keys to the kingdom, but he who held the writers, held the kingdom itself.

⸻

A well-dressed kid about my age with an unyielding enthusiasm similar to my own approached me in the William Morris waiting room and introduced himself as Lanny's assistant. Lanny Noveck was the literary agent I was to meet. On the way to Lanny's office, my doppelgänger in Armani talked about two things: how much he liked my writing, and how much he liked William Morris. He referenced specific scenes and characters in my *Molly Dodd*. He quoted my own dialogue to me. Then he talked about how totally jazzed he was to have made it out of the mailroom and how completely psyched he was to be assigned to such an amazing agent as Lanny. As we turned a corner and walked down a long hall, we passed in front of several desks staffed with similarly jazzed and psyched assistants and newly minted hotshot MBAs and JDs who had also recently made it out of the mailroom. They all smiled at me as I passed. Several greeted me. I was introduced to another assistant outside Lanny's office who, after shaking my right hand, immediately seized the warm depleted Evian from my left and rapidly replaced it with a properly chilled one. My head spinning, I was then whisked into an impressive office where three agents stood to greet me.

If you've ever been through fraternity rush, you'll know exactly what this process feels like.

Lanny looked like a man named Lanny. He was at ease, paternal, the kind of guy who brings you comic books when you're sick, who teaches you why Gulden's spicy brown mustard is the best condiment for hot pastrami on rye, the kind of guy who was so connected he didn't need to make a big deal about it. One had to fight the urge to call him Uncle Lanny. Although he had only been at the agency for seven years, Lanny was William Morris incarnate.

The meeting itself laid out as these meetings typically did. *What do you like to watch? What would be your dream show to work on? Where do you see yourself in five years? Have you found a decent place to live yet? Where's your favorite place for sushi so far?* There were no incorrect answers. After a potential client was given the impression that he was being suitably screened, the agents then declared that they were "big fans" and the future was discussed. The credentials of the agency were presented. Names were dropped. Success stories told.

All I could think was "Wow! This could actually happen!" It was like listening to the homecoming queen hinting that she wanted to sleep with you and then describing in vivid detail what she was like in bed. I tried to say only enough so as to remain animate, afraid that if I said any more I would rapidly transform into Jeffrey the Babbling Idiot and blow the whole thing.

The primary selling point for the big agencies was the promise of packaging. In other words, if a young writer was represented by Morris, he or she would be put together with a respected director, high-level writers, celebrity actors—the young writer would be rolled into the package offered to the studios. So when I say names were dropped, I mean names like Bill Cosby—stars. Since Morris had quite an impressive roster of stars, one could feel very confident that a Morris TV writer would be a working TV writer. If anyone still had any doubt about the big agency's supremacy in television, all he had to do was look at the 1988 schedule. In the 8:00 time slot: *Sledge Hammer!* on ABC, *Tour of Duty* on CBS, and *Cosby* on NBC—all William Morris packages, programmed on all three networks throughout the same slot. A grand slam!

Finally, these kinds of meetings ended with agents declaring that their specialty was "breaking in" new writers. That it was, in fact, their own area of expertise and no one in town was better at it than they. By the time these meetings drew to a close, most young writers thought they were ready to sign any kind of contract that was put in front of them.

JEFFREY STEPAKOFF

I arrived in Hollywood just as the machinery of finding, shaping, and marketing new writers was gearing up. Soon after my meeting at William Morris, the same questions I was asked and the same benefits I was promised would be posed and pitched with increasing frequency throughout the offices of television literary departments at all the major talent agencies. I didn't know this yet, of course. What I did know was that William Morris was every bit as impressive as I had dreamed. I also knew that I genuinely liked Lanny. He was—there's just no more accurate way to say it—a good guy. It was heady stuff to have my work considered by people like this, people who wanted to *represent* it, put their names on it; and even more so to hear palpable descriptions of a life where I could pay the rent by making more of it.

I wanted to sign something right then and there before they changed their minds. The only reason I didn't was because of this nagging feeling I had about that crazy lady I had met earlier in the day. "You'll end up signing with me, you'll see," she had predicted, and I could still hear her voice in my head. I wanted to take some time and think about it all. The William Morris guys were gentlemen in every sense of the word about what I wanted to do.

In fact, "Gentlemen" was the very first word on the agency contract that they sent to my stolen office at Universal the next day when I was at work. "Gentlemen: This will confirm the following agreement between us," the authorization papers read. "I hereby engage you for a term of. . . ." The attached note explained that they respected my desire to think about it, but they wanted to be clear about their interest. There is little in life that equals the simultaneous thrill and terror of reading one's first agency papers. The exhilaration that comes from being wanted is at the same time tempered by the contractual nature of the expression. With the exception of an apartment lease, it is, for most young writers, the first time they are asked to make a long-term and binding commitment—with consequences that go far beyond any lease. No matter how much a new writer thinks he'd cut off his left pinky to receive an offer of representation, once the massive contract documents are actually placed in front of him, he begins to sweat. Some writers even bring the contract to lawyers. But the fact is, if an agent doesn't get a writer a "bona fide and appropriate offer" of employment within ninety days, the WGA-mandated Artists' Manager Basic Agreement of 1976 (the AMBA contract) stipulates that the agency papers are null and void. Amazingly, though, this reality doesn't keep writers from sweating out the decision to sign. And the fact that I was still haunted by that intense agent in the strip mall increased the quantity of perspiration on my brow.

I asked everyone I could for advice. The consensus was that this was a very good problem to have and I should shut the hell up, realize how lucky I was, and, obviously, go with the better known of the two agencies. I pretty much reached the same conclusions on my own, but still, there was something about that woman . . . something about her assuredness and demeanor . . . something that I couldn't let go. . . .

One of my buddies at Universal, Kevin Reilly, a fellow motion-picture marketing peon who I helped stuff *Harry and the Hendersons* T-shirts into envelopes (and the future president of NBC), introduced me to a girl he was dating named Jamie Tarses (the future president of ABC), whose father had actually created *Molly Dodd*. She didn't mince words. "If Beth Uffner wants to represent you, you have to go with her. You *have* to," she said. Jamie went on to tell me something that was not yet public knowledge. Beth was about to join forces with a growing literary boutique called Broder, Kurland, Webb.

It was explained to me that unlike the big agencies, namely Morris, ICM, and CAA, whose business models were to package all of their various talent—actors, writers, directors, producers, editors, musicians—into a television series, literary boutiques were agencies that concentrated almost exclusively on TV writers. Although the big agencies were beginning to adjust their strategies to account for the increasing primacy of the writer in network television, this was akin to turning a battleship. Sensing an opportunity in the rapidly changing market, individual agents and small teams of agents began to center their attention on writers. And the really savvy ones limited their lists to TV writers. The idea of a specialized talent shop was nothing new. There were many small to midsize agencies that focused on specific kinds of actors. If you wanted young, classically trained talent, you went to J. Michael Bloom. If you wanted Jack Nicholson, you went to Sandy Bressler. What was novel here was the notion of applying this kind of specialization to writing talent.

After Bob Broder and Norm Kurland were joined by Elliot Webb in 1983, BKW quickly and quietly became one of the most successful talent agencies in town. Their major clients? TV writers. With talent like the Charles brothers, Barry Kemp, Glenn Gordon Caron, Earl Pomerantz, and Donald Bellisario, and a hand in shows like *Cheers, Newhart,* and *Moonlighting,* the boutique was, agent for agent, just as profitable as any of the big three, and by some accounts, more so. While highly publicized stories about movie stars and the superagents who got them record amounts filled the industry trades as well as the consumer publications, literary boutiques like BKW consciously stayed out of the limelight, preferring their 15 percent back-end stake in several TV shows that might earn half a billion dollars each in syndication to a 10 percent commission on a handful of $15 million movie stars.

When Beth joined them in 1988, Broder, Kurland, Webb, Uffner (BKWU) and a few other similarly sized boutiques would radically change the landscape of the business. Beth's forte was finding and shaping neophyte writers. Her list was a sort of feeder program for her partners' more established clients. Beth fed her new clients to her partners' bigger fish who were getting shows on the air, creating the perfect paradigm for the packaging of series programming. Not only was the agency in a position to stock its packaged shows with its own writers from top to bottom, but even more importantly, young writers could be trained and groomed on those shows, eventually becoming future showrunnners who would command their own BKWU packaged series.

While the big agencies could promise young writers that they would be put into a package with star actors, literary boutiques could promise young writers that they would be packaged with established writers. As the writer-showrunner supplanted the actor as the must-have element in a TV package, boutique representation became the first choice for many TV writers, new and established. Many writers still went with the big agencies, of course, especially those who also wanted a screenwriting career. But many of these same writers, in particular the younger ones, often left when they discovered that a) the agency was too large to focus on their individual needs, and b) the agency was primarily committed to servicing the name actors who intrigued the writers in the first place. The literary boutiques prided themselves in taking a career-view to representation. They were able to provide a great deal of personal attention to their writers because they chose not to take on actors who required a notoriously high amount of maintenance. Writers rarely took up their agents' time by repeatedly calling and complaining about the size of their trailers. This allowed the literary boutiques to stay firmly focused on the goal—not just to draw a 10 percent commission on salaries for a few years, but to groom and place future showrunners.

I followed Jamie's advice. After I couriered two bottles of Glenlivet to William Morris with a thank-you note, I called Beth Uffner and said yes.

Immediately thereafter, now that I was finished obsessing about and finally making what I thought was the biggest decision of my life, I was struck by the absolute and utter ridiculousness of my current state of affairs. I finally had an agent. Great. Now what? I was so busy focusing on representation that I neglected to give due consideration to the rather serious matter that there was, in fact, no industry in which my agent could represent me!

The strike was getting worse. Way worse. During the last week of June 1988, the Writers Guild turned down the latest of several offers from management. This last one, which the studios promised was their best and final offer, was rejected three to one by the nine-thousand-member guild. Both sides firmly dug in their heels. As the work stoppage lengthened, the pain it was causing increased. Daily pickets were growing heated. Universal announced more layoffs and summarily closed the commissary. The WGA had handed out more than $2 million in interest-free loans, the majority of its strike fund. Writers were beginning to face the fact that they might not be able to pay their bills. The specter of writers losing their homes became more and more real. A splinter group had formed within the guild that wanted to settle. The group was garnering more and more support every day, raising the possibility of a dramatic battle within the WGA itself. Since divisiveness is precisely what management wanted, studio representatives fanned the flames every way they could.

The studios publicly and privately stated that they would stop at nothing to keep shows in production. Management promised that they had plans in the works to have several shows back in production right after the July 4th holiday. But they stopped short of explaining who would write these shows.

While I was trying to decide between agents, my boss's boss, the head of Motion Picture Research, put me in touch with an old fraternity brother of his who happened to be working on the lot—as Universal's senior vice president of Current Television. This executive had positive words about both agents, as well as my spec scripts, which he asked to read. Right after management's promise to keep TV shows in production, this executive called me for a meeting.

Being summoned to Universal's executive office building, "the Black Tower," is an otherworldly experience. A trip to the fifteen-story glass monolith, built to make Lew Wasserman's authority clear and indisputable, gives you the definite sense that you're going to meet the Wizard. The senior vice president of Current Television had an office on an upper floor with a commanding view to the north. You could see all the way from the picketers down below, across the entire smog-filled valley, to the San Gabriel Mountains. The office was furnished like most Universal executive suites, with formal studio hand-me-downs. The executive, easygoing, laid-back, stood in stark relief to both his stuffy office and the tense town below.

I sat down, cracked open the cold Perrier that had been thrust into my hand, and listened as he got right to the point. He offered me a job: $10,000 to write a script for *Charles in Charge*, a sitcom starring Scott Baio.

How could he offer me a writing assignment in the middle of a writers' strike? Well . . . he proceeded to tell me a story about when he was a kid in college and he took a job as a scab baggage handler during a strike. It was a colorful story about how he needed money for college, for his future. He wanted to work. They didn't. He wasn't uncompassionate, but why should he show allegiance to a group to which he didn't belong?

His story resonated with me. I sure wanted to work. This wasn't my strike. Why should I show allegiance to a union to which I didn't belong? In fact, the WGA wouldn't even *let* me join. In order for me to enjoy the privileges of membership, I first had to be offered a job, and the WGA certainly was not offering me a job. To the contrary, they were keeping me from getting one.

For the most part, Hollywood is a union-shop town. This

means that in order to work, you have to be a union member or become a union member. But in order to become a union member, you first have to be offered a job by a company that has signed a collective bargaining agreement with the union. The way this usually works is that if a studio or showrunner wants to hire a new writer, they tell the WGA, and the writer pays a $2,500 initiation fee and becomes a union member. But because there was a strike on, the studios had not signed the current bargaining agreement and were not signatories of the guild. Therefore, the studios were free to hire whoever they wanted and the union was closed to new members.

No one had asked me about whether or not the guild should strike. No one had offered me the right to vote on the matter. But a major studio was offering me a real, high-paying professional writing assignment. My very first one. Why the hell shouldn't I take it?!

Well, there was a good reason, actually. According to the WGA, if they ever found out, I would be "blackballed," barred from future membership, unable to *ever* work as a professional writer in Hollywood. But the Universal executive assured me that there was no way the union would find out—as long as I never told anyone about the offer. As of this writing, with one exception, I never have.

I had a major decision to make, and this one I had to be very careful not to talk about to anyone.

FOUR

Green Envelopes

*"An agent is a bulldog. You don't want him
sitting at your dinner table. You want him outside,
tied up in front of the house, barking like crazy."*
—A TV WRITER-PRODUCER

"I look at my writers like annuities."
—A TV LITERARY AGENT

U nlike New York, Los Angeles is a relatively easy city in
which to be poor. For one thing, as many of the nation's homeless who have made pilgrimage to the People's Republic of Santa Monica can tell you, it's warm and
sunny in Southern California. This cuts down on some basic
cost-of-living expenses and simply makes a struggling life
more bearable. Unlike nearly every other city in the country,
no one (okay, almost no one) is from Los Angeles. People,
young people, come from all ends of the earth to pursue a
goal, a dream, that can only be realized in the City of Angels.
Consequently, there is a massive subculture of interns and assistants, coffee-getters and lunch-deliverers. Though there is
no question that living below the poverty line sucks, in L.A.

there's a certain nobility in it—it is an accepted and expected part of the proverbial dues-paying process. This process bonds people, creating a tight-knit community. As though pulled together by some unseen force, industry people always seem to find each other in L.A. They are drawn together like iron ore clinging to a magnet after it's run along beach sand.

After a few weeks, the romance of indentured servitude in Brentwood wore off, so I packed up my few belongings, left my garage, and crashed in the spare room at my buddy Delbert's piece-of-shit apartment on Genessee in West Hollywood. A fellow drama student from Carnegie who had graduated a year before me, Delbert was an actor-waiter who spent his time reading Sartre, smoking Camels, and tattooing a great deal of himself with funds garnered from the pawn shop on Santa Monica. He was a great drinking buddy, a loyal friend, but a dreadful roommate. I soon sublet an amazing split-level apartment a few blocks away on Hayvenhurst from a yoga instructor who was leaving for Nepal. She was more concerned about finding an agreeable caretaker for her cat than the rent, so she made me a deal I could afford.

If I wasn't working at Universal, hanging out at Canter's Deli with Delbert, or trying to keep that wayward cat alive, I was getting together with other aspiring TV writers. Through the Carnegie Clan I immediately met a lot of people in the industry. I went to parties at Belinda Wells's (John's ex's) home in the hills on Camrose. I met new friends who were assistants and interns for meals and drinks. I took classes at UCLA's extension program, where I met many young writers, one who more than a decade later would end up hiring me. In fact, this kind of networking had a role in nearly every writing job I would ever have. Most TV writers have a similar story.

Having been treated like quite an oddity for blowing off a sensible future to pursue an eccentric endeavor like writing, I was thrilled to have finally found so many other like-minded spirits. However, despite all the support and fellowship that L.A. had to offer, I was hungry, figuratively and literally. More than anything else in the world, I wanted to work as a writer. And to someone who was living hand to mouth for a shot at that dream, ten thousand dollars seemed like all the money in the world. While interning, I stayed very well informed about the various catered meetings throughout the marketing department at Universal. I was always on hand to help clean the kitchen and conference rooms. Half of Tom Hanks's tuna sandwich would be a nice lunch. Sid Sheinberg's remaining Chinese chicken salad made a great dinner. The leftovers from the regular Friday executive meeting sometimes got me through a whole weekend. But as much as I appreciated the free meals, after my offer from Universal Television, I began to wonder exactly why I should forgo the opportunity to eat food that hadn't already been picked over by the rich and famous. Ten thousand dollars could literally change my entire life. I thought about the offer, constantly and carefully.

Being a screenwriter in early Hollywood was, by most accounts, great fun. The Screen Writers Guild, formed in 1921, was in reality more of a social club than a labor organization. Meeting in an old house on Sunset, parties were thrown, plays were performed, and it's safe to say that alcohol was in abundance. The early SWG was not too different from a collegiate alumni association like Carnegie Mellon's West Coast Drama Clan, which I joined in 1988 when I came to L.A.

But by the 1930s, while Hollywood seemed safe from the hardship that troubled most American industries, this was, in fact, not the case. Rather than trim their own massive salaries or the cost of tickets, studio bosses forced huge wage cuts on labor, including writers. Writing for the studios was hard and often thankless work. Hours were long. There were no royalties or residuals. Credits were assigned not on the contribution of the writer, but as the studios saw fit. Writers were often lent back and forth between studios, like costumes or lighting equipment. And the studios were very committed to keeping things this way, even if that meant threats, bribery, or doing business with mob-connected labor leaders.

Hollywood writers soon realized they needed more than a club. In 1933, ten writers met at the Roosevelt Hotel to reorganize the Screen Writers Guild into a "guild with teeth." It soon began to work, and studio management was not pleased. Many writers at this time had affiliations with radical theater groups back in New York that supported or simply explored communist ideals. And most writers, even the most successful and those from wealthy families, saw themselves as workers and identified with the struggle of organized labor. However, by 1947, when the House Un-American Activities Committee (HUAC) began investigating the Hollywood labor unions, it was one thing to be a worker, and quite another to be a Communist. Red-baiting, an accusation of Communist sympathy, became a weapon that studio management could use to keep organized labor in check. Many writers who were threats to the studio system were subpoenaed, dragged before the HUAC and asked (among other things): "Are you now or have you ever been a member of the Screen Writers Guild?"

Some, like writer Budd Schulberg (*What Makes Sammy Run*) and director Elia Kazan (*On the Waterfront*), "named names" and implicated their left-leaning colleagues as Communist sympathizers. Others, like the "Hollywood Ten," a group of ten artists—nine of whom were writers—refused, were cited for contempt, and served prison time. Hundreds of writers, like Ring Lardner, Howard Koch, Dorothy Parker, Lester Cole, John Howard Lawson, Clifford Odets, Arthur Miller, Dashiell Hammett, Arthur Laurents, and Lillian Hellman were "blacklisted" by the studios, which refused to employ them. In 1952, the Screenwriters Guild allowed the studios to remove writers' names from movies they had written. Some writers were able to work under pseudonyms or "fronts" (using friends who took credit for their work) like Dalton Trumbo, who wrote *Roman Holiday* but whose friend Ian McLellan Hunter took credit for it as well as won Trumbo's Academy Award for it. But others had their careers and their lives irreparably destroyed.

It was during this tumultuous time that television exploded in popularity. Much of early TV, which was produced in New York, was basically just filmed theater. Variety programs, like Milton Berle's *Texaco Star Theater,* and Sid Caesar's *Your Show of Shows* resurrected vaudeville. Anthologies like *Playhouse 90, Kraft Television Theatre,* and the *Philco* and *Goodyear Television Playhouses* literally presented plays, many of which writers dug out after the works didn't sell on Broadway. Though some writers during this period—such as

Rod Serling, Reginald Rose, and Gore Vidal—are still highly regarded dramatists, early television writers received even less respect, artistic and financial, than their brethren who were writing for motion pictures. John Brady reports in his book, *The Craft of the Screenwriter*, that Paddy Chayefsky received nine hundred dollars when his teleplay *Marty* aired in 1953, but fifteen times that amount—plus a percentage of the profits—when it was made into a movie. For an entire TV season of work, writing *nine* one-hour shows, Chayefsky was paid just seventeen thousand dollars. Television may have been "golden" during this age, but it certainly wasn't a gold mine for those writing it.

Hollywood's hope that television was just a fleeting highbrow fascination was not to be the case. As the price of TV sets dropped and popular programming became more sophisticated, TV caught on in a big way. In 1950, there were more than 10 million TV sets in this country. When Hollywood finally realized that the damn thing wasn't going to go away, the West Coast studios decided they had no choice but to join the party. It wasn't long before Hollywood took over the party.

Unlike live TV in New York, early television in Hollywood had more in common with B movies than with theater. Early filmed television shows were formulaic. Westerns and cop shows became staples of the new medium. Shoot-outs and chases became expected conventions. Scripts were often written simply to take advantage of existing movie sets on backlots. Nonetheless, people watched. By 1955, two thirds of the country owned a television.

When Desi Arnaz put three film cameras in front of his wife's live stage comedy, *I Love Lucy*, and essentially invented the sitcom, it wasn't just audiences that were now captivated. The Hollywood studios quickly realized that the real beauty of filmed entertainment was that it could be rebroadcast, ad infinitum. And every time a show was rerun, the studios incurred no additional expenses but received additional revenue. The writers of those shows, however, did not. This was the basis for the writers strike of 1953, which resulted in a contract that paid TV writers their first residuals. A year later, several groups, including the Screen Writers Guild, representing writers on both coasts, merged to form the Writers Guild of America.

The WGA led the next work stoppage in 1960, which was much longer and turbulent than previous strikes, mainly because the studios were able to keep making TV shows. Warner Brothers alone had more than a hundred television scripts written. This was doable without union writers because most of the scripts were simply recycled from other shows. Producers just changed the character names on a script that had already been shot on one western and used it for a shooting script on another, and the same went for cop shows and lawyer shows. No one really noticed. That was the quality of the vast majority of television being made at that time. But this would change.

The late sixties saw the rise of higher-quality programming, which was due primarily to the rising involvement of the writer in not just writing the show, but producing it. Many TV writers were now writer-producers, or "hyphenates." Although this greatly improved the quality of TV, it created some unique problems for the guild. During the strike of 1973, while the majority of the membership supported the guild, accomplished writer-producers like Norman Lear, Richard Levinson, Charles Fries, William Sackheim, Leonard Stern, and Aaron Spelling felt like traitors. They supported the guild, but they were also producing for the same companies the guild was striking. Over the next decade, this conflict of interest quietly grew.

By the mid-eighties, a strong and increasingly vocal faction within the WGA began to emerge, much of which was composed of regularly working writers, many of whom were hyphenates. According to *Variety*, in 1985, of WGA-West members with credits in the previous ten years 80 percent earned less than $5,000 a year writing. By 1988, about 10 percent of the guild's members were paying 50 percent of its $5.3 million in annual dues. From the mid-eighties until today, the yearly working membership of the WGA has remained at about 50 percent. And of that group of working writers, a very small minority works steadily most of the year, as opposed to freelancing a job or two. And of *that* group of steadily employed writers, an even smaller group continues to work regularly, year after year. Some are hot screenwriters. Most are television writers who work on staffs. A strike has different effects on a writer who sells a project or two every few years and a television writer-producer who is suspended from a long-term multimillion-dollar contract. This discord within the guild was one of the main reasons another strike in 1985 barely lasted two weeks and was generally disastrous for writers.

In 1988 management expected the same thing. They were wrong. Although the guild's divisiveness was there from the start of the dispute with the studios, this time the WGA leadership dug in its heels.

JEFFREY STEPAKOFF

The primary demands from the WGA were for greater residuals from one-hour dramas and from the burgeoning foreign television markets. Unlike most walkouts in America, which take place for better working conditions, health benefits, pensions, and higher pay, writers strikes have almost always been centered on residuals. Of course those other issues are on the table as well, but the real hot button for writers is not so much initial compensation as it is participation in the ongoing revenue stream of what they create. And this is much more than a simple matter of dollars. It's also a philosophical issue. How much should a creator share in the future of what he or she creates? How much should be the sole property of the corporation that employs the creator? These are questions with which most industries never have to deal.

You see, residuals are really a form of ownership, like a dividend a company pays owners of its stock. Getting residuals means that after a writer is paid his or her initial compensation for writing a script, he or she is paid again every time that TV episode is used again—whether rerun in prime time, on cable, on a local station in Thailand, as part of in-flight entertainment, as part of a "clip show" broadcast, on DVD, shown in the produce section at Kroger, on screens at gas-station pumps, or downloaded onto a computer, cell phone, or iPod. Anytime, anywhere, in any form a writer's work is rerun, reused, or repurposed, that writer receives a green envelope from the WGA in the mail a few weeks later. Depending on how a script was used, checks can be anywhere from a few cents to more than $25,000. You never know. You can imagine the thrill every time one of those green envelopes arrives in the mail.

Emboldened by victories in previous strikes and the conflict they once again sensed within the guild, the studios budged very little during the initial negotiations. With critical stakes on the line—residuals and the future of the guild itself—the writers also remained obstinate. Consequently, the strike dragged on, escalating into something bigger than either side ever imagined. And gone were the days when the production companies were mom-and-pop shops run by avuncular studio heads who would help everyone sort out their differences. By the middle of June 1988, the strike had become the longest labor stoppage in Hollywood history. The L.A. economy had lost hundreds of millions of dollars. The entire state of California was bleeding as the $6.5 billion entertainment industry had ground to a halt. And most alarming, viewers started to find other things to do. For the first time since the invention of the medium, viewing habits were broken.

At the end of June, with bargaining hopelessly deadlocked, the studios decided it was time to take drastic measures. Well aware of those hundred reworked scripts during the 1960 strike, the studios felt pretty confident that they could replicate that effort. But to fully appreciate the mind-set of management, you have to remember the prevailing attitude toward organized labor in the eighties. Reagan's firing of 12,700 air traffic controllers, followed by the collapse and disintegration of their union, was still fresh in the minds of most people. Reagan was easily able to find and hire replacement workers, and within a few months thousands of new controllers were trained and working.

In the fall of 1987, just a few months before the WGA walkout, the National Football League players went out on strike. In response, the twenty-eight team owners hired replacement players. Regular games were played and televised. Attendance and ratings suffered only slightly. The public supported management over the football players who were widely seen as overpaid prima donnas. The football strike lasted just twenty-four days and was a complete catastrophe for the players union.

By the summer of 1988, the Hollywood studio heads took a look around and decided, "Screw the WGA! Who needs union writers? Let's go find some people who want to work!" The studios and production companies scoured the planet for material and people who could write material. Sitcom scripts from England and Canada were considered. The studios looked into hiring foreign writers. People like me were offered their first jobs.

On June 24, the Alliance of Motion Picture and Television Producers (the studios) announced that production would be starting up and new shows would be made for the fall season. Most people speculated that scabs would be used. A few days later, on June 29, NBC's head of entertainment, Brandon Tartikoff, publicly proclaimed that "come hell or high water," there would be original programming on his network. Tartikoff promised a "Bastille Day" announcement on July 14 that would lay out his new fall schedule in detail.

The entire town wondered if the studios could actually do this. Could they really make TV without union writers? Many figured, no way, this just wasn't possible. But others thought, why not? After all, how hard could it possibly be to find willing and able labor to write television?

The industry held its breath. And so did I.

In 1988 Oliver North was indicted for conspiracy, the Soviets withdrew from Afghanistan, and Wayne Gretzky was traded to the L.A. Kings, but I didn't notice. None of my friends noticed. When you write, or aspire to write, TV, "current events" means what's going on in the TV business.

For most of the country, the Writers Strike of 1988 was a news footnote at best. But if you lived in L.A. that summer, you followed the strike the way people in Washington probably followed Watergate in 1972. I spent much of my time at work listening to news reports on the radio, swapping rumors on the phone, and meeting friends to share gossip.

In all "industry towns" there is a certain myopia that applies to that city's dominant business. In Milwaukee I'm sure brewmasters talk beer, and in Silicon Valley programmers surely yak about chip speed. But I soon learned that in Hollywood, one way or another all talk is shop talk. Indeed, every single aspect of the business, from who's hiring who, to who's writing what—and, in the summer of 1988, what was going on with the strike—are all discussed not only with great focus, but with a reverence that surpasses the attention given to cancer research. I would have heated conversations that lasted well into the night about topics like Aaron Spelling's fourth acts and the genius of David Chase's "espadrille" scene in that *Almost Grown* pilot. It is impossible to work, or aspire to work, in television without getting entirely wrapped up in this world. It becomes your entire world, so much so that everything outside of L.A. seems, at best, quaint. And in reality, irrelevant.

In a human-interest piece I saw on the local news that summer, a reporter walking along Melrose Boulevard asked people the same simple question: "How's your script coming along?" He asked all kinds of Los Angelenos from all kinds of socioeconomic groups, and something like 80 percent of them answered with a sincere account of the status of their spec TV and film scripts: "Great! Almost done. Should be able to quit my job at the law firm any day now."

Here's another example. For the July 4th weekend, I went to the beach with some friends, and *all of us* pulled out television scripts to read. Not books. More than a dozen young people, all reading TV scripts.

> ***Writer Friend:*** How's that *Roseanne*?
>
> ***Me:*** Interesting. (Meaning I don't know what to make of it.) It's like the anti-*Cosby*. How's the *Hooperman*?
>
> ***Writer Friend:*** Brilliant, fucking brilliant. Top of act, he's got the protagonist sticking his head in a toilet tank to rinse the shampoo out of his hair when the plumbing breaks. Talk about laying pipe, talk about establishing character—and he's done it all in the teaser, for Christ's sake!
>
> ***Me*** (in an earnest hushed voice): Bochco is the master. Did you hear he was working on a pilot before the strike about a genius kid doctor?
>
> ***Writer Friend:*** Someone should write a show about us, you know, people our age.
>
> ***Another Writer Friend*** (looking up from a *Family Matters* script): My friend was an assistant on *Growing Pains* and she says that Neal Marlens says that nothing interesting ever happens in your twenties. That's why there are family

> shows about kids and shows like *thirtysome-*
> *thing*, but nothing in between. No stories to tell
> about twenty-year-olds that anybody cares
> about.
>
> ***Me & Writer Friend*** (accepting this as gospel and
> going back to our script reading): Oh, huh, I
> guess that's right.

Unable to make a decision about whether or not to scab, I fi-nally decided to ask someone for advice, someone who was not wrapped up in this world: my father. I'll be honest. To say that my dad was, well, less than supportive about my interest in writing would be putting it mildly. Having spent his lifetime in sales management for a furniture manufacturer, my father knew as much about a writing profession as Willy Loman. I think it would be accurate to say that he was nothing short of heartbroken when I left Ogilvy & Mather, which wanted to pay for me to get an MBA, so that I could go into serious debt getting an MFA. I'll be even more honest. I could have asked a lot of people for this advice. I believe I chose my father be-cause I figured he'd talk me into taking the money. He didn't.

"Look, if they want you now, they'll want you when this thing is over," is what he told me.

This was the first time my father expressed actual belief in my ability to write. I followed his advice, called the Universal exec, and passed.

On Bastille Day, July 14, Brandon Tartikoff made his announcement—but with no fall schedule as he had promised.

Two days later, the major studios presented their plans to put a couple dozen network and syndicated programs back into production. Some of these were reality-based shows, some were rehashes of network news, and some were revivals, like *The Hardy Boys Mysteries*, made by using old scripts from the 1977 series. And a few were actually original scripted shows.

During the strike of '88, during what Robert Thompson and many other critics now call "Television's Second Golden Age," no new scripts were written for *L.A. Law*, *China Beach*, *The Wonder Years*, *thirtysomething*, or *Cheers*. But *Freddy's Nightmares*, *The Munsters Today*, and *Charles in Charge* went into full swing. Perhaps the greatest consequence of the strike was to prove how irreplaceable writers had truly become in television.

I wasn't the only one who passed on opportunities to work. Not a single WGA member ever crossed the picket line (at least publicly). Though, as the strike wore on, a growing bloc of writers let it be known that if the union leadership didn't settle soon, they would not only cross, they would leave the guild. On July 14, the same day as NBC's botched proclamation, twenty-one WGA members asked the National Labor Relations Board to nullify the WGA's rules that kept them from working. These writers were the lead dissidents in a group called the Writers Coalition (formerly the Union Blues). What this group had in common was that they all worked regularly. Most were high-income hyphenates, writer-producers like Robert Singer (*Midnight Caller*), Bill Blinn (*Starsky & Hutch*), David Milch (*NYPD Blue*), and Lionel Chetwynd (*To Heal a Nation*). You have to understand. These were guys who *ran* things. While they certainly saw themselves as writers and identified with the cause of writers, they drove 7-series BMWs, lived in multimillion-dollar homes in the Palisades, and sent their kids to Harvard-Westlake. These guys weren't exactly like the writers of the past.

On August 1, 631 WGA members (according to Chetwynd) signed letters stating that they wanted to leave the union by opting for court-approved "financial core" status. But two days before this happened and the WGA was busted, the guild leadership settled with management. In the end, it wasn't the studios that concluded the strike. The internal struggle between regularly working and occasionally working writers eventually forced the union's hand.

After 1988, it was clear that the era of writers as simply workers was over. Consider John Wells. In 1988, Wells was earning about $400,000 a year. He had just become an executive story editor, your basic working TV writer. Eleven years later, in 1999, he had a net worth that I guess would be in the nine-figure range, and he became president of the WGA. He had a stake in several shows on the air and the resources to develop more. He was a writer, yes. In many ways a writer's writer. But he was also someone who made hiring and firing decisions about everyone working on his shows, including fellow writers.

Look at the significance of this. After 1999, Hollywood writers were essentially represented by management. Yet this was not the conflict of interest that it might seem to be. Writers had never had this kind of representation before, mainly because writers could never have attained this kind of control and wealth before. Wells was not so much a powerful anomaly as he was the poster boy for the New Hollywood Writer.

Today, most working television writers participate in the management of their shows. Whether they are called story editors, producers, or consultants, today's TV writer has a say in everything from story to casting to editing. What most people I meet never seem to understand about television writers is that writing is just one aspect of what we do.

The 1988 strike really had no clear-cut winner. Writers gave up a little in foreign residuals and received a little in the cable markets. The new contract was essentially a compromise. Still, over the next ten years, from 1988 to 1998, writers' earnings doubled. This was due not so much to specific contractual gains made during the strike but to the rising importance of the writer in television, a business that was about to explode.

In general, TV writers get paid in three ways: 1) for work that might become something; 2) for work that is being done; and 3) for work that has been done.

"Work that might become something" basically means a development deal. Simply put, this is when a writer is paid to develop or think up ideas that might someday become a television show. Writers receive anywhere from a few hundred thousand dollars to more than ten million (plus additional compensation if their projects actually go forward) for this kind of work. As the demand for TV writers and new shows increased exponentially during the nineties, so did the amount of writers offered development deals and the amount of money they were paid.

"Work that is being done" means writing a television

script and/or working on a series staff. Writers are paid a fee for every script that they write. These fees go up every year when new contracts are negotiated. In the late eighties, for network prime-time shows, this was about $11,000 for every half-hour script and about $18,000 for every one-hour script. As of this writing, those fees are $20,956 and $30,823 respectively.

Staff work is the bread and butter of most working television writers. This kind of employment means providing a wide range of writing and producing services required to run a series. Nearly all writers who work on a staff do so under an agent-negotiated contract that guarantees payment per episode for a specified number of episodes. The WGA stipulates minimum payment levels for staff work but, as in professional sports, very few people really get the minimum. Although all writers receive the same stipulated payment for scripts, staff salaries are highly negotiable. Here are the basic staff positions and their ballpark compensation levels:

TV Writer's Title	Average Compensation per Episode
Staff Writer	$ 7,500
Story Editor	$ 9,000
Executive Story Editor	$10,000
Coproducer	$12,500
Producer	$17,500
Supervising Producer	$25,000
Coexecutive Producer	$35,000
Executive Producer	$60,000

Again, these are averages. As writers move from show to show, their "quotes" (what they earned on their last job) almost always rise. If a writer is in demand—if he or she has multiple offers from different shows—there is no cap on what a studio can pay for that writer's services, or what title that writer can be offered. Many writers earn well over six figures an episode. Bruce Ferber was paid $6 million just for his writing-producing work on twenty-eight episodes of *Home Improvement*—that's more than $214,000 an episode. He got script fees and residuals in addition to that.

Writers on the staffs of network shows also receive program fees. At about $500 an episode, it's a kind of hazardous-duty pay.

And for "work that has been done," writers collect residuals and a variety of other fees, including recurring-character payments and character "spin-off" payments. If a writer creates a new character who appears for the first time in that writer's script, the writer is compensated $443 every time that character appears in additional episodes, whether or not the writer wrote the additional episodes. If that character "spins off" into a new series, the writer is paid $1,598 per episode for each half-hour show produced and $3,036 per episode for each one-hour show.

A single episode of television can earn a writer income in perpetuity. Let's say a writer was hired to write a one-hour drama episode in November 1997 for a network in prime time.

- The writer would initially be paid $25,116 in three installments.

- In March 1998, the episode receives a network prime-time rerun, for which the writer receives $16,640.

- Two months later, the series is sold to foreign free television, for which the writer receives $5,823.

- Subsequently, the series is sold into syndication, where the episode has its third, fourth, and fifth runs over the summer of 1998. The writer receives $4,992 for the third run and $4,160 each for the fourth and fifth runs.

- In September 1998, the series is sold to basic cable for a license fee of $750,000 per episode. A residual of 2 percent of the license fee, $15,000, is due to the writer.

- Then, in November, various episodes of the series, including the writer's, are licensed for in-flight usage at $25,000 per episode. A residual of 1.2 percent of the license fee, $300, is due to the writer.

- So the writer has earned $76,191 for a single episode in one year. And as long as the product is reused, most of the residual payments continue forever.

If you consider that most writers on staff are credited with about four scripts a season, you'll see that a writer on staff of a popular show earns $304,764 for the scripts he or she writes. Add that to say, $20,000 an episode (an average writing producer's salary) for a normal season of twenty-two episodes, and the writer is now up to $744,764. Add on program fees and recurring-character payments and you can see that a typical mid-range TV writer on a staff earns close to $800,000 for one season's staff work, about nine months. Add to that a standard pilot development deal, say $250,000, and you can see how twenty-five-year-olds earn more than a million dollars a year writing TV.

Most lucrative of all, writers have back-end participation in the shows that they have developed or created. In short, most writers receive 5 percent to 17.5 percent of the revenues their shows earn when sold into syndication. Some highly successful writer-producers can get as much as 25 percent. (More specifically, today writers receive a percentage of the MAGR—the modified adjusted gross revenues—meaning that distribution and overhead fees are deducted before the profit participants are paid. Throughout the nineties, most studios, particularly Sony, paid writers a percentage of the pure AGR—the adjusted gross revenues—which did not have these fees deducted.) In addition, included in the revenue side of the equations are moneys from ancillary markets and products. Think about what a cut of the merchandising proceeds from hats and T-shirts and coffee mugs can be worth to the writer-creators of the *Star Trek: The Next Generation* franchise.

Finally, in addition to the staff salaries and script fees, the studios and production companies are also contractually obligated to pay another 15 percent of those wages to the WGA Pension and Health Fund. In other words, when a studio pays a writer $100,000, that studio must also contribute an additional $15,000 to the fund. Currently, with more than $1.8 billion dollars in assets, the WGA pension fund is one of the most quietly well-funded pension plans in the United States.

After 1988 it became much more lucrative to be a TV writer. However, paradoxically, the 1988 strike caused irreparable damage to the network TV business. When the fall season started late in December 1988, 9 percent of the audience did not return. Entire families that used to gather around TV sets after dinner disappeared entirely from the Nielsen radar. This began the acceleration of network audience erosion that has continued to this day.

One of the greatest beneficiaries of the strike was the newly developing cable networks, which began to grow as many viewers, in search of something to watch, bought cable for the first time. Nineteen eighty-eight was the first year that a cable network had a large enough audience to qualify for an entry into the Emmy Awards, which allowed it to compete with the major broadcast networks. HBO received several nominations that year and won its first Emmy. In 1979 about 90 percent of the audience watched the big-three nets. By 1988 that number had dropped to 70 percent. By 1996, less than half of the prime-time audience, 49 percent, watched the big-three networks.

As network ratings dropped, advertising revenues dropped. The networks, whose only real source of income came from that advertising, studied several possible new business models that could ensure profitability. One of these was to look at several successful nonscripted shows like *America's Most Wanted* and *48 Hours*, which the studios developed in 1988 as a defensive response to the strike—and consider making more like them. These were shows that did not use writers.

So an interesting thing happened during the decade after the strike. As writers grew in importance due to their greater involvement with producing as well as writing TV, and thus became much more costly, seeds were carefully planted to develop programming without them.

FIVE

Written By

*"It occurred to me that maybe it was a good thing
not to be the first stop—getting what everyone thought was
the best material. Maybe nobody really knows what's best.
Maybe best is making your own choice, on its own
sole merits, not its buzz or bloodlines."*

—BARRY DILLER

Turned out my dad was right. The day the strike was over I called the Universal vice president. I told him that I would now love to work for the studio. I don't know if it was just enthusiasm for my work or guilt, but he sent my spec scripts to several producers on the lot. Rick Okie, the supervising producer of *Simon & Simon*, responded to (which means "liked" in agentspeak) my writing.

Now, if you step back and think about it, this was a pretty amazing thing. My quirky romantic half-hour comedic spec, *Molly Dodd*, about a single woman looking for love in New York City, got the attention of the producer of a one-hour drama about two brothers that solve crimes, carry guns, and have frequent high-speed car chases. But what I would soon learn is that this sort of thing happened all the time in TV, mainly for two reasons. First, what we'd all like to believe: Good writing transcends form. And second, what is often a greater truism: You never know what people are going to like. Over the coming years I learned that this simple fact, more than anything else, defined the television business.

When I worked in advertising, I saw our clients create products that everyone knew consumers were going to like. One client created a new insecticide that worked better than the competition's and could be used safely on your tomatoes. It was a slam dunk, and everyone knew it was going to be from the start. I saw another client create a new fast-food breakfast, one of those artery-clogging sausage-and-egg deals, which they offered for half the price of the competitors'. Again, we all knew it would be a home run, and we were all right. In TV, there are no such sure things. There are guesses, hunches, gut responses. People's careers, mortgages, kids' tuitions, entire lives, and an entire industry—all predicated on pure subjectivity. That, I began to see over and over again, is television.

When I started my internship, the human resources exec who hired me suggested I read William Goldman's *Adventures in the Screen Trade*, a book she felt defined the movie business. Well, as right as I thought Goldman was that "nobody knows anything," I thought this was even truer in the TV business. In TV, where there is no tracking, no testing and changing, nobody ever knows what will work because nobody ever knows what anybody is going to like. And not only do programming executives never know what audiences will like, but writers on staff never know what the studio will like. New writers never know what showrunners will like. If before the executive sent my script around the lot someone had given me a list of all the dozens and dozens of shows in production at Universal, *Simon & Simon* would not have been one that I would have guessed would have "responded to" my *Molly Dodd*.

This sort of thing drives new writers crazy. When I got together with other writers who were also trying to break in, the number-one topic of conversation was always specs. An unbelievable amount of effort has always gone into the prognostication of the spec market, though it does little good.

Every season, certain specs are "hot." Every young writer I met seemed to know what these were. Particular shows, even if they're not broadly popular, become hip in the L.A. community. Word gets around of the shows and scripts most liked by showrunners. Agents look at what's working in the spec market and on the air, try to anticipate what will work next, and add their views to the mix. When I first got to town, endless stacks of *Cheers* and *Murphy Brown*s were written and sent around town. A few years later, it was the *Seinfeld*s. Then the *L.A. Law*s and *NYPD Blue*s. Followed by *The Sopranos* and *Sex and the City*s and *The Shield*s, and right now, I'll bet *Entourage*s and *The Office*s are flooding Hollywood. Yet despite this lemminglike rush of hot scripts—maybe because of it—many producers inexplicably want to read the offbeat *Molly Dodd*s. You just never know.

Complicating matters even more, writers never know exactly what genre of script readers want. Some showrunners will only read movie scripts. Some want plays. Some will only read scripts in the same genre as their series. Some want the exact opposite. Readers not only have different tastes, but different needs for their staffs. Some want a female voice for their hard-edged drama. Some want a dramatic touch to their goofball sitcom. And every season, every reader, it's something new. This is the main reason that the first thing an agent does when she falls in love with a writer's spec is to make him write another one. Immediately after signing me, Beth Uffner had me spec an *It's Garry Shandling's Show*. Delbert thought it was very funny. I'm not sure anyone else did.

And in addition to all the various schools of thought about *what* to spec, new writers immediately hear a wide variety of rules about *how* to spec. I often heard that you're not supposed to write a "typical" episode for the show. You know, not the one where Sam and Diane sleep together. I heard that you're not supposed to do anything too out of the ordinary, not a crossover episode where characters from one show appear on another. Oh, and the golden rule that everyone always hears: You're not supposed to write a spec of the show on which you really want to work. All new writers quickly learn the supreme decree that showrunners never want to read a script for their own show.

But here's the problem. Just like most everything else in television, none of these rules really hold up. Over the coming years, I would see these rules successfully broken, again and again.

What I eventually figured out is that what most showrunners really want is a writer who has a fresh and distinctive voice; but at the same time, they want a writer who can suppress his or her fresh and distinctive voice and conform to the voice of the series. But since no one quite knows how to find this, let alone explain what it actually is, the one thing everyone agrees that they are looking for in a spec is good writing.

Now, the good news is that this is actually a fairly discernable thing. In a sea of arbitrariness, good writing is perhaps the one thing that has objectively agreed-upon standards. Whether or not those who are supposed to know and care about these standards actually do is another matter, but the standards are there. TV writing is a highly structured craft. Scripts must be a certain number of pages. Every show has its own specific page count, fifty for a *Dawson's*, seventy for an *ER*. (*Gilmore Girls* is off the charts.) Act breaks have highly established requirements for each genre and form. Half-hours generally have two acts; one-hour dramas have four. Everything from the inciting incident in the teaser to the way exposition is laid out to the stakes of the climax are all fairly agreed-upon components. So while the *story* you write is assessed purely subjectively, the *storytelling* can be judged fairly objectively. This is why, I believe, the best advice I ever got on specs was what Wells told me to do, something I soon learned few writers ever heard: "Just spec a show that you like." In a world where you never know what anybody else is gonna like, that turned out to be some damn good advice.

Very little is cooler in life than driving up to the front gate of a Hollywood studio and stating your name. The inevitably heavyset guard gives you a nod, a day pass, and a smile that means, "Good luck, kid." Although I had an internship at Universal, I took the morning off for my pitch meeting with *Simon & Simon*, took advantage of the pass, and drove directly to a primo parking spot on the lot. Still wearing suit and tie, I made my way to the main TV production office building.

But as cool as it was to be going to a real meeting, I felt what would become a familiar pang in my gut.

This was, in fact, my second meeting with the *Simon* producers. There are essentially two kinds of meetings in Hollywood. Meetings where people want to get a look at you—the "meet 'n' greet"—and meetings where people want to see what you can actually do. The first kind is easy and often even pleasant. The room is always filled with smiling happy people who are always "big fans." These people always want to know the same sorts of things, where you're from, how you like Los Angeles, what you think of the traffic, what you like to watch on television, and so forth. Essentially, the purpose of these meetings is to, as the name suggests, meet you, greet you, and determine, if they were to hire you, if they could be locked in a small room for long periods of time with you. You have been invited to this meeting because someone has read your work and wants to see what you're like, or because someone has heard good things about you, read the first five pages of something you wrote, and wants to see what you're like.

The other kind of meeting is where actual work is done. A few days earlier, I had a meet 'n' greet with the producers, which allowed them to get a look at my carefully chosen shirt, declare that they were big fans, and determine that at least I did not *openly* display any psychotic behavior. Having passed the requisite assessments, I was then invited back for a second meeting to "pitch" the show. The basic idea of this, the pitch meeting, is to try to sell a story to an existing series, which then, hopefully, becomes a script assignment.

I pitched *Simon & Simon* when it was in its eighth season. More than 150 episodes had already been produced. Before my pitch meeting, I went to the production office on the lot and borrowed as many tapes as I could. For three days and three nights I watched shoot-outs and boat chases, explosions and fist fights, and men in Ray-Bans and cowboy hats kicking in doors, jumping off roofs, and fearlessly facing all kinds of jeopardy without ever losing their capacity for witty banter. Oh, and more auto-theft rings than I care to remember. I could easily have been watching any of a dozen shows that were still in production at that time, old-school TV shows like *Mac-Gyver*; *Magnum, P.I.*; *Hunter*; *Murder, She Wrote*; *The Equalizer*; *T. and T.*; *Matlock*. As opposed to quality writer-driven shows, these older series were strictly predictable, well-made plays. Just a year or so earlier, most of the prime-time network schedule was filled with such offerings, many from the massive Universal Studios sausage factory: *Hart to Hart*; *Spenser: for Hire*; *Houston Knights*; *Jake and the Fatman*; *The Law and Harry McGraw*; *J.J. Starbuck, Private Eye*; *Ohara*; *Mike Hammer*; *Scarecrow and Mrs. King*; *Hardcastle and Mc-Cormick*; *Crazy Like a Fox*; *Remington Steele*; *Riptide*; *Airwolf*; *Hawaiian Heat*; *T.J. Hooker*; *Stingray*; *Matt Houston*; *Partners in Crime*; *The Dukes of Hazzard*; *Knight Rider*; *CHiPs*; *The A-Team*; *B.J. and the Bear*; *MacGruder and Loud*; *Tenspeed and Brown Shoe*; *The Fall Guy*. The list reads like an embarrassing though kitschy-cool collection of lunchboxes one has squirreled away in his parents' basement. (Okay, I don't have *all* of them.) These shows did not shock or offer insight. Nor were their stories particularly memorable. It's fair to say that no one gathered around the water cooler to discuss the cutting-edge material on last night's *Manimal*. Cocktail parties of the day rarely featured discussions about the riveting and topical dialogue between Jake and "The Fatman" Mc-Cabe. In the pre-TiVo world, these were shows that you could fold the laundry to. They provided comfort through the familiar, the better ones in an entertaining way. They were not writer-driven but plot-driven. So while a new kind of quality television was sprouting up around Hollywood, an old kind of show was simultaneously dying off. I didn't realize it at the time, but I was about to become a sort of TV missing link.

One of the most distinctive aspects of old-school TV was that much of it was written by freelancers. In the sixties, when a full season was thirty-nine episodes, a writing staff might consist of only one producer and one story editor. They would hear pitches from freelance writers and assign scripts to the stories they liked. But as writers became more involved in producing shows, this would change. By 1997, freelancers wrote only 15 percent of all network television shows.

Toward the end of my meet 'n' greet, I was told how to prepare a pitch: "Bring in some stories that you like, preferably ones we haven't done before. Bring in a good jumping off point and act breaks; there's no need to flesh out the whole story." This is how much of TV was made at this time. Although I had nodded knowingly during my instruction, I really didn't know squat about jumping and fleshing. Nevertheless, I figured, if I came up with enough material, surely something would stick. My list of ideas was long, very long.

A secretary named Violet stepped away from her Tetris game and offered me my bottled water while I waited in the producer's outer office. I noticed that these offices were furnished exactly like the executive suites in the Black Tower. As I waited, I wondered if Lew Wasserman had determined that brass banker's lamps, dark leather upholstery with nailhead trim, and formally framed pictures of horses were conducive to high levels of creativity. Or maybe, to the contrary, perhaps he wanted all his employees to stay on budget and think like accountants.

As I entered the room, I was warmly greeted by the writer-producers, mostly men, mostly older men, some older than my dad. These were not the lords of television. These guys were not Bochco or Cannell or Spelling. These were the writing proletariat. These guys worked for a living. Consider Rick Mittleman. Looking more like a weathered race-car driver than an erudite scribe, he had worked on everything from *McHale's Navy* to *Get Smart*, from *Nanny and the Professor* to *Bridget Loves Bernie*. He had even written for *The Flintstones*! And these guys were nice. Legs were propped up. Baseball games discussed. Jokes bandied about. The story room felt like a Kiwanis Club meeting. These guys were comfortable, like men who had modest mortgages.

I sat on a sofa in the supervising producer's office and presented my stories. I pitched ghosts and lottery-ticket winners and twins. I pitched black-market babies and frame-ups and money that falls out of an airplane. I pitched all sorts of dreck that they had heard a million times over the last eight seasons. Although I'm pretty sure they were relieved that I didn't pitch a story featuring midgets, I could tell from their faces that this was not going so well. But what I didn't know at the time is that pitching rarely goes well.

The act of telling a story before actually writing it is a skill that some Hollywood writers have turned into a high art, while others break out in a rash even thinking about it. I quickly discovered a real fondness for the meet 'n' greet, and found that pitching required not just extensive preparation but a good amount of Benadryl.

There is another reason—which I was learning firsthand—that pitching fell out of favor: It's pretty ridiculous. Look at the process. You're supposed to come into a room full of writers who spend every waking moment of their lives living and breathing the world of a series and that series' characters and tell them a story they haven't thought of before. You have to convince them that you possess a deep empathetic understanding of their beloved characters, which to them sounds like someone they just met at a party telling them what to do with their kids. And even if you really do luck into an area they have not yet thought of, this calls into question *why* they haven't yet thought of it. This doesn't exactly create the most conducive environment in which to work.

In the late eighties, as the quality of television got better, it became more and more difficult to nail a good story, especially on your own, especially as an outsider. And shows began to learn that just because someone was good at pitching, it didn't mean that he or she would be good at writing. In fact, pitching is essentially a *sales* skill set and is in many ways antithetical to the process of writing. Although the WGA implemented rules that force staffs to buy two freelance scripts a season, presumably to give new writers a shot, shows began to get around this by simply assigning scripts to assistants as a form of compensation. And many shows started "auditioning" new writers for their staffs by finding someone whose work they already liked and then simply *giving* him a staff-developed story to write as a freelance script. That is precisely what *Simon & Simon* did for me.

The head writer, Rick Okie, a Yale graduate and former CBS executive, took me under his wing. We worked out a story together. I was given a contract for "story and teleplay," meaning I was guaranteed $18,750 to deliver a story, a first draft, and a second draft—a complete script.

There are countless ways that writers go about the initial story-development process. Some work alone, some with one other person, some with entire rooms full of people. Some jot down scene ideas on note cards. Some work on dry-erase boards. Some just shoot the shit for hours on end and have assistants construct a story line from the stream of consciousness. When I first heard this process described—"breaking story," everyone calls it—I thought this seemed like a rather violent way to reference what I imagined to be a fairly cerebral process. But after doing it, I understood that the name made perfect sense. When you work on a story, you basically spit out whatever comes to mind and then rip it all apart. Then you examine the pieces that are left, get rid of the junk, take the good stuff, and construct a story. Stories aren't carefully baked or lovingly hatched. Good TV stories are cracked like eggs, snapped apart like fortune cookies, smashed into tiny pieces with the ruthless wrecking ball of absolute impartiality and then custom-built from the ground up. Breaking story is in fact an aggressive task, not, I quickly discovered, for the faint of heart.

I spent several days breaking story for my episode with Rick. He taught me how to subdivide a story into acts, four of them, with a climax at the end of the first three, and then into individual scenes, five or six per act, represented by a one-line active description that we wrote onto note cards. My episode was about Rick Simon's (the protagonist's) long-lost son showing up. So my note cards featured lines like, "Rick meets son," "A.J. fabricates excuse to keep kid around," "Kid snatched," "Major Action/Pursuit: Rick saves kid from jeopardy," "Mom shows up for heart-to-heart," and "Bittersweet parting—it's not his kid but wishes it was." Armed with my twenty or so cards, which could be shuffled as the need arose, I then fleshed out the story into a four-page prose document, my official story outline. Although the script form of an episode is highly standardized, story documents can and do take any form, from thirty-page narratives to a few sentences scribbled on a Baja Fresh napkin. Even the WGA dares not offer a minimum definition of what constitutes a story, let alone the official delivery form of one. Ten years later, I would work for Joe Dougherty, an Emmy-winning writer who offered me the best definition I've yet to hear about constructing a television story: "A story outline is like a map. It should be detailed enough so that you know where you're going, but vague enough so that you can make discoveries along the way."

On Friday, September 2, 1988, I got the go-ahead and started writing. It was Labor Day weekend and it was unholy hot. I wrote the first two acts in two days and two nights to the sounds of West Hollywood's nonstop party, which rode the Santa Anas into my open windows. When my neighbor, a typically pleasant-natured but unbearably gregarious-when-intoxicated 250-pound bearded transvestite, brought a little piece of the party into our courtyard right under my window,

I drove to my office on the Universal lot, where I finished the last two acts.

On Tuesday, September 6, I handed Violet my first draft. She didn't understand. She thought it was a more developed story. When I explained it was my first draft, she looked at me warily, then shrugged and took it. I got a call from Rick a few hours later. He was very enthusiastic and especially appreciated how fast I got it in. However, when I passed this news on to my agent, she proceeded to chew me out: "So you can write fast, that's great. But no one needs to know that! Next time you can sit on it for a week and work on something else! And I hope you're not wearing that tie to these meetings!"

A week or so later, on a Saturday afternoon, Delbert and I were hanging out in my sublet trying to scrape together enough money to get something to eat. Delbert had pawned his nineteen-inch television the prior week. I had a few bucks coming every week from my internship, but that barely paid the sublet and utilities. Every month was a struggle. As we considered an ad in *L.A. Weekly* that offered to pay cash for plasma, the mail arrived. I noticed a letter from Beth Uffner & Associates, which I ripped open. Inside was a check for more than $5,000, for the story part of my script deal. I had never seen a number this big on a check before, and neither had Delbert. Though I am loathe to admit this, yes, there was yelling. High fives were exchanged. My bearded neighbor came running to make sure everything was all right. I knew money was coming, but I think because of the amount I heard being bandied about, it didn't seem real until the check actually arrived. Needless to say, there's nowhere to cash a check for five grand on a Saturday afternoon, but that didn't keep us from trying. In the end, we ducked into Canter's and threw down the American Express card I got when I worked for Ogilvy & Mather. We then proceeded to get properly intoxicated on Wild Turkey at the Formosa Cafe, the chosen site of such rituals for many decades.

I got some minor notes and did a second draft. Rick also took a pass at the script but the vast majority of what I wrote stayed. Watching my episode film was thrilling. From the minute I walked onto that soundstage, it was immediately apparent to me how powerful the pen was in television. I had written "They sit on a red sofa" and sure enough there on the set was a red sofa. A simple choice between the words "DAY" or "NIGHT" in a script have a power one typically associates only with a deity. On the other hand, if you're a baby writer, like I was, when you show up on the set, people eye you wearily. And if you're a freelancer, it goes like this:

> *Security Guard:* Can I help you?
>
> *Me:* Oh, hi, I'm Jeffrey Stepakoff.
>
> *Security Guard:* (What the fuck do you want?) Hi, can I help you?
>
> *Me:* I'm the writer.
>
> *Security Guard:* Your name's not on the call sheet.
>
> *Me:* I'm a freelancer. Rick Okie told me I could come to the set.
>
> *Security Guard* (recognizing the name of the executive producer and changing his tone): Go see Larry, the Second AD.
>
> *Me* (to Larry): Hi, I'm Jeffrey Stepakoff.
>
> *Larry:* Shhhh . . . we're blocking.

Me (turning red and whispering): Sorry.

Larry: (What the fuck do you want?) What do you need?

Me: I wrote the episode.

Larry (looks at the script he's holding, reads my name, looks at me, looks at the script, finally makes a decision): Wait here.

Larry goes to the first AD, points to me, and points to my name on the script. The first AD sees me watching, nods at me, smiles broadly, and can be seen asking Larry, "What the fuck does he want?" Larry shrugs. Finally, the first AD gives Larry an order. Larry quickly grabs a director's chair, jogs back to me, opens the chair, and hustles me into it.

Nothing quite changes the tone of a set like having the writer present, even a baby freelancer. The crew doesn't know if you're a peon or management. But they do know the power of the pen, and even baby writers can wield that.

On November 19, 1988, barely two months after I got my first TV writing assignment, my first episode aired. There were articles in local papers about me that day. In the *Pittsburgh Press*, under a photograph of me looking like a deer caught in the headlights, were the words "Like a dream come true," which I must have uttered in a phone interview. My agent and Hollywood producers were quoted as saying all sorts of embarrassing things about me. Emmys were referenced. Ridiculous dollar figures were quoted. A well-known producer said I was "the best writer to come down the pike in five years." My entire future was predicted and priced, even though my very first episode hadn't even aired yet. I tried so hard not to believe my own press, but I am ashamed to admit, it was not easy. I was dizzy.

At 6:02 P.M. Pacific Standard Time (9:02 P.M. Eastern Standard Time), my name flashed on the television screen for exactly three seconds: "Written by Jeffrey Stepakoff." Fifty-five minutes later, the phone started to ring and it did not stop. I turned on the answering machine. At 7:57 P.M., when the show concluded its broadcast in the Central time zone, my phone went crazy again. At 9:02 P.M. in L.A., along with about twenty writer-friends all crammed into my new 600-square-foot apartment, I got to see it for myself. About 15 million people saw what I wrote that night. About 15 million people saw my name and knew that I was a Writer. After about thirty-five phone calls, the tape in my machine ran out. (I saved that tape for years.) My friends and I went up on the roof of my new apartment just off Sunset and drank Jim Beam by the search lights from the police choppers until dawn. I did it. *I really did it.* From this day forth, for me and my friends, I was now living, breathing testament that it could be done. What else can I say? It was one of the greatest days of my life.

SIX

Breakfast at the Polo Lounge

"Television is just a toaster with pictures."

—MARK FOWLER, REAGAN'S FCC CHAIRMAN

The studio, Beth told me, really loved my episode. They were—by now I was familiar with the expression—big fans. But I already knew this, because not only had the upper-level current executives called me to say how much they loved my work, but the junior-level ones did too. And the most amazing thing about it was that they were all complimenting the same parts of my script.

They all loved the same bits of dialogue, all referenced the same action sequence, and all said that the guest character I created felt very "authentic." In fact, they all spoke with such stunning similarity that I wondered if they had had a meeting to discuss and agree upon these things. I later learned that in fact they had. I later learned that these talking-point assessments of my work were indeed quite handy, for executives all over town could now love my script without ever having to actually read it, and love me without ever having to get to know me. This was my first direct experience with buzz and the momentum it creates.

In Hollywood, momentum is everything. And in Hollywood there is only momentum, one way or the other, meaning that you are either succeeding or not succeeding. You see, no one does just okay in TV. People either *love* your work and are *big fans*, or they want nothing to do with you. You're either in or out. If you hear they thought your script was "interesting," they hate you. If they didn't "respond" to your work, they hate you. If they had any kind of reaction other than to absolutely *love* what you did, you're screwed. And if you don't hear quickly that you're loved, you're not, because in Hollywood, everyone *loves* to spread good news—that's how momentum works. In Hollywood, no news is always bad news and bad momentum. Momentum also changes on a dime, but it never sits on that dime.

I was offered a multiyear overall contract with Universal that would put me on the staff of *Simon & Simon* and then other Universal shows when *Simon* ended. The offer was for $250,000 a year.

Beth, however, would not let me take the deal. We had words. I liked the show. Okay, sure, I thought it was a little cheesy, but it was fun to write and fun to work on. I was high as a kite on the experience of writing something and then seeing it made a few days later. I wanted more and I was being offered more—and they were gonna pay me for it. A shitload of money, by the way. But Beth would have none of this. I found myself pleading with her the way I used to plead with my mother to let me stay out late. And just like my mom, Beth flat-out refused. She insisted that she wanted me to work on a "quality" show. "That's nice that they want you," she said. "But we're passing."

"Passing!" I explained to her that just a few months ago in Pittsburgh I was walking five extra blocks by one restaurant where lunch was $3.25 to another restaurant where lunch was $2.75 because that fifty cents made a difference. "This is a degree of security," I insisted.

"You want security?" she replied. "Go sell insurance."

The truth is, Beth expressed nothing less than disdain for the show. She was annoyed that they were offering me money. To her, they were trying to steal me. She wasn't involved in getting me my first script. She wasn't involved in where it was now headed. We had a pretty heated fight. I lost. I'll never forget the phone call to my father. "Dad, I was offered a quarter million dollars a year to write TV. But I turned it down."

"What!" he exclaimed. "Why!?"

"Because Beth says it's not a quality show."

My agent called me back about two hours after our battle. She was curt: "Tomorrow afternoon, one o'clock, Bistro Garden on Ventura, you're having lunch with David Milch. You know who he is?"

"I know who he is," I lied.

"Get with the program, Jeffrey. He ran *Hill Street* with Bochco."

"Right."

"Call me afterward. Don't wear a tie. And I told him not to take you to the track, so if he tries you tell me."

I didn't know it at the time, but I think I had the job before I even went to that lunch.

MTM Enterprises gave me an office on the second floor of the main administration building, often called the "flash cube" building because of its shape, on the CBS/MTM Studios lot on Radford. I had an extra-long sofa that was great for napping, a standard-issue desk with return, and three long windows that overlooked the *thirtysomething* soundstage on the back lot. I brought in my own computer, a Mac SE loaded with MacWord, because there was no scriptwriting software on the market yet and I never could get the hang of writing a script with DOS commands on the studio IBMs. I also got a parking space, complete with my name printed on a small sign in front of it. A friend took a picture of me standing next to the sign. My Honda's parking space was right next to one used by a large white Bentley with a license plate that read RESIDUAL.

My assignment was to develop and write a one-hour script for Milch about life in a college town. David had a deal with MTM to create a new show for ABC called *Capital News*. Compulsive or ambitious, depending on your perspective, Milch also had several other projects in various stages of development, and this "College Town" show was one of them. David had already hired famed novelist Jim Harrison (*Dalva*, *Legends of the Fall*) to write a draft of the project (Harrison called it Teeter-Totter), but Milch also put me to work simultaneously writing my version of the show.

Much has been written about Milch in everything from the trades to popular magazines. He's a bit of a mythical figure in Hollywood. After earning an MFA in writing from the University of Iowa, David taught English at Yale, where

Pulitzer Prize winner Robert Penn Warren was his mentor. He was also a habitual gambler, an alcoholic, and a hard-core heroin addict. In 1982, his former college roommate, *Hill Street* writer Jeffrey Lewis, introduced him to Bochco, who assigned Milch the premiere episode for *Hill Street*'s third season. The episode, "Trial By Fury," is widely regarded as the best *Hill Street* episode ever made and perhaps one of the best hours of television ever made. After the script won the Humanitas Prize, Milch took the prize money, which came from the Catholic Church, and bought himself a stake in a racehorse. Tony Soprano meets Sophocles is the best way I can succinctly describe him. The only person he was even remotely afraid of was Beth Uffner. He never did take me to the track.

I had breakfast with Milch several days a week at the Polo Lounge in the Beverly Hills Hotel on Sunset. He was always seated when I arrived, always had the same table, and was always reading *The Daily Racing Form*. We talked about sex, drugs, and defecation, as well as Nathanael West and the latest *Paris Review*. These were all among David's favorite topics. The general plan for my script assignment was for me to bring in ideas for the "College Town" project, primarily based on my personal experiences during college, discuss them with Milch, and get direction. But the truth is, this was less of a job and more of a seminar, a sort of life tutorial, really.

After breakfast I would drive over the hill, across Mulholland, speeding back to my office on the MTM lot. Meeting with David was never a dull experience. I was always ready to write after our conversations. (On one morning I was so affected by our breakfast discussion that I nearly ran over Wilford Brimley as I was driving out of the hotel. Suffice to say, the expression on the face of the portly actor, staring at me through the windshield as he was splayed out on the hood of my little red Civic, was less than enthusiastic.) I spent much of my time writing scene ideas on note cards and taping them to the walls. In a few weeks, my walls were covered. I had very little idea what I was doing, of course, but the walls sure looked cool. In the afternoons, David would grab me and we'd walk and talk. Sometimes we'd talk character dialogue. David did not use a computer to write. He did not use a type-writer or a notepad. He *dictated* his scripts, often the day the episode was shooting. He spoke them aloud while anxious as-sistants typed or scribbled down what he said. And I mean word for word what he said, right down to the punctuation. "Johnny: What the fuck happened to that horse in the fifth, question mark. Pete: Stepped on a bottle cap, comma, you prick, period."

Milch frequently offered me cash. He almost always had a large wad of cash in his pocket, and sometimes he'd just spon-taneously whip it out and ask me if I needed any pocket money. Sometimes he'd peel off hundred-dollar bills and drop them on the desk of an assistant. "Your horse just came in," he'd say, often just a few minutes after berating them about something. Milch went through more assistants than Murphy Brown. I heard he would offer actors cash on the set if they would get their lines right on the first take. Once he came into my office and asked me if he could borrow it for a minute. I stepped out and a weathered and rather unseemly gentleman in a trench coat walked by me and stepped in. They shut my door, reopened it a few moments later, and left. Milch patted me on the back and went on his way. Why he wanted me to see all that I'm not sure.

The truth is, I had no reference point for any of what I saw or really any of what I was doing. I had just spent two years and put myself twenty-five grand in debt to learn something that wasn't helping me a whole lot here. There were no classes in graduate school about story breakfasts at the Polo Lounge or David Milch or what it would be like to work with someone like him. Then again, perhaps that point wasn't lost on Milch. Perhaps that's why my whole experience at MTM felt, more than anything else, like I was being educated.

Many people have called Milch a genius. I have no doubt that this is true. In an exposé about Milch in *The New Yorker*, for example, Bochco says: "David is a genius in the literal definition of that word." And yet, Milch told me that when Bochco gave him some script notes with which he didn't agree, Milch snuck into Bochco's office and urinated all over the place. Bochco then fired Milch and shortly rehired him, but only after Milch agreed to write "urine-free" on Post-it notes and stick them in the areas where he didn't relieve himself. Whether this particular anecdote is true or not, I can't say for sure. And I suppose it's remotely possible that I'm even combining some of the various elements from many of the tales of debauchery that I heard. But let me assure you, while these kinds of things may sound like collegial pranks, they were more. David once shot out the lights on a police car's roof with a shotgun. "Haunted" is the word that most comes to mind when I try to describe Milch. This was not a man who simply had a colorful past that he parlayed into a marketable eccentricity. This was a man who had real demons.

I tell you all this because meeting Milch made me understand, for the first time, *why* someone really makes a career writing television.

Money, of course, is one of the primary reasons writers get into TV, but often it is not why they stay. And never does it entice them to do their best work. Hollywood has a long history of luring good writers with the promise of easy money. James M. Cain, Raymond Chandler, John Fante, Daniel Fuchs, Horace McCoy, Clifford Odets, Maxwell Anderson, Dorothy Parker, John Dos Passos, Theodore Dreiser, Dashiell Hammett—all wrote in Hollywood. However, these writers never worked in television. They wrote movies over which they had little control. Their screenwriting endeavors were really second careers, in most cases used to support other forms of more satisfying writing. Faulkner didn't write in Hollywood because he loved the movies. He did it purely for the dough. Same with F. Scott Fitzgerald.

But from what I saw, David Milch, and many other great writers that I met around MTM, were not just writing for the money like a lot of those old screenwriters did. Even with his gambling and other vices, David was rich. I mean, filthy rich, and every year he worked he got richer. In the late nineties, he received more than $15 million to work at Paramount and more than $60 million for his stake in *NYPD Blue* (according to *The New Yorker*), and even after undergoing repeated heart surgeries, Milch didn't buy a yacht and sail the world. The guy worked his ass off to create and run *Deadwood*. Milch and writers like him that I met at MTM were driven by something besides money.

I was fascinated, partly because I grew up in a world

where, frankly, everybody I knew had to work. Not working wasn't an option, unless you wanted to, you know, do something noble, like black-box theater in New York. I was also fascinated because even though I'd only written one produced episode of TV, I was starting to understand what was driving these guys.

Remember the end of *Annie Hall*? Alvy writes a play that mirrors his failed relationship with Annie, but in the end, *unlike* real life, the characters make up and stay together, after which Alvy turns to the camera and shrugs: "Whadda you want? You're always trying to get things to come out perfect in art because it's real difficult in life." I think that summarizes why writers get addicted to TV writing. The chance to get things just the way you want them, to see this thing in your head, what was once a dream, fully and perfectly realized. And you get to do it again and again every week. Although I'd only done it once, I wanted more. Just like Milch, I had the bug. Sure, money's great, and I'm told heroin is too, but as ridiculous as this sounds, I truly can't imagine anything more intoxicating than making TV shows every week.

～

I'm sure another reason my job felt so much like a tutorial was because for all practical purposes, I was working at what most in Hollywood actually considered to be a school for writers. MTM Enterprises was established in 1969 by Mary Tyler Moore and her then-husband Grant Tinker to produce *Mary Tyler Moore* for CBS. Scholars, critics, and professionals alike consider MTM to be singularly responsible for the birth of "quality television." But more than anything else, the studio was renowned for being, what Tinker called, a "writers' company."

Pretty much from the day I started there, I heard stories about how Tinker would go out of his way to find writers in whom he believed, then leave them alone to do their work, protect them from outside interference, and, most significantly, put them in charge. Tinker created the modern prototype for the TV showrunner, the writer-producer. He also created a corporate culture, a program, really, where young writers were taken under the wings of the more experienced, taught craft, exposed to production, and given time and room to grow into future showrunners. He did this partially because it was the best way to run a business—you know, invest in the future—and partially because, in 1969, TV was pretty sucky. Something radical had to be done.

When I was a little kid in the late sixties, the TV in my house was almost always set to the same station: Channel 2, CBS. Seriously. Night and day that's all we watched. My dad would walk across the room, turn on the set, and that was it. From *Gilligan's Island* to *My Three Sons*, from Carol Burnett to the moon landing, it was always CBS in our house. Walter Cronkite was a member of our family. And not just ours. It was the same story all across America. Right after *I Love Lucy* in the fifties until well into the mid-seventies, CBS was the dominant network. It was not uncommon in some seasons for CBS to have eight of the top ten shows.

Now, here's the kicker. CBS was not number one because its shows were so great. To the contrary, they were number one because their shows were inoffensive. *The Andy Griffith Show, Petticoat Junction, Green Acres, The Beverly Hillbil-*

lies, Gomer Pyle U.S.M.C., Mayberry R.F.D., Hee Haw, The Glen Campbell Goodtime Hour, CBS single-handedly mastered the "hick TV" genre not because people loved this stuff, but because guys like my dad simply did not want to get off the sofa to change the channel. Think I'm kidding? NBC even had a name for this thinking, which literally became programming policy at the networks. NBC exec Paul Klein called it the "LOP policy," meaning "Least Objectionable Programming." The theory is that people will watch anything on television as long as you don't offend them so much that they have to change channels. When FCC chairman Newton Minow chewed out America's broadcasting executives, calling television "a vast wasteland," this was the kind of TV he was talking about.

And along with this policy, there was another reason why TV during the sixties was pretty awful—it all came from the same place. In the early fifties, before airing *I Love Lucy*, CBS gave ownership of the show to Lucy and Desi's new independent production company, Desilu. All CBS wanted was the advertising revenue. They did not envision the reruns of the episodes being worth anything. They were wrong. In 1957, at the height of the golden age of television, a third of all shows aired by the major networks were produced by independent production companies. These were small innovative companies that had to think outside the box to survive. But when the networks realized the value of reruns, they put a stop to all that and began to air only shows that they had made themselves or had a stake in. By 1968, independent production companies made just 4 percent of network television programming.

In 1970, seeing that networks were becoming a "vertically integrated" oligopoly—that is, doing business only with themselves and thus hurting the quality of the product—the FCC created the Financial Interest and Syndication Rules, or "Fin-Syn," and it changed everything.

The idea here, in the FCC's words, was to "foster diversity of programming through the development of diverse and antagonistic programming sources." In a nutshell, this meant prohibiting the networks from making and syndicating (selling reruns of) their own shows, thereby allowing independent production companies to compete.

So now the networks were back to just one revenue stream: advertising. TV's profitability was directly related to how many people were watching, and that number would soon max out. No longer was TV a growth industry. Suddenly, the idea of programming the least objectionable dreck to the biggest, laziest audience wasn't such a great policy. Searching for new ways to maximize profits, the networks began to think about focusing on the most valuable parts of their audience, instead of just trying to get the biggest. Thus began the focus on demographics, delivering the most desirable groups of viewers to advertisers. For starters, this meant urban eighteen to thirty-four-year-olds, those with disposable income. And not surprising, it was quickly discovered that this group, for which the car companies were willing to pay a premium, were not all that into *The Beverly Hillbillies*.

Now, two big things converged here. At exactly the same time that the networks realized they had to start making shows that would attract affluent audiences, a new generation of independent producers was empowered by the FCC's Fin-Syn rules to do just that. Suddenly, objectionableness became desirable.

Two independent production companies led the charge to create controversial or so-called relevant programming: Norman Lear's Tandem Productions, creators of *All in the Family*, and MTM. These little companies were everything that the big factories like Universal were not. Realistic character and relatable storytelling were always more important than laugh tracks and car chases. And at MTM in particular, writers were quite literally the foundation of the company. Tinker started the company by finding two writers whose work he admired, James L. Brooks and Allan Burns, of whom both had written for the highly regarded comedic drama *Room 222*, and asking them to create a series for Mary Tyler Moore. He gave the writers unprecedented freedom to develop the pilot as they saw fit and then ultimately to run the series with similar autonomy. When *Mary Tyler Moore* was sold into syndication in 1977 for more than $50 million, the wisdom and value of investing in writers was clear.

The eponymous show also created a franchise that spun off numerous hits: *Rhoda, The Betty White Show, Paul Sand in Friends and Lovers, Phyllis, Lou Grant.* And it created a model for how to develop original programming that would lead the studio to important dramas like *Hill Street* and *St. Elsewhere.* Although many of the company's shows were not ratings monsters, advertisers loved them because of the upscale demographics. Mercedes advertised on *Hill Street*; safe to say this was not the case with *Simon*.

MTM was a tightly held company that was not beholden to shareholders. It played by its own rules. During the 1985 WGA strike, for example, when the major studios locked writers out, MTM continued to pay its writers their full salaries. Comedies were shot on film instead of cheaper videotape. Sophisticated dramas were created that might take years to develop a loyal audience. And the company was entirely free to sell these shows to any network it chose—or not to. If a network had a problem with a series, MTM execs would go to the mat.

Most of the producers of television at this time, from the big studios to the little production companies, had a similar function. Remember, TV shows are deficit-financed, meaning the studio makes them at a loss, rents them to the network, which makes money selling advertising, and only recoups its investment when (or if) the show goes into syndication. Understandably, whenever there was a creative difference of opinion—say with a casting choice, or a story line, or even the hiring of a particular writer—studio executives would throw their weight around. And the studio usually won. If the network wouldn't acquiesce, there were always other networks. If all the networks were scared of a project, the studios could always sell new episodes to local stations (called first-run syndication), as Norman Lear discovered with *Mary Hartman, Mary Hartman*. Of course, the network was free not to pick up a show, cancel one already on its schedule, and buy from other production companies, but because of the Fin-Syn rules, it could not tell everyone to go to hell and just make its own shows. So even though the studio had all the blood in the game, the network had to play by the rules of the game.

This scenario created a system of checks and balances, a healthy and productive forum for discourse, where the longevity of a series was weighted more than its overnight ratings, where the overall quality of a series trumped selling out a character for a salacious story that might produce a big but short-lived audience. The result was, more often than not, quality TV. This was the case for big factories and small independents alike, and the real winner was the consumer, the viewer.

The major studios, however, were not quite as zealous about protecting their shows as independents like MTM were. This was partially simply a difference in corporate culture, and partially because the studios had numerous revenue streams.

During my internship, I was in a meeting where the president of Universal Pictures, Tom Pollack, remarked that if the movie division couldn't resolve its financial troubles with good product, the company would still be fine because they always had the studio tour, and if that stopped being profitable they could always sell the backlot to a condo developer. (I'm sure these thoughts were bandied about in the same half-serious way at 20th Century and MGM before Century City and Culver City became residential communities.) The small independents, however, didn't have the luxury of destination studio tours and real estate with its own zip codes. The independents understood that the only way they could compete with the big studios was to create not just a successful show or two, but a business that could consistently churn out hits year after year. Hence, Tinker created more than a company. He created a culture of training, the repercussions of which extend well beyond MTM.

The creators and showrunners of many of TV's greatest and most popular shows learned their chops at the studio, including: Glen and Les Charles (*Cheers*, *Newhart*); Ed Weinberger (*Taxi*, *Phyllis*, *The Cosby Show*); Stan Daniels (*Taxi*); James L. Brooks (*The Tracey Ullman Show*, *Rhoda*, *Lou Grant*, *The Simpsons*, *Mary Tyler Moore*); Allan Burns

(*Rhoda, Lou Grant*); Gary David Goldberg (*Family Ties, Brooklyn Bridge, Spin City*); Barry Kemp (*Newhart, Coach*); Hugh Wilson (*WKRP in Cincinnati, Frank's Place*); Jay Tarses (*The Days & Nights of Molly Dodd, Buffalo Bill, The Slap Maxwell Story*); Mark Tinker (*St. Elsewhere*); John Masius (*St. Elsewhere, Providence*); Bruce Paltrow (*St. Elsewhere, The White Shadow*); Anthony Yerkovich (*Miami Vice*); Dick Wolf (*Law & Order*); Tom Fontana (*Homicide: Life on the Street, Oz*); Glen Gordon Caron (*Moonlighting, Medium*); Marshall Herskovitz (*thirtysomething, My So-Called Life*); Joshua Brand and John Falsey (*Northern Exposure, A Year in the Life, I'll Fly Away, St. Elsewhere*); and Milch and Bochco. Former MTM writers and those that trained under them are still responsible for some of the best shows on the air. Important TV writers whose names you'll still see in credits, like John Romano, Lydia Woodward, Russ Woody, Mark Frost, Jeff Melvoin, Earl Pomerantz, David Mirkin, Barbara Hall, Doug Steinberg, and Kerry Ehrin, all trace their lineage back to MTM. Would *Boston Legal* have ever existed—not to mention *Ally McBeal, Picket Fences, Boston Public, The Practice*, or *Chicago Hope*—if Bochco hadn't hired and trained David E. Kelley?

Three simple principles—hire good writers, train more, protect them and their work—are responsible for MTM's success and its impact on modern television. This was the time-honored role of the studios, especially the independent ones. However, these doctrines would soon no longer apply.

Along with thinking about shows that did not use writers and focusing on demographics, the networks employed a third strategy to ensure profitability. In the wake of the 1988 strike, arguing that the loss of audience to the growing cable markets was making the network TV business unsustainable, the networks began a well-funded lobbying campaign to overturn the Fin-Syn rules so the nets could once again own what they aired instead of renting it from independents. In the mid-nineties, the networks would be successful.

Not only would this ultimately facilitate the end of MTM, it would lead to the end of all independent television production companies. In 1992, right at the end of the second golden age of television, there were sixteen new series produced by independent studios and production companies. As of this writing, there are none.

When I was watching all those great quality shows back in my apartment in Pittsburgh, I had no idea how much MTM and other independent production companies had to do with them and the TV renaissance. I don't think many people did. But as I started working in the business, the demise of the independents would soon affect my life in a very big way.

SEVEN

The Funny Business

"We use all parts of the buffalo."

—Showrunner Jeff Greenstein to the writers in his story room

The best way to get a job writing television is to already have a job writing television. Once someone has hired you, you are now immensely hireable. Agents who wouldn't return your phone calls suddenly call you at home just to let you know that if you ever need anything their door is always open. Executives whose names you've read in the trades stop you on the lot after a meeting just to say hi. Once you get your first job you are suddenly a proven commodity. Not necessarily proven to be successful, but proven to be considered possibly successful by someone proven to be successful. And the system is set up to market such a commodity quite effectively.

Once I was working for Milch and also had a produced episode under my belt, I was off. I suddenly had big fans all over town. I took meeting after meeting. There is an entire infrastructure of agents and executives in the television business whose primary task is just to keep up with writers. They call it "tracking." Your spec scripts are photocopied. Everyone "reads" you. Assistants, who are often writers trying to break in or wannabe executives, pass copies of your work to their friends, who study it and talk about you and your work at parties. Your name goes on lists (marked A, B, or C) in closely held files and up on dry-erase boards in conference rooms as you are officially "approved" by studios and networks. You're in. Your name becomes a part of that loud buzzing noise you hear all over L.A. You become a piece of the golden puzzle that every executive studies during the day and dreams about at night—how to put together the right elements to make a hit show. Like Sisyphus and his boulder, the pursuit of such a prize drives men and women to near insanity.

I found the whole thing at once thrilling and deeply unsettling. I mean, a year ago I was poor. Now I found myself eating a lot of spicy tuna rolls with Hugo Boss–outfitted young men and Donna Karan–bedecked young women who were referencing scenes in my spec scripts and talking about my future.

At one lunch at Teru Sushi on Ventura, after executive Bill Sheinberg finished an extensive critique of what I had ordered—he was impressed with my choice of tako (octopus) but not so much with the Philadelphia roll—he told me that his door was open if I wanted to bring him my ideas for new series. The son of a salesman, I nodded confidently and thanked him self-assuredly, but let me tell you, inside I experienced an acute queasiness that was not entirely from the tako. (I ordered this stuff, by the way, because the day before I was thrown out of the famed Sushi Nozawa down the street, and I mean literally shown the door, because I ordered a California roll.) Frankly, I was spending every day just trying to come up with riffs of dialogue and the occasional story to keep Milch happy. Not an easy task. Milch was very displeased with Jim Harrison's pass at the script, grumbling about alcohol abuse and literally tossing it at me when I bravely said I liked it. I had quite a job on my hands already and, hell, I just got here. *How could they already be talking to me about my own show?!* But in fact, young writers like me with virtually no experience all over Hollywood were starting to hear similar proposals as the TV business began to heat up.

I received invitations to write episodes for a variety of different shows. I accepted some. I wrote a *Beauty and the Beast* for Witt/Thomas and CBS that didn't go so well. I wrote an episode of a new sitcom for 20th and ABC called *Have Faith*, which went great but the series got canceled. I wrote an episode of a drama called *Sons and Daughters* for Paramount and CBS which also went fine, but by this time my attention was focused on staff jobs. My job with Milch and MTM eventually ended without much ever coming of the script. It didn't really progress the way that Milch wanted it to, and his attentions went elsewhere, mainly to his series that got picked up by ABC, *Capital News*. But that was fine with me because I had been invited back to Universal to work on a pilot for a new series, *Major Dad*. It's pretty rare to hire young writers to work on pilots, but they wanted to take me off the market before the staffing season started.

My agency was packaging the series, meaning that they collected a packaging fee and had a stake in the back-end of the show so I didn't have to pay 10 percent commission. Essentially the show was created around Gerald McRaney, called Mackie by his friends, and it was in one's best interest to be his friend. This was a man who gave huge hunting knives, the kind with which you slaughter a deer, as Christmas presents, and who was rumored to carry a .357 with him at all times. For some reason, and I strongly believe it was simply because I was from the South, Mackie and I got along great. I'm not sure anyone ever told him that he was doing comedy, which, oddly, worked just fine. The truth is, there was very little that was real funny about rocket launchers and MREs, but ever since *Cosby* you could put a laugh track under just about anything and make a profit. And from what I could see, Universal was damn good at this.

As strange as the process of writing drama was with Milch, comedy was even stranger. Rick Okie was assigned by Universal to executive produce the show along with Earl Pomerantz. Rick remembered my work on *Simon* and introduced me to Earl, a quirky, big-hearted Canadian who reminded me of Gilbert Gottfried. I was hired to help punch-up the pilot, and when the show was picked up, I was hired as a story editor— but I soon learned that my title meant nothing except to connote pay class. Most sitcom staffs function as meritocracies, meaning the best story or the funniest joke wins. Unlike other jobs where you follow a long process of paying dues and climbing a ladder, in TV if you're good you can go straight to the top pretty quickly.

Major Dad was my first experience with the story room, or as most writers call it, the Room. Sometimes a conference room, sometimes, like on *Major Dad*, just the boss's office, this is where the staff's writers congregate to brainstorm stories and collectively write. In the case of sitcoms, a lot of time is spent punching-up the script, making it funnier by improving and adding jokes. Work in the Room is probably the most important work on a TV series. It is the heart of a show. And yet this was the first I'd ever really heard of it. Just like I had no reference point for bosses like Milch, they don't teach you anything about the story room in school. This was probably because so little actually gets reported about story rooms, since they're off-limits to everyone except a show's writing staff. Outsiders of any kind, even actors and executives, no matter how powerful they may be, are never allowed in the Room while legitimate story work is in session. I had heard that Bochco wouldn't even let an assistant into the Room.

Writers' rooms casually developed in response to the demands of the modern television production schedule. Story rooms did not exist in the early days of television. A playwright did not need a lot of help punching-up an existing stage play purchased by *Playhouse 90*. As far as I can tell, there is no mandate from the WGA that a story room exist on a TV series. Likewise, there are no rules that specify the behavior in the Room. So anything, and I mean *anything*, is fair game for finding a story. I saw people talk about the most embarrassing, most personal things in their lives, things they would never publicly reveal, things they might not even tell a spouse, but that often led to material for episodes.

As odd as I found the Room to be on *Major Dad*, this was just the tip of the iceberg. The culture of story rooms is usually set by the showrunner, and some of the story rooms in which I would later work were . . . well, I'll get to that, but here's the sort of thing I first encountered.

During a story-room session where eleven writers were punching-up a script I wrote, Earl couldn't understand a speech I wrote for the major (Gerald McRaney), who was instructing his daughters in the proper military way to fold a shirt. I tried to explain it several times, which was difficult because of the pressure in the room. Finally, without missing a beat, without any forethought or trepidation whatsoever, my boss ripped off his shirt, handed it to me, and exclaimed "Show me!" For the next few minutes, using Earl's shirt, I explained in detail how to fold while Earl dictated the speech to a secretary. For the next few minutes, eleven male and female writers sat there and watched Earl's hairy man-breasts while he did this. I don't know if he was just so focused on getting out that script that he didn't care that he was partially naked, or since being naked is a figurative requisite for writing comedy he figured—what the hell! All I know for sure is that nobody at Ogilvy & Mather advertising ever took off clothing in a meeting. I'd never been in a situation where the person in charge was so invested that he literally gave the work the shirt off his back.

First an obsessive-compulsive genius-junkie, then a comic-stripper. At the time, I figured it was just a weird coincidence that I had ended up with such oddball colleagues, but this was only the beginning.

Although the dynamics of the story room vary from show to show, production schedules do not. All sitcoms follow a very structured production schedule, which gives shape to a writer's week as well as the story process. About two-thirds of sitcoms follow a Monday-to-Friday schedule. Some, like *Major Dad*, follow a Wednesday-to-Tuesday schedule. They all go something like this:

Day One: A brand-new script is read at the table by the actors. This is fittingly called the "table read." It's a fun and bonding way to begin the week's work on a new episode. (That is, if a script has actually been written by this time.) The read-through is attended by all the writers, directors, representatives from various production departments like hair and makeup, sets, and properties; if the show has children in it their parents, guardians, and tutors are present, covering executives from the studio and network attend, and even agents are often present. It's the first time the writers get a sense of how the episode will play, and whether or not it's funny. After the read (assuming that confidence is high that a final script will soon appear even remotely resembling the draft that exists on Day One), the actors meet with the director and start learning lines. The crew begins to construct sets. During hiatus week when you're not shooting an episode (usually one week out of every four), the writers map out future episodes. So now, based on one of those ideas, one of the writers will go off and write the script for the next week. Another will go off and develop or write the one for the week after that. The rest of the writing staff goes to the story room, orders lunch, often puts in orders for dinner, too, and settles in. Ideally, the script will be in such great shape that the writers can spend the entire day (and night) doing nothing but punch-up. This is a process in which the entire staff goes through a script line by line and simply tries to make it funnier. On *Major Dad*, Day Ones, especially on episodes that came later in the season, rarely had the luxury of strictly doing punch-up. I worked on episodes that had nothing but a two-paragraph concept at this point. If you didn't know before the read-through, you know now what kind of structural work you have to do. Often scenes are restructured and rewritten. Often new scenes are developed and written. Sometimes entire acts (and even entire scripts) are reworked. Again, depending on the state of the script and how the showrunner likes to do things, the entire staff will often do this work as a group. An assistant or two usually sits at the computer typing up the agreed-upon changes. Sometimes the script is projected on a screen for all to see as the assistants input the changes. It is not uncommon for a staff to split up into groups and work on the script in teams. If the material needs a lot of rewriting, this is often the only way to do it. Although I have heard of shows (often run by family men) that finish the work before six even on Day Ones, most sitcom staffs work well into the evening on this day.

Day Two: On this day, the writers basically pick up where they left off the day before. This is usually the last chance for actors, the studio, and the network to get in their licks. Standards and Practices usually responds by this point as well. These are the fine folks at the network charged with ensuring that nothing illegal, immoral, or unethical gets onto America's airwaves, aka, the censors. If the notes come in, they are addressed, i.e., they are ignored, negotiated, or appreciatively folded into the script. If anything has come up in the rewriting that might require unexpected production changes, this is the last chance to make the various departments aware. On *Major Dad* I saw entire sets constructed in twenty-four hours. It was amazing. At the end of the day, or before the sun rises on the next, a revised script is published, couriered, and delivered to all concerned parties. Sometimes, at least on *Major Dad*, if a script was working, Earl would send us home early. If not, we'd work through the night once again, breaking occasionally to do important things for the creative process, like have golf-cart races through the backlot.

Day Three: Again, the writers continue where they left off, but this day is usually earmarked for polishing and punch-up. I worked with writers who did nothing but show up on writing staffs for this one day. These so-called punch-up doctors might only get one or two jokes in the final produced episode, but they're often some of the most memorable. Everyone knows sitcoms that are remembered for that one classic line. Needless to say, someone who can deliver that kind of line on a moment's notice is in high demand. Some of these people make more money for a day's work than most of the other writers on staff make per episode. I was teamed up with a writer on *Major Dad* named Peter Tilden. We were assigned several scripts together. A radio personality, Peter didn't study screenwriting at a fancy school. He didn't come up through MTM. I don't think he spent his time going to the Robert McKee classes and obsessing about becoming a story structure expert. But Peter was funny. I mean, he could find the funny in anything. Any situation, any prop, any line in any script, Peter could see certain things, turn a phrase, express an unexpected perspective that was just hysterical. He didn't work at it. It was just him.

These are the kind of people that you often find in a sitcom room.

Day Four: The writers attend the final dress rehearsals. Sometimes, on previous days, if the script is in good enough shape, the writers might attend "blocking rehearsals" in the hope of getting an idea of how the script is playing. No matter how funny a joke may be in the Room, you really have no idea of how well it will work until you hear the actors perform it. Day Four, ideally, is when you are going to get a proper sense of the entire episode. Every conceivable effort is made to have the script completed and working by early morning Day Four. There is hell to pay if it isn't. I worked on episodes where the staff stayed up all night on Day Three to have a script in the actors' hands by the time they awoke. However, what often seems like genius when you're writing under pressure at 3:30 in the morning is not quite as brilliant when the actors read it a few hours later. One time in the middle of the night on *Major Dad*, we needed a funny line for the major—actually, we just needed a funny word: "Sure, I'll just quit my job in the Marine Corps and begin my new career as a _____." Twelve smart, talented, highly paid writers sat on the floor of Earl Pomerantz's office at Universal for well over an hour and did nothing but pitch funny occupations. Somehow, the idea of Gerald McRaney as an alligator wrestler made us laugh so hard we just had to use it. A few hours later, though, at the final run-through, it didn't seem so funny. Certainly not to Mackie—*"An alligator wrestler?"*—who wanted to know what the writers were smoking at 3:30 in the morning. Writers often continue to punch-up the script while or after watching the final run-throughs.

Day Five: Show day. The show is taped (or filmed) before a live audience. All the writers are present, almost always on the stage floor. Some even still punch-up a line or two during the performance. Show day always reminded me of theater. In fact, I always thought that the sitcom taping was to L.A. what Broadway was to New York. Our tapings were always filled with tourists from all over the country, just like a Broadway show. The whole thing feels like a party. There is a great band. There is a warm-up stand-up comedy act, followed by a high-energy introduction of the stars. Then you watch the scenes being taped (or filmed). Then you watch the same scenes over and over. Truth be told, it gets kind of boring watching the same material over and over, but the show never stops being interesting because the show, the real show, is not the material at all but the *making* of the material. When you go to a sitcom taping, what you are watching is not only the actors performing on the stage, you are watching all the people on the floor in front of the stage, the writers and producers, the director, the executives, and all the agents. More business is probably done on the floor of sitcom tapings than anywhere else in Hollywood. And as an audience member, you get to watch it all. Part populist entertainment, part cinema verité, part tourist attraction, the sitcom taping will probably shed just as much light on our civilization as the ancient theater reveals about the Greeks.

After the show the writers sleep, then two days later the whole process starts again.

⁓

As you can see, rewriting, especially as a group, is a major part of the sitcom writing process. Nearly all sitcom writers become acutely aware of this the day they turn in their first script. I know I did. As a playwright, I learned that the written word was holy. I sat through many read-throughs of my plays where actors and directors would politely, deferentially, ask permission to drop a comma or add an adjective. After my story was approved for my first TV script, I spent a week off alone writing it with the same care and love that I wrote my plays. Great attention went into every single syllable. I had friends repeatedly proof it. The script was *perfect*, ready to be shot—or so I thought. I turned it in to my bosses at the end of the day on a Friday. A few days later, they told me I did a great job, thanked me, congratulated me, and told me to join all the other writers for the script's first story session, where twelve of us proceeded to rewrite the entire script from page one. Oh, the story was pretty much left alone, and a few of my jokes stayed, I think. But we went through my precious work page by page, line by line—sometimes even word by word—and rewrote it as a group. I smiled and tried to join in, but it's hard to be funny when your beloved words are being torn apart like fresh bread at the dinner table. This was my coming-of-age week.

Earl kept the bones of my plot intact, heard everyone's best pitches for better lines and funnier jokes, and made decisive decisions about what stayed and what was changed. The result was that my script was made better—better than I had realized that it could be. And I learned not to take my work, or myself, too seriously. This was a hazard of playwriting training, one that sitcom work helped rid me of.

I saw that in TV, words are disposable, jokes can get better through the rewrite process, stories can be improved by additional perspectives, and it's never done until it's in the can (filmed). But I also saw on other days that sometimes you *do* get it right the first time, stories can be destroyed by second-guessing, and sometimes too many perspectives can be the worst thing for a script. Sometimes, it turns out, scripts work just fine on Day One, but by Day Five—when the studio, network, and actors have all chimed in, when you've heard the jokes a hundred times—the scripts simply aren't as good as they were when you started the week. A good showrunner like Earl is usually the difference between improvement and screwing the thing up, but it's still no guarantee of progress during rewrite week, because there is always a rewrite week even if the script doesn't need one. Even if a sitcom script ain't broke, it gets fixed, because that's what the staff has been hired to do and that's the tradition.

When I wrote *Major Dad*, sitcoms were king. Sure, there were the *China Beach*es, but when regular folks talked about TV, they talked about situation comedies. That's what people mainly watched. For example, during the 1988–89 season, eight out of the ten top shows were sitcoms: *The Cosby Show, Roseanne, A Different World, Cheers, The Golden Girls, Who's the Boss?, Empty Nest,* and *Anything but Love.* And *Dear John, Growing Pains, Head of the Class, Amen,* and *Night Court* weren't far behind. In addition, perhaps with the notable exception of *ALF,* which also wasn't far behind, most of these sitcoms were also pretty good. Several were great. I would even go so far as to call many of these quality shows. This would be the trend up until the mid-nineties. In the 1995–96 season, 60 percent of the top twenty highest-rated shows were sitcoms: *Seinfeld, Friends, Caroline* *in the City, The Single Guy, Home Improvement, Boston Common, Frasier, Grace Under Fire, Coach, Roseanne, The Nanny,* and *Murphy Brown.* However, as of this writing, in the 2005–2006 season, just one comedy, *Two and a Half Men,* made the Nielsen list of the top twenty shows.

What happened to sitcoms? A lot of things. But for starters, many of these shows were made by independent production companies.

Although my agency represented Earl and packaged *Major Dad,* Beth also represented the executive producer of my favorite show on television, *The Wonder Years.* At least once a month, I dropped hints that I wanted to meet him. Finally one day when I was bringing her daughter back from a day at the arcade, I pleaded with her to set up a meeting. This was something I always seemed to be doing with her, pleading. This was something that many of my friends just didn't understand. Most working writers didn't even ask their agents for things, they told their agents what they wanted. But that's not how it was with Beth. One year I gave her a holiday gift, and after thanking me she told me which store in Century City to buy next year's gift. It made perfect sense. They had stuff she liked and at good prices. Pushy but pragmatic, she was born to be an agent.

The other thing that was amazing about Beth was that nearly all her other clients felt the same way (perhaps with the notable exception of *ER* executive producer Lydia Woodward, who, previously an agent herself, didn't take shit from Beth). She finally did set up the meeting for me with the

Wonder Years executive producer, Bob Brush, who was just as scared of her as I was. Even though he had started his career writing for *Captain Kangaroo* and chain-smoked Nows, he constantly wore his sunglasses indoors and had a Keith Richards troubled cool about him. So swapping stories about Beth not only made me like him, it made me feel a little less like a wuss.

By this point in my career I was starting to realize that these meet 'n' greets were about more than my choice of shirt and a wide-eyed display of awe at both Los Angeles and the work of the person who was meeting and greeting me. I was now being interviewed for staff positions. So not only did people want to make sure they could tolerate me for long periods of time, they wanted to make sure that I could actually contribute something of use to a writing staff. Now, trying to predetermine this in a meeting is pretty much like interviewing someone you just met to go into a barroom brawl with you. Despite what they say, you have no idea what they're gonna do when the chips are down. All you can do is look for the most qualified person who, even more importantly, you think you can trust.

The more I went on these meetings, the more I recognized a similar look in showrunners' eyes, even hugely successful writer-producers who I greatly admired. They were all trying to figure out what I'd do on the battlefield. Would I help take the hill, pee my pants, or shoot them in the back? With some nudging from Beth, I quickly picked up that my task in these staff meet 'n' greets was to strike a tone somewhere between irreverence and deference. *Trust me, I have my own way of writing, but my secret dream is to make it*

just like yours. Truth be told, I'm edgy, but manageable.
The idea was to be cool, but never cooler than the meeter-
greeter.

I got an offer to write a freelance script as a staff audition.
I passed the audition and got the job.

EIGHT

Life and Times of a Story Editor

*"The only way to change people's minds
is with consistency."*

—JACK WELCH

"Imitation is the sincerest form of television."

—FRED ALLEN

I n 1988, the year I graduated from school, I earned $40,577. In 1989, I earned $152,425. In 1990, at age twenty-six, I earned $275,692. That year, like many other working TV writers had done, I met with Encino CPA Barry Entous and formed a California corporation. It was called Pet Rock Productions, because when I was a kid I always carried a rock with me. My friends thought I was, you know, quirky, eccentric, because they didn't have terms like OCD in the mid-seventies in Georgia.

At a party thrown by a Carnegie alum, I met a very nice girl who was working as a researcher on *China Beach*. Although she had an undergraduate degree from MIT, she decided what she really wanted to do was write plays. So she went to grad school at UC Davis and studied the craft. After also meeting an alum of that school, Carol Flint, who was a writer on *China Beach*, she had come to the same conclusion that I had, that TV was where it was at for writers. So now she was trying to break into it. We found we had a lot in common, and we were pretty much living together within a few days. It wasn't long, however, before my tiny apartment was too small for the two of us—all our books alone took up half the place—and we started looking at houses.

In the spring of 1990, I bought a 1,160-square-foot, two-bedroom, one-and-a-half-bath house in Mar Vista for $440,000, and my girlfriend and I moved into it together. It was small and old, but it had a pool, and if you stood on your tiptoes in the westside yard, you could make out the Pacific Ocean. I put a hot tub in a corner of the backyard and got a golden retriever named Maggie. I bought a Mazda Miata, one of the first ones in this country, which was a very big deal in Los Angeles. A new Ghurka No. 5 shoulder bag, in khaki canvas, was almost always on the front seat. Although many of my home furnishings came from IKEA and all the requisite artsy-ironic pictures came from Z Gallerie, I indulged in the dream entertainment system with the big-screen TV, laser-disc player, and KEF surround-sound speakers. Since I used this primarily for business-related purposes, my corporation actually owned it. I had frequent pool parties where Mrs. Gooch's filet mignon and fresh corn from Gelson's were barbecued and served to a decidedly under-thirty industry crowd. The writing staffs of numerous prime-time shows were always well represented. Someone would tell a joke, next week it would be on a sitcom. Someone would tell a story, next month a drama episode about it would be aired. The rest of the guests were young writers who were trying to break in, researchers and assistants, several of whom would end up creating and running their own shows and being future multimillionaires. Whenever someone had a show on the air, we would all gather around the TV, watch together, and celebrate. Except for the polo shirts my mother sent me, my clothes came mainly from The Gap and Banana Republic, although I did have to buy a tux—a Mani, the same one that Tom Hanks wore in *Joe Versus the Volcano*—and a suit, an Armani, blue, double-breasted. I wore the former to industry award events and the latter on the high holidays, which were spent at the Synagogue For The Performing Arts, a growing industry temple where the rabbi was a celebrity, the cantor had been Rodney Dangerfield's opening act, and agents trolled for new clients during the Torah portion. I studied karate at the dojo behind Sports Club/LA, the same place Nicole Brown Simpson and the kids trained. I met friends for brunch at Patrick's Roadhouse and for late-night chicken and waffles at Roscoe's. I took my girlfriend to Michaels, Maple Drive, Chinois on Main, Granita, Chasen's, and 72 Market Street (may the latter three RIP). There were spur-of-the-moment weekend trips. Mud baths at Two Bunch Palms. Swim-up blackjack at the Trop. Tubs of iced Coronitas on the beach in Huatulco. And mostly, there was the work. Developing, writing, and producing a new television episode every single week, forty-five weeks a year. I lived every minute with a sense that I had made it to the absolute center of the world, that there were truly no limits, that anything was possible. I had every reason to believe this, since all the evidence regularly pointed out that this was, in fact, true. Wells's words from that CMU lecture frequently resonated in my ears. *Three hundred people making a product for 300 million.*

⁓

The Wonder Years writers' offices were in a condo complex in a questionable residential neighborhood in Culver City. It was one of those dumps you see all over L.A., three two-bedroom units upstairs over an open garage area below, the kind of place you see on the news that pancakes after an earthquake. At the Universal factory, even as a baby writer, I had my own office in a nice building near the commissary. Scott Baio was in the office next to me. *Hey, Chachi, what you working on, buddy?* I had all that classic Universal office furniture. I had a union secretary named Ellen who took care of me. If you saw me sitting in there, you'd think I was a kid visiting his father the insurance executive. So to leave my house and drive to a bedroom in a condo every day was bizarre. On the other hand, it was also great fun.

Story editor Eric Gilliland (future showrunner of *Roseanne*) had the bedroom across the hall; story editors Mark Perry (future showrunner of *One Tree Hill*) and Mark Levin (future showrunner of *Earth 2*) were down the hall in their bedrooms; two assistants, Rita Hsiao (future writer, *Toy Story 2*) and Jeff King (future writer, *Josiah's Canon*), worked in the living room; and the kitchen area was sort of a communal break room. It's tempting to describe our office as a locker room, but that wouldn't really be accurate. It was more like summer camp. I brought Maggie, my paper-training puppy, into the office every day. Levin decided he would take up the saxophone, which he frequently played. There were wrestling matches in the living room, practical jokes played in each other's office-bedrooms, and NERF basketball was a way of life. Bob Brush's office was over the set, which was in a warehouse in another part of Culver City, so we were pretty much on our own except for the occasional story meetings. Sometimes we worked one-on-one with him to develop an outline that one of the writers would then write. Sometimes we worked with Jill Gordon, the coexecutive producer/big sister, to flesh out a story. The process was always changing, but it was usually extremely laid-back. Unlike sitcoms where the form mandates regular group writing, in a film show like *The Wonder Years*, pretty much anything goes. And it did.

The Wonder Years was part of a unique genre that was often called a "dramedy." In the late eighties, a lot of these kinds of shows appeared, like *Slap Maxwell*, *The Days and Nights of Molly Dodd*, *Frank's Place*, and *Hooperman*. Borrowing elements from both sitcom and one-hour, these were half-hour, single-camera shows shot on film. Although they reached their height of popularity during this time, the idea of telling a story without regard for whether or not the form demanded comedy or tragedy was not new to television. *Room 222*, the show Allan Burns and James Brooks worked on before *Mary Tyler Moore*, was one of the first. *M*A*S*H* was another. *Moonlighting* is also considered to be one. Most dramedies were very funny. Some were even written with the classic set-up/punch-line rhythm that we used on *Major Dad*. This was partially because of how they were marketed and partially because so many sitcom writers were working on them. But shows of this hybrid form also had dramatic story lines and emotional moments akin to what one would find on the best dramas, and because of the lack of contrivances like the laugh track, dramedies did not feel hokey.

The dramedy form lent itself perfectly to the kind of closed-ended sitcom-like stories the show was conceived to tell. I think this material in this form is one of the reasons the show worked so well. I also think timing had a lot to do with it. The show just clicked with its audience, both kids and their baby-boomer parents. It was the perfect time for this show. Not all TV series have the good fortune to be born at the right time. Another reason the show was so successful was because of the opportunities afforded by the narration. Even if we had a huge problem with a story in an episode after it was filmed, we could almost always get it to work in postproduction. If a scene was off, we would simply rewrite the voice-over, have Daniel Stern quickly rerecord the narrative, play "The Long and Winding Road" over it and a shot of Kevin and Paul walking home at sunset, and we had people in tears. But probably the greatest single reason the show worked as an ongoing series is because of the tone in our offices. Somehow that summer camp sensibility, which included a lot of discussion about growing up, made its way onto the page and onto the screen. I would see this sort of thing, the spirit of the writer's office ultimately defining a series, for better or worse, again and again.

In the end, *The Wonder Years* worked for a million reasons that all came together just right—it was a case of catching that proverbial lightning in a bottle. I will never forget the experience of sitting on a train and listening to the people next to me talking about how much they loved last night's episode of the show, talking about how much it was just like something that had happened to them when they were kids. It was an episode that I had written. Being a professional, I played it cool and didn't tell them that it was mine . . . for at least like two minutes.

While I was working on *The Wonder Years*, *The New York Times* interviewed me for a feature story about TV writers. Above a huge picture of me in the Arts & Entertainment section was the headline—SITCOM WRITING: RICHES PLUS RESPECTABILITY. The article, published on August 5, 1990, was one of the first major exposés about the explosion in the global television industry and how young people were suddenly flocking to L.A. to write TV. The story focused on "the link between comedy and money that the media has seized upon: it is possible for a twenty-four-year-old television story editor to make nearly $200,000 a year, and that's just for starters." The story was really the first harbinger, the first public one at least, of the new Hollywood that was coming.

Astonishingly, up until that time, very few people really understood what I did. My father flew out to L.A. on several occasions just to try to get his head around it. I still think he came out just to make sure I wasn't dealing drugs. "They pay you for making up stories all day?" Some people actually thought that the actors just made up their lines. Most people I met thought a story editor was a film editor. "I thought you wanted to write, maybe you'll get lucky someday," people would say to me. Moreover, no one, especially my family, seemed to believe what I was earning. What TV writers were paid was, quite literally, an inside secret. There was this tacit sense that we weren't supposed to make a big deal about it. After the article, it seemed that the floodgates opened. Over the next few years, writers began to pour into Los Angeles. Ivy League schools in particular began to send their graduates to Hollywood. Students from Harvard, Princeton, and Yale all found highly organized West Coast alumni clans that helped them get footholds in the television business. Soon, the "Princeton Mafia" or the "Harvard Hasty Pudding Clan" made up entire TV staffs. The most educated, or at least the most expensively educated, young people in the world started flocking to Hollywood. And many of them not only found work very quickly, they found themselves at the center of a decade-long seller's market for TV writers. The figures that were quoted in that 1990 article were nothing compared to what writers would be earning ten years later.

Just a few months before the article came out, I got my first sense that the winds of change were beginning to blow. An older writer who had become a friend and taken me under his wing had advised me to put together a "five-year plan." He said he had done it and it helped him visualize his future and stay on track. I did mine. I wrote that I hoped to get an over-all development deal with a studio. Instead of a deal that is linked strictly to a series in production, this is a deal where a studio locks up a writer for several years. The writer might provide services for existing shows or the writer might develop new shows. When I showed it to him, he said everything looked good except one thing. He said he didn't believe in development deals because although they often paid well, they tied your hands creatively. They kept you from working for other studios. Essentially, he said, they were a form of selling out. He said he would never take one. A few weeks later, he signed an overall development deal with a major studio. It was huge. Really huge. He purchased a $2.3 million house, a mansion, really, that I helped him move into. At that point it was the biggest house I'd ever seen before in my life. There were, I don't know, seven, maybe eight bedrooms. A wood-paneled office. A sweeping staircase like something out of Tara. A kitchen with appliances I didn't even recognize. A spectacular pool. And a view of the 405 and the entire Valley off in the distance. It was breathtaking. I remember hearing that an 80 percent mortgage at about 12 percent (the going superjumbo thirty-year rate) would bring the monthly payment to around $19,000. That's nearly a quarter of a million dollars a year for a house payment. And he bandied these numbers about as though they were chump change. As much as it blew me away at the time, the fact is, when compared to what the studio was paying him, and what the studio was making off his work, and what the studio might make off the work he might do, those numbers *were* chump change.

Now, this was confusing to me. A few years earlier Wells had told me that he was offered six hundred grand to work on a P.I. series, *Ohara*, I think it was, but he took substantially less to work on new high-brow series that he really loved set on an army base in Vietnam. And there was Milch and the writers at MTM. Money was not the main reason these guys were writing. But something was changing in the nineties. Part of it was the amount of money being offered. Part was the speed with which it was being offered. Part of it was the experience level of the writers to whom it was being offered. Television was not necessarily getting better; it was getting more lucrative. The composite effect of all this, when combined with the palpable changes taking place in the industry, made me smile a little every time a writer after that point told me what he would never do.

⁓

In 1991, I went to work on *Sisters* as an executive story consultant, another step up in credit and pay from my previous position. At this point, I was no longer just courted by executives, now the agents started. Yes, I already had representation, but along with competing for the same new talent, agencies often steal each other's working clients.

Now, entire teams from Creative Arts Agency would crowd into my small office on the Warner Brothers lot. I was taken to frequent lunches and dinners in restaurants that food critics spoke about in hushed terms, restaurants my friends and family back home were reading about. I felt loved. I felt well fed. I felt guilty. Even though I hadn't been doing this very long, I had been doing it long enough to know that Beth wouldn't be crazy about me dining with other agents, which is why I wanted to tell her.

After one obnoxiously expensive meal at the Hotel Bel-Air with an agent who I later heard was well known for poaching other agents' clients, like a sheepish child, I called to let her know it was "just lunch." Her response—and I must confess, I can still hardly believe that this is what she said, but this is what she said—was: "You tell [agent] that if he doesn't stay away from you I will nail his knees into the ground with railroad spikes." I did not dine with other agents again. Well . . . actually, I did one more time, and that didn't turn out so well. I'll get to that shortly.

Although *Sisters* didn't win snazzy statues like my previous series, it was clear to me very quickly that one-hour dramas were my favorite genre. I knew this when I saw it snow for the first time in L.A. It was in September—probably the hottest month in L.A. because the Santa Anas really kick up—in Burbank on the Warner Brothers backlot. I walked from the *Sisters* writers' offices to the set—one of those suburban streets you've seen a million times in movies and TV shows—and it was covered in fake snow. Props guys in shorts were dumping heavy canvas bags of the white stuff in front of several massive ten-foot-high fans, which were blowing it all over the place. And those poor actors—Swoosie Kurtz and Sela Ward—standing in the middle of it all, wearing hats, gloves, and heavy winter jackets, sweating their asses off and pretending to shiver every time they heard—"Action!"

You never got to do this kind of storytelling in sitcoms. To the contrary, you were literally writing to the existing sets. As a film show, we had more leeway with *The Wonder Years*. There's a certain magic you always felt walking to a location shoot at midnight. We shot a lot of the exteriors on *The Wonder Years* in Burbank Hills, and even if you parked blocks away, you always knew where the cast and crew were working because of the lighting. There was always that one 20,000-watt Fresnel up on a crane, creating a moonlight effect on the constantly wet-down pavement. But one-hour dramas, even pure character-driven ones like *Sisters*, had the budget and the resources of an entire backlot, which allowed you to write anything from a winter day in Chicago to a huge rally at city hall to a house fire. It was great.

When I worked on *Sisters* I was one of five writers. Two were executive producers Ron Cowan and Dan Lipman, a writing team that also lived together. And the other two were executive script consultants (a small step above story editors) and also a team, Chris Keyser and Amy Lippmann. Writing teams are very common on TV staffs. Many are married or live together. Many writers feel they can be more productive and more marketable with a partner. The perceived advantage for a show is that they get two voices for the price of one. On the other hand, sometimes shows don't want too many voices. And sometimes, one voice is working and the other is not. In comedy, where group writing is the norm, teams assimilate easily. In one-hour, where the episodes have more authorship, the sum of the two voices is the relevant factor. In half-hour, many teams will work together, one at the computer, one pacing, and write the entire script as one. In one-hour, most partners divide up the script, working on different scenes or different acts. Some one-hour partners even split up a script according to the type of scene. I started to notice that some writing partnerships were great, especially the ones where one partner's strengths made up for the other's weaknesses, and vice versa. But I also worked with writing teams who brought their personal lives, including problems they were having with each other at home, into the Room. Sometimes these conflicts actually led to usable stories. But more often they didn't.

The five of us almost always broke story together on *Sisters*. We'd hang out in the EP's office and just yak. On the wall, as in nearly all one-hour Rooms, were two dry-erase boards. These tracked the arcs of the characters—what happens to them, their emotional growth—through the season, as well as the status of the episodes, such as which writers are working on them and what stage the episodes are in. Some of our story sessions focused on the character arcs through the course of several episodes. Some of our sessions resulted in a loose story that would be assigned to me, Chris and Amy, or Ron and Dan. When a story was assigned, the writer of writers would then break out the beats of the story alone and post these on a dry-erase board. I had one in my office.

The process of breaking out a story this way is called "boarding." It helps the writers visualize how an entire episode will play. The classic way to do this is to draw three vertical lines down the board from top to bottom, equidistant apart. This creates four columns, one for each act. In each column you write a line or two explaining what each scene will be. These scenes are numbered. Each act usually has about six scenes (some shows have five per act, some as many as ten, depending on pace and style), so the average script usually has about twenty-four primary scenes.

Most one-hour dramas have an A-story, a B-story, and a C-story. The A-story, as the name implies, is the main narrative of the episode. It has the most drive and its scenes typically bookend the acts. If a show has a "teaser," the first scene in an episode that comes before the credit—and most one-hours today do because of the mandated imperative to quickly hook an audience—a scene from the A-story usually leads off. The B-story is the secondary or supporting story line, which can stand alone or intertwine with the A-story. The C-story is a runner, a few skeletal scenes, often created for no other reason than to give the cast members who are not in the A or the B something to do (not only to keep them involved and happy or to sometimes give them requested time off, but also to justify their episodic rate for the week). I found that I liked episodes where the story lines all resonate off each other or inform each other. I liked episodes where even if characters do not interact across story lines, we, the audience, see their parallel or related development, which will pay off when they do come together. And I liked episodes where even if the story lines are entirely separate from each other, the A, B, and C are still thematically linked. There is plenty of good one-hour TV where none of this occurs, but for my taste simply plugging arbitrary story lines into an episode, like ordering from a Chinese food menu—one from column A, one from column B—feels, well, arbitrary. In very broad strokes, in most one-hours, the A-story accounts for about twelve scenes, the B-story for about eight, and the C-story for maybe four.

After boarding an episode, it would be fleshed out into an outline and then scripted. I always felt that the two young script consultants, Chris and Amy, wrote the best episodes of the show. Curiously, even though they did not create it, they seemed to nail the voice of the show. Before joining the staff, they had previously written an episode for *L.A. Law*. However, David Kelly, who was running the show at the time, told them he was not going to put them on staff because he would just end up rewriting them. He encouraged them to go find a show where they could learn and actually see their work produced. Although they were bummed about this initially, it turned out to be excellent advice. In 1994, they left *Sisters* to create and run their own show, *Party of Five*, for the fledgling Fox network.

Although there were only three entities writing the show,

we also had a nonwriting executive producer on staff, a highly experienced producer who had also served in this capacity on several popular series during the 1980s. Just as the name suggests, the idea is to attach someone with producerial experience to a show, ideally to free up time for the writing producers to spend more time writing. As we will later see, throughout the nineties, nonwriting EPs became frequent additions to TV shows, because when executives left a job at a network, they were given something called a "POD" or producer overall deal, which was not only a way to compensate executives who were squeezed out, but also a way for the network to exercise control over a show.

Over the coming years I would work with several nonwriting producers who were great additions to staffs, usually when there was a clear demarcation of duties. However, this was not always the case. Often, making an executive who does not write an executive producer in a writer's medium can be like putting a military officer who doesn't read music in charge of a symphony.

Although most nonwriting executive producers, in fact, see their jobs as conductors, and see their compensation as payment for providing such services, I think it is important to point out that not all do.

On one of the shows on which I worked, after I finished developing a story with the other writers, creating an outline and then writing two drafts of an episode, the nonwriting executive producer approached me privately and told me that he wanted to put his name on my script. He smiled and said not to worry, he would pay me back the money he received for his portion of the script fee. The residuals we would sort out later.

I didn't get it. It sounded like he was saying that he wanted me to agree to have him share the "written by" credit or maybe to give him the "story by" part. He tried several times to explain to me what he was telling me to do but, I swear, I just couldn't understand. So he had to spell it out. He explained to me that he took a credit or two every year or so on scripts, so that he could qualify for the Writers' Guild health insurance.

I had never encountered anything like this before. I finally understood and said no. Maybe it wasn't the smartest thing to do politically, and I was learning that to survive on a staff you had to think about this stuff. But it sure felt good.

⁓

Sisters did not pick up my option for the following season. They called my agent and told her it just wasn't a good fit.

Getting fired sucks. For one thing, the same buzz-driven momentum that moves you forward, changes direction at the drop of a hat. But aside from that, it hurts. You see, the trouble with all the hoopla and fuss that everyone makes about you is that you start to believe it. Just like the agents and execs who define you by the bullet points distilled from the buzz, you start to do the same to yourself. And when you buy into the positive stuff, you have to likewise buy into the not so positive. I got the news weeks before my contract expired, meaning I didn't have to keep coming in but I still got paid. I was earning $5,500 a week at that point just for my staff work, and I can tell you that despite popular belief, there is little joy in collecting money when you're not doing something to earn it.

There was also, however, a deep sense of relief. When they told Beth it wasn't "a good fit" they were being polite. Let me give you an example. In a scene that we were working on in the story room, Alex (played by Swoosie Kurtz) had just installed a security system in her home. The writing executive producers wanted the alarm to go off in the middle of the night, Alex to jump out of bed, pull a gun, and almost shoot her daughter, Reed (Ashley Judd). And right before the accidental shooting took place, they wanted the recorded alarm to not only scream "Intruder! Intruder!," they also wanted it to say things like, "Nice hair, sweetie," and "Do something!" when Alex walked by. Well, I couldn't get on board with this. I couldn't understand how you could expect the audience to stay in the moment when you not only had a comedic beat, but you completely broke reality. This was a realistic drama. You can't just one day decide to start breaking the fourth wall. *"How could you have a recorded security system talk to a character? That's not real!"* I said in a variety of different ways. Even though my bosses loved it and simply could not stop laughing at how cute it was, I just couldn't let it go. It seemed so clear-cut to me. I argued this and argued this simply because, at the time, honestly, this one little moment on a modestly rated TV show seemed to me like the absolute most important thing in the world.

After getting fired, I watched the show and, naturally, there it was, the security system talking to the character:

> *Panic Master:* Code Red! Code Red! Intruder outside master bedroom! *Do something!*
>
> *(Alex shoots the security alarm a look and then talks to it.)*
>
> *Alex:* I'm trying to!

139

Yeah, it was cute, but like I thought, it was also silly and completely defused the tension in the scene. But you know what? The show did not, in fact, fall apart. The show wasn't canceled. Viewers didn't write in complaining. Nobody talked about it in the trades. I began to realize that the only way to have a career writing TV is to know when to shut up.

Beth sent me on a variety of meetings. To be honest, a twenty-nine-year-old with a bunch of money in the bank doesn't pull off that wide-eyed "I'll kill to work here" enthusiasm very well unless it's for a show for which he really felt that way. I did not have meetings with any of the shows I felt that way about for the 1992–93 season.

In a meet 'n' greet with *The Fresh Prince of Bel-Air*, I spent much of the time interviewing Winnie Hervey, the EP, about the working hours and conditions. Although Beth said I was a shoo-in for the gig, I did not get an offer.

While I was trying to figure out what I would do the following season, late in the afternoon of April 29, 1992, a man named Reginald Denny was pulled out of his truck at the intersection of Florence and Normandie and hit with a brick. Evidently, a lot of people in the city were very upset about the verdict that came out that day in the Rodney King trial. But I didn't notice, because not only was I consumed with life as a TV writer, I was also breaking up with my girlfriend. I heard about the beating on the radio of the U-Haul that we'd just rented so that we could move her out of the house. While the city literally burned around us that night, with LAPD and the National Guard using the Santa Monica Airport right behind my house as a staging area, we had our big breakup.

As I said, she was very nice. A kind of backslapping pal, she was a great friend to a lot of people, including me. But she was extremely frustrated. More than anything in the world, and I mean that quite literally, more than anything she wanted to be a TV writer, and it was not going real well. I would come home from a shitty fifteen-hour day on *Sisters* and she would want me to read and help her with her spec scripts, which I did. But, frankly, they never quite knocked my socks off. I didn't *respond*. Still, I introduced her to William Morris, who signed her and represented her as a one-hour drama writer. This did not go well. She wrote a script for a Bochco show; this did not go well. Went on pitch meetings; they also did not go well. I figured this had to be more than just bad momentum. One day when she came home nearly in tears because she was so nervous during a pitch that she spilled Diet Dr Pepper all over the leg of the executive producer of *Star Trek: The Next Generation*, I thought to myself, for Christ's sake, get a job, stop hanging out by the pool, and go be a dental hygienist or something!

Well, she did get a job. I did not work in television that season, but she did. Days after splitting up, she went on the staff of a new sitcom. And they loved her. Everyone *loved* her. She was a star. Within a year she was a coproducer on a hit series, and a year later a coexecutive producer on another hit series. The next year she *cocreated and ran* a hit series. The year after that, she cocreated and ran another even more successful show, one of the best and biggest hits of the decade, *Dharma & Greg*. She quickly became one of the best and most sought-after writer-producers in television.

As you might imagine, I did some serious soul-searching.

I thought a lot about what had happened since I arrived in town. Unlike other occupations where you stay with the same company for thirty years and eventually get a gold watch, writers move around a lot in TV. Writers frequently leave or get kicked off one show and move on to another. I started to think of a TV writing career as like being in a large fraternity party and frequently moving from room to room. Every room has its own little mini party, with new people and new material. In addition, the overall career span is very short for most TV writers. The WGA estimates that in an average season 20 percent of the entire workforce turns over as established writers leave the business and new writers join. But I started to think that maybe with me, something was going on that was more than just the regular rhythms of the business.

Until 1992, I kept getting jobs, great jobs. And while momentum and good fortune were certainly responsible for giving me many of those shots, I was succeeding on my own skills when I took them. I had *written* my way onto both *The Wonder Years* and *Sisters*; both gave me audition scripts before putting me onto their staffs. And my first staff scripts were very well received. Not wanting to lose me, *The Wonder Years* even exercised their option on me for two years when they got their midseason pickup. So the decision to leave before that contract was up was ultimately mine. Beth felt I should only work someplace where I could be a runaway success, and Bob wasn't as enthusiastic about my later scripts as he was about my first ones, and it was pretty much the same story on *Sisters*. I began to realize there was a pattern here.

I was capable of doing the writing. The issue, I think, was

that I hadn't quite figured out the balance between the writing and the living, the writing and the being a writer. Part of this was all the distraction coming from the buzz and the money. In truth, I had a very large line of credit at several establishments in Vegas, which I visited quite often, sometimes just for the afternoon. Why not, I thought. Milch spent half his life at the track and much of it at the craps table. But of course, I was no David Milch. I was just a schmuck from Atlanta trying to figure out not so much how to write TV, but how to be a TV writer.

And part of this was an inability to fully appreciate that being a TV writer meant working on a TV staff, which, as it turned out, was more of a job than I fully understood. I left the windowless offices at Ogilvy & Mather because I wanted to write, not work. Well, as it turned out, writing on a TV staff was in fact not just fun and games and writing cool stuff, it was also tolerating and negotiating—knowing when to shut up. At times, it was being rewritten. And at times, it was getting an assignment you didn't love and finding a way to love it. Writing TV on staff was often, in fact, work.

The truth is, when you took away all the trappings, I was still just a kid behaving as such. Mine was not an uncommon story during this period in Hollywood. What I would realize over the next two years is that if I was gonna work in this rapidly changing business—hell, if I was gonna have a *life*—I would have to change too.

NINE

The Hollywood Gold Rush

"There are many ways to talk about television. But in a 'business' perspective, let's be realistic: basically, our job is to help Coca-Cola sell its product. To make the advertising message well received, the audience's brain must be available. Our shows are here to make the brain available, to entertain it, to relax it, to prepare it between two messages. What we're selling to Coca-Cola is available human brain time. Nothing is as difficult as getting this availability."

—PATRICK LE LAY, CEO OF TF1, THE MAIN FRENCH TV CHANNEL

f this were a movie, this is that point in the second act when you'd see a montage, a series of intercuts between things that were happening to me and things that were happening to the industry, as both progressed. Here is the prose version of that.

Most people living in L.A. between 1992 and 1994 felt a certain Job-like quality about their lives. It was if the universe was challenging us, testing our resolve to stay. On February 10, 1992, a "100-year storm" swamped the 101, killed eight people, and caused over $150 million in damage. A couple months after the April 1992 riots—which killed fifty-four and caused over a billion dollars in damage—on June 28, 1992, at

4:47 A.M. the 7.3 Landers earthquake rocked the city. It was followed a few hours later by the 6.4 Big Bear quake. In January 1993 another torrential storm and subsequent flood again caused more than $150 million in damage. In October 1993, the Malibu fires caused more than a billion dollars in damage, followed by related floods and mudslides of near biblical proportion. And at 4:30 A.M. on January 17, 1994, the Big One hit. The 6.7 Northridge earthquake was so powerful it literally knocked me out of my bed. Smelling like a heavy dirty rug that had been beaten hard for a good long time, the broken city shook and growled with aftershocks for weeks. The quake killed sixty-one people and caused over $42 billion in damage. And all of this took place in the middle of a massive recession, partly caused by the collapse of the region's aerospace industry, that saw more than a half million people leave metro Los Angeles. Add to this the daily perils of life in L.A.—smog, traffic, killer bees, and regular insanity like O.J.'s June 17, 1994, slow-speed chase—and life in L.A. during this time felt like some sort of Darwinian rite of survival.

However, if this was indeed some sort of test or rite, I passed. I knew a lot of young writers and industry folks who joined the other half a million, threw up their hands and got the hell out of Dodge. But I met even more young writers who were pouring into the wanton city during this time. Between 1993 and 1998 the Writers Guild admitted 3,077 new members, the vast majority of whom went to work in television. You see, despite the worst that nature could conjure, and despite whatever personal reasons were driving us, we stayed in and came to L.A. mainly because there was never a more exciting time to be a television writer. What can only be described as a modern-day gold rush was now under way, and we were at the epicenter of it.

⁓

Right after the 1988 strike redefined the role of the writer, two events took place that redefined the entire industry: the Berlin Wall came down and the satellites went up. The opening of foreign markets, combined with numerous new ways to deliver TV to those markets, spearheaded the explosion. The sudden collapse of the Soviet Union in the early nineties had an unforeseen and radical effect on the TV industry. Overnight, privately owned TV stations replaced state-owned monopolies in places like Russia, Israel, Malaysia, Greece, Finland, Norway, and all the former Soviet satellites in Eastern Europe. Huge, global satellite networks popped up and started broadcasting. Cable companies laid millions of miles of coax all around the planet. Even the most remote locations in the most far-off countries could now receive television. And there was only one kind they wanted—American.

Hollywood syndicators—companies that represent TV shows—began to actively court these previously closed markets. And representatives from these new stations flocked to trade shows like NATPE (National Association of Television Program Executives) and MIPCOM in Cannes in search of American programming. By the mid-nineties, entertainment became this nation's second-largest global export, surpassing traditional factory and agricultural products. By 1996, international sales of U.S. entertainment products would total $60.2 billion, and television made up nearly half of that. In that same year there were 1.4 billion TV sets around the

THE HOLLYWOOD GOLD RUSH

planet, three times as many as there had been just sixteen years earlier. The entire world suddenly had an insatiable appetite for American television.

And just as this explosion took place in the foreign markets, the domestic market started heating up as well. In 1972, HBO had launched the first pay cable network service. First using underground cable and later satellites to deliver the signal, HBO provided paying viewers with entertainment content. In 1976, entrepreneur Ted Turner broadcast his local Atlanta UHF station, WTCG, Channel 17, all across the country on RCA's Satcom 1 satellite, creating a basic cable channel. Turner's station was relaunched in 1979 as WTBS, the first so-called superstation. In 1987, Rubert Murdoch launched an entire fourth network, Fox. By the early nineties, there were hundreds of new channels and, like the foreign stations, they all needed content: TV shows.

In addition, scores of new local stations, many not affiliated with a broadcast network, also popped up in this country, and they were also in need of programming. And those local stations who *were* network affiliates still needed to fill their non-network timeslots. Suddenly, TV shows became one of the hottest goods around.

Two venues in particular took off like never before: basic cable and free television. *The Wonder Years* sold into basic cable when Nickelodeon purchased it in the mid-nineties, right about when the prices started to go through the roof. Fox Cable Networks paid $400,000 an episode for *Dharma & Greg*. Lifetime paid just over $600,000 an episode for *Party of Five*. TNT paid more than $800,000 an episode for *ER*. TBS paid $1.15 million an episode for *Seinfeld*. On average, a standard hit show started earning about $100 million dollars for its production company in basic cable. Since this is the range in which most shows are deficit-financed, a strong basic cable sale can help a production company break even on its investment. All reuses of the series after that puts it in the black.

But the real money is in "off-network syndication" on free television. Simply put, syndication is the sale of a television program to multiple television stations without using a broadcast network for delivery. For example, *M*A*S*H* is no longer broadcast on CBS, but it is still syndicated in local markets all over the country. Twenty years after it was made, the series still makes millions of dollars for its original producer. (Some shows are produced for "first-run syndication," like *Oprah* or *Earth: Final Conflict*. These shows were broadcast for the first time in syndication and sold to individual local markets, not mass broadcast on a major network, like ABC. Though some can be very profitable, like *Baywatch*, first-run syndies still don't make the kind of money that off-net syndicated shows, like *Everybody Loves Raymond* or *Friends* do. Some shows can also be "off first-run," like Paramount's *Star Trek* franchise. This means that after they initially air in first-run syndication, the episodes are further syndicated around the country.) Off-net syndicated programming can take many forms. Some shows are "strips" that run every day. Others run once a week. Some deals include "barter" rights, in which the syndicators get a portion of the ad revenue generated by the local stations. Syndication deals allow shows to be exhibited for a set period of time, known as a cycle. After the cycle is up, the deals must be renegotiated. Many popular shows are picked up for numerous syndication cycles generating enormous wealth for the companies that made them years earlier. And the small stations share in the wealth through the enormous advertising revenues garnered by rerunning these hits.

Seinfeld is a good example of this newfound wealth that poured into Hollywood through off-net syndication. In 1998, the syndicator, Sony Pictures Television, sold the series to all the Fox local stations in nineteen major urban markets in the country. Each local station paid about $480,000 per episode for the right to air the series. There are 151 produced episodes of *Seinfeld* available. This means that the show brought in more than $1.4 billion in revenues, shared by the studio and profit participants, such as Jerry Seinfeld and Larry David. (Larry David, by the way, reportedly earned more than $200 million for his stake in the show.) But that was just the first major cycle. In the beginning of 2004, every one of those nineteen local stations renewed its license fee for the show, guaranteeing that *Seinfeld* will be seen all over the country through March 2011. The second cycle will generate about the same amount of money as the first, plus additional revenue for barter advertising. And this is *on top* of whatever the show also earns in basic cable. So, in the end, *Seinfeld* could end up being worth well over *$3 billion*. Not bad for a television show about nothing. The promise of this kind of money coming from something as intangible as an idea in Larry David's head drove entire companies to near madness.

From 1992 to 1994, trying to exercise greater control of my life, I took a bunch of interesting and eclectic assignments. (Okay, some more odd than interesting.) Instead of working on staff, I freelanced numerous TV episodes, a few of which I have managed to keep off Internet Movie Database. I wrote several video games. I developed an Internet series for Paramount Digital Entertainment. I went on the road with Yakov Smirnoff, the Russian comic, and helped turn his act into a sitcom. My time writing *What a Country* material in Laughlin, Nevada, is a subject for another book.

Some people take up things like skydiving when they go through "a period of growth." I took Judy Carter's famous stand-up class, which required me not only to perform my act at venues such as the lounge of a Holiday Inn in Granada Hills, but culminated in ten minutes at the Improv. The skydiving would've been much less frightening.

After ending up in a fleabag room off Hollywood Boulevard, penniless and in deep trouble, Delbert realized that he was an alcoholic. I attended some meetings with him where people discuss such things. The Beverly Hills men's meetings were especially memorable. I've never seen so much cigarette smoking and cookie eating in my life. Huge celebrities, who I cannot name, joined guys like Delbert telling tales of drug and alcohol abuse that were mind-boggling. I firmly believe there were people in attendance for no other reason than to hear some of these stories. And I know there were several agents in the room who were there only to scam clients. As often happens between twelve-steppers and their former friends, Delbert and I stopped spending a lot of time together.

In 1994, I fell in love with the girl who I would marry. Leaving my house and my pool, my soon-to-be fiancée, Elizabeth, our dog, Maggie, and I rented a cozy house on 25th Street between Pico and Pearl in Santa Monica. It was, for lack of more specific words, a magical place.

Under the palms and jacaranda trees in the backyard, there was a sprawling, well-tended garden replete with grapevines, seasonal greens, and a million different varieties of heritage vegetables. We dined out there year-round, lawn picnics during the day, candlelit suppers at an ancient wooden table at night. Most notably, the house had a guest suite with its own entrance downstairs, which became my office. Immediately upon moving in, I began to focus intensely on my writing and I was soon quite prolific. After numerous freelance assignments, I eventually wrote new spec scripts and a screenplay.

One of my gigs was to cowrite a pilot for Paramount and ABC with a tough but gracious writer named Michael Piller (cocreator of *Star Trek: Voyager, Star Trek: Deep Space Nine,* and *The Dead Zone*). Although ABC did not pick up our show, the experience changed my life, because one night Michael brought a bottle of La Tache burgundy (Pinot Noir) to dinner at our home. It was the '87, which I was told wasn't even one of the more profound years, but still, I had been drinking red wine for years and I had no idea such a thing existed. Michael and I worked on several more projects together. He also taught me how to buy wine, which we started doing together regularly, at Sotheby's, Christie's, and Butterfields.

Rather than going to Vegas several times a week and blowing money at the Frontier's craps tables, my life now became one of long, reflective hours spent writing alone in my basement office during the day, and long and memorable dinner parties with friends, writers and actors, and showrunners and movie stars, which went well into the night.

It was a very happy, dreamlike time.

At one dinner party with two other couples, one of the attendees had had more than his fair share of the '86 La Turque that Piller helped me acquire. Jack, a buddy ever since my days in motion-picture marketing, wanted to know why the pretty young woman next to him, a very close friend of ours, had chopped her hair so drastically short.

The young woman tried to explain that she had just finished acting in a film called *Boys Don't Cry*, in which she had to play a boy.

In a city where half the residents are "actors," Jack could not seem to comprehend that she had actually *made* the movie and it was really going to get released.

"Well, stick with it! Maybe you can get some friends together and get the thing produced!" he slurred. "You gotta have perseverance in this town, *Mrs. Toupee*."

She smiled politely, as did her husband.

The next day, Jack called us. "I just watched a rerun of *Life Goes On* and I have to say, that guy at your house last night with the shorthaired girl looked exactly like Chad Lowe."

"That was Chad Lowe, Jack."

You can imagine Jack's reaction when the shorthaired girl walked onstage to receive her first Oscar a short time later.

⚶

Television wasn't the only medium competing for the services of TV writers during this time. After *Beauty and the Beast* was nominated for an Academy Award in 1991, it became readily apparent that animated films were no longer just cartoons. They had great artistic and financial potential. To be sure, animated feature-length films would soon provide the content that would feed many of these companies from top to bottom. From rides at their theme parks to fodder for their TV shows, animated films poured great newfound money into the business.

When the studios saw the value of feature-length animation, they started bringing in professional screenwriters to work on them, as opposed to just using storyboard artists. But the studios quickly realized that screenwriters worked alone. They did not know how to work collectively in a room with board artists on a regular basis, a task necessary for the ongoing development of an animated movie. TV writers, however, were quite accustomed to this.

I spent 1994–96 working at Walt Disney Feature Animation. Rita Hsiao, a former *Wonder Years* assistant who was working full time in feature animation, recommended me to Disney. After they read my *Northern Exposure* TV spec, they asked me to develop a movie for them. I was presented with three options, the first two of which were fairly fleshed-out stories that seemed to be pretty far down the development pipeline. The third was just a premise. It was explained to me that Michael Eisner was very passionate about making a feature film about bears, presumably because of the possibilities of selling plush bears in the company's retail stores. That's pretty much all I got, bears. And of course, given the CEO's passion for the project, I elected to find my own passion for it, which was not hard. Actually, once I signed up I did receive some notes that had been kicked around with Eisner. There was a page that said "King Lear/Joseph with Bears" and another that said "Antigone." These included a few paragraphs inserting bears into the classical themes. I would later learn that this was Disney's philosophy of storytelling. Find a well-known tale, borrow the bones, Disney-fy it. Hey, it worked.

Being a student of drama, I was in my element, though at one point I developed a *Jazz Singer* version of bears, which the executives loved, but it ended up being a bit weird for Disney. I spent months developing characters and a story for these furry critters, which was the first iteration of an animated feature later entitled *Brother Bear*, released at the same time the ubiquitous plush bears were released in retail outlets worldwide.

While I was working on the teddy bear flick, Disney asked me to join the team that was developing *Tarzan*. They had a script that was written by a screenwriter, but the directors said they weren't pleased with how it turned out. So, working closely with the directors and board artists, I spent nearly a year reconceiving and rewriting the film. It was great fun applying classic story craft to hand-drawn pictures. I had a brand-new office that was painted in bold primary colors. I hung out with storyboard artists, some of the most unappreciated storytellers in our culture. Most had low six-figure salaries, long-term contracts—some were signed up for as long as seven years—and they were required to fill out time cards. I worked with artists who had been at Disney so long they had worked with Walt. We'd have long, laid-back discussions about the same story point for weeks. Whether or not to kill Kerchak, Tarzan's ape dad, went on for months. The vast majority of my time was spent rewriting story sequences, little one- to two-page scenes. I'd rewrite the same page or two for weeks, over and over, while board artists drew new pictures for the scene. For this I was paid $6,750 a week. The studio happily paid my membership to the International Alliance of Theatrical Stage Employees Local 839 (aka, the Cartoonists' Union), which I was required to join because Disney Animation did not want the WGA anywhere near their place. I came in at 9:30 A.M. every day and left at 5:30 P.M. every day. I ate leisurely at the shiny happy Disney commissary during my lunch break. I played lots of foosball, pinball, and Ping-Pong with the board artists. I did not work weekends or holidays. There was no stress. No Room. No pressures of production. Our actors were all drawings, and unlike their live-action brethren, they caused very little mischief.

However, after a couple years of writertopia, hanging out under the giant Sorcerer's Hat, I realized I missed the pressures of TV. It took ten years for *Brother Bear* to go from page to screen. There was no pressure at Disney Feature Animation because it took a decade to make a ninety-minute story! As fun as it was, and it was a blast, I missed not only writing something and then seeing it produced and aired just days later, I missed the excitement that only comes from the pressure of production, from being on a TV staff. At the end of 1996, I was ready for it again, in a big way.

⌐⁓⁓

By no coincidence, 1996 was also the year I got married, on a warm night in December, on the pool deck overlooking the ocean at Shutters on the Beach. This was also about the same time that what is widely regarded as the great tipping point in television took place: when the FCC finally repealed Fin-Syn (the Financial Interest and Syndication Rules) with the passage of the Telecommunications Act of 1996. Networks were now allowed to own their own shows. Networks could now make money off the syndication of the shows they aired.

With this major regulatory hurdle now gone, television was no longer treated like a public trust, which is how the FCC initially conceived it, but as any other product in a free marketplace. Now, networks were no longer obligated to serve the public by carrying certain types of mandated programming. Some estimates put the value of the airtime given to broadcasters with this act at $70 billion. The implications were profound. In fact, the end of Fin-Syn is widely regarded as one of the defining industrial events of the twentieth century. The repercussions have shaped how we get, who controls, and the content of our news, information, and entertainment.

As soon as the rules were repealed, nearly overnight, a tidal wave of mergers and acquisitions, start-ups, and consolidations took place. NBC immediately formed its own studio, NBCP (NBC Productions), so that it could supply and profit from its own shows. CBS formed CBSP (CBS Productions). Paramount and Warner Brothers, joining Fox, immediately launched their own in-house networks, UPN and the WB. CBS merged with Westinghouse, and then, a few years later, with Viacom. TimeWarner acquired Turner Broadcasting System for $6.5 billion. Not to be outdone, the Walt Disney Company purchased its own network too—ABC, for $19 billion—more than three times what General Electric paid for NBC just seven years earlier. It was an extraordinary time for Hollywood, a historic time for American industry. The entire known world seemed to shift on its axis. At exactly the same time that all these new markets, foreign and domestic, clamored for TV shows and drove up the price of syndicated programming to previously inconceivable levels, new entire networks—also in need of programming—joined the fray.

⚶

While the accumulation of great wealth by ostentatious Wall Street traders received thorough coverage in the American press during this era, TV lit agents, especially those at the boutiques, quietly amassed eight-figure fortunes. Though agency packaging fees on TV programs had been around since the early days of television, never before had they become so prevalent or so valuable. A 5 percent packaging fee on a $1.5 million-an-episode network license fee for twenty-two episodes generates $1.7 million a season for an agency. If an agency had a few shows like that every season—on top of their standard 10 percent commissions on talent—they could have nice regular paychecks.

But as hit shows became more valuable, the studios started charging astronomical amounts when they negotiated or renegotiated license fees with the networks. For example, Warners demanded a license fee of $276 million a season from NBC for *ER* when it went into its fourth season. Imagine the packaging fees an agency gets from a quarter-billion-dollar-a-year license fee. Not to mention the riches generated by a 10 percent adjusted gross back-end on the billions of dollars in syndication revenue from a *Seinfeld*.

If a studio were to balk at demands from an agency to pony up a packaging fee—a very reasonable response when you consider that these fees are essentially a tax on a production, the only production expense that doesn't somehow appear on screen—the agency could just take their writer and their writer's show down the block. But this didn't happen. To the contrary, studios and production companies tripped over each other, literally fighting for the privilege of paying whatever they had to pay to get in business with writers and the shows they were creating.

Along with the new writers who were arriving, a new breed of agent now came to Hollywood as well. Up until this time, most of the major literary agents, like eighties television shows, could be described as "old school." Deals were made easily and quickly. Beth would call me in the afternoon, tell me a show was interested, and before she went home, she'd have a multiyear deal all worked out. She considered the studio's needs as well as her client's. Think I'm exaggerating on the impact this woman had on people? Another Beth client, Rob Long (who ran *Cheers*), wrote an entire book about her called *Conversations with My Agent*. In it he says she was "just a giant in the business. She has a complete uninterest in money or deals; she's always focusing on having a show on the air that's good." I'm not so sure I would say that she was entirely uninterested in money, but her primary agenda was not to let any nonsense from any party stand in the way of a good TV show. I'm sure she knew that packaging fees from good TV shows that went into syndication was the way to retire rich, which is what she did in the mid-nineties.

Before she retired, though, as part of my plan to make fundamental changes in my career and my life, I knew I had to start with my mother-agent. A couple of young and rising agents at Creative Artists Agency had been aggressively pursing me, and I agreed to a lunch with them, where I told them that I would seriously consider having them represent me. I think I asked for a few days to think about it, which in my mind meant that I'd hem and haw for a few weeks like a high school kid trying to decide which college to go to.

I swear, I wasn't back from that lunch for more than two hours before Beth called me and wanted to know why the hell I was talking to CAA. I learned two things that day: 1) assistants all talk to each other all over town, and 2) Beth really did know everything. Naturally, she proceeded to chew me out, and I felt like an idiot. Her partner, Bob, called me and said that if I had a problem with Beth, he'd rep me. Bob was an amazing agent, but I felt even guiltier and stupider. I stayed with her for several months but, not surprisingly, I did not get invited to her Passover Seder that year, and let's just say that some of the love was gone. Though I did not go with CAA, my consideration sped up something that I really did need to do. After a brief stint with a former ICM heavyweight, Jack Dytman, I signed with a new young agent named Dan Brecher in 1995.

Until this point, most TV lit agents either started as execs or came up through the famous agency training programs, such as the ones at William Morris or ICM. Beth was an executive at MTM. The new breed of agents that came to Hollywood in the nineties came from other places. Yes, many also went into those training programs—like Gavin Palone, who roared through the ICM program to become an agent at age twenty-two—but many had already had other professional training or even other careers first. Many were coming out of Ivy League law schools and MBA programs and fighting each other for the privilege of serving in mailrooms. Many were also skipping the mailroom and going right to work as junior agents. Naturally, all this new business not only created a massive need for writing talent, but also for people to represent that talent.

Right before Beth left the agency, a new junior agent joined the firm. After graduating from Amherst and then Harvard Law School, Ted Chervin worked as a federal prosecutor in New York City going after mafia members and drug dealers—think Vin Diesel in Armani. He then came to Hollywood and made partner at the agency very quickly.

After working on Wall Street in mergers and acquistions at Bankers Trust, my guy, Dan, had just finished his MBA at Wharton and was asked by former UTA (United Talent Agency) partner Robb Rothman to be his junior agent at another well-regarded literary boutique, the Rothman Agency. Robb represented numerous upper-level writers and showrunners, including many from *The Simpsons*. Within months Dan had an enviable roster of talented new writers, many whom he just went out and found. Within a few years, a lot of these writers were creating and running shows. Dan soon made partner. In my mind, Ted and Dan typified the new breed of agents, many of whom also came from law and business schools. These young turks brought with them the same kind of orientation and sensibility as their friends who argued in courts or who went to Wall Street. Many of these new agents not only had the same skill sets that litigators and traders had, but the same personalities, too. They were hotshots of the highest order. TV writer and author Hadley Davis described the new atmosphere at her lit agency, Broder-Webb-Chervin-Silbermann, as that of a Wall Street investment bank. "You have the sense that Ted and Chris [Silbermann, another new partner] get to the office at three A.M., trade Hong Kong gold, and do one-handed push-ups until the rest of Hollywood wakes up," Davis told me. My agent at Rothman Brecher was the same. His voice was always hoarse from negotiating deals sixteen hours a day. Dan applied his business school background to assess my value in the market and then negotiated very aggressively. Though he kept trying to get me to go back on the TV-staff market before I was ready, he had me paid significantly more money than any previous writer at Disney Feature Animation. He literally helped make a new market. And as I moved back into television, my quote quickly doubled. Indeed, the new agents who were coming to Hollywood seemed more like they came from the training program at Solomon Brothers than the one at William Morris. And unlike the old-school agents who were literally from a different generation, these new TV lit agents had a lot in common with their clients. Saying she was a "full-service agent," Beth would try to fix me up with girls she thought would be good for me, like her daughter's nanny. Where Beth was maternal, Dan was a contemporary. Where she was an authority figure, he was a close friend (and still is). In fact, I came to think of Dan not so much as an agent, but as an equity partner in my career.

Along with the writers and agents came a new breed of executives as well. Hollywood has always attracted the young and determined, but never before had so many very young people been in positions of such high power before. As advertisers grew increasingly focused on marketing new products to younger audiences, executives who were part of these audiences, and thus personally understood their likes and dislikes, quickly grabbed the reins from older, long-entrenched executives. Over the course of a couple years in the mid-nineties, a sort of industrywide coup d'état took place. Just as I found with the agents, these new execs I met were my age, had had similar experiences, and were interested in the things in which I was interested. This takeover had a direct impact not just on how business was done, but on the kinds of shows that were created. The takeover ultimately changed the entire nature of television programming. The vast majority of schedules on most networks (perhaps with the exception of CBS for a while) soon became targeted specifically at the well-under-thirty-five crowd. Soon entire networks would aim their entire schedules at the youth demo.

At thirty-two, Jamie Tarses was the youngest president of a television network—ABC—in history. Shows like *Friends*, which she was personally responsible for developing, were a direct reflection of the kinds of sensibilities these new execs brought to the business. I distinctly remember a meeting I had with the thirty-three-year-old VP of creative affairs at Warner Brothers, David Janollari, who was also instrumental in developing *Friends* from the studio side. We talked about TV shows we liked, but mainly we talked about back-packing in Thailand. It was cool. Everyone who was taking over at the nets and studios were like-minded spirits of the same generation. Kevin Reilly, thirty-four, became the exec VP at Brillstein-Grey and would soon become the head of NBC. In his early thirties, Eric Tannenbaum became head of television at Columbia TriStar. At twenty-eight, Susanne Daniels became the first head of prime-time series for the WB, and at twenty-six, Jordan Levin became head of comedy development and current programming for the WB. A few years later, in their early thirties, they would be the network's copresidents.

In all industries it is common for executives to know each other. At the top levels, they often know each other well. But these new young entertainment execs were much more than business associates. Even though they worked for competing companies, these new executives dated each other, partied together, went to Cabo and Hawaii together, lived together, and in some cases, married and divorced each other. At the same time that the major networks and studios were being consolidated by just a handful of companies, the individuals who took over the entertainment divisions at those companies all came from a small, tight-knit coterie, an exclusive club of sorts.

Not surprisingly, the new agents were also very tight with the new executives. Like college drinking buddies, they were all hanging out together. There were spats and rivalries like you'd find with any close group of friends. But mostly there was an understanding, a collective pact, that there was an unprecedented opportunity not only to make a fortune, but to redefine popular culture. It was a very exciting time. I attended parties where groups of new young agents and execs would all be in attendance. Around 1995–96, it seemed like everywhere you went that one hit from the Rembrandts (the *Friends* theme) was playing in the background, like some sort of anthem. Shop talk was de rigueur, no matter what the venue. The new executives had a vision of what television could be. And the new agents had access to the people who could bring these visions to fruition.

Right as all these new executives, agents, and writers came

to town, right as all these new networks and studios popped up, and right as all these new domestic and foreign markets opened up, there was convergence—an explosion, that resulted in the widespread employ of the aforementioned development deal. Although these high-paying arrangements, which make writers exclusive to one studio for a long period of time, were fairly rare historically, during the mid-nineties, development deals started being passed out like new WGA cards.

The only way all the independent production companies could compete with the massive new studio-networks, like Disney-ABC, was not just to hire writers, but to take them off the market and away from the competition for as long as possible. The objective of the game for anyone who wanted to be a real player soon became to lock up as much writing talent as possible.

Suddenly, writers all across town began to receive offers for these kinds of deals, where they would be given massive amounts of money to think up new ideas exclusively for one company. Sometimes these deals had a production component, meaning that the writer was required to work on a show for a period of time, say year one, and then develop for a period of time, say year two and year three. Often writers were asked to develop new ideas but also remain on a series as a "creative consultant." I would soon work on staffs with many creative consultants who were on development deals. When they showed up, they often had a hard time opening the doors to their offices because weeks of scripts and memos had been slid under their doors and were piled up on the inside. Suffice to say, most consultants spent most of their time developing as opposed to consulting. Often, agents made deals that allowed writers just to develop, literally to just sit and think. Often a promising new idea for a series would start to make its way through the complex pipeline toward production, only to be sent back when it hit a bump—studio notes, trouble with an actor, failure to negotiate acceptable licensing fees—for "further development."

During this time, it became standard procedure to give the third-tier writer on a thirty-fifth-highest-rated show millions of dollars to sit in a room for a couple years with a NERF basketball and try to think up the next *Veronica's Closet*. And those writers who were fortunate enough to actually be on a legitimate hit were offered even bigger deals to stop working on it and just think. There were approximately five hundred development deals a year made in Hollywood during this time. Most writers averaged a couple million dollars a year to develop. Some were paid a lot more. A friend who was even younger than me, David Rosenthal, earned $2.5 million a year from Fox Television to just, as one former colleague said, "think funny." It was not unheard of for some writers to earn five million a year or more. In 1998, Jeff Astrof and Mike Sikowitz, Ted Chervin's clients, former executive story editors on *Friends*, college buddies who had just moved to L.A. for the Warner Brothers comedy writing program seven years earlier, were given $10 million over four years by Warners to think up ideas for new shows.

As crazy as it seems, if a studio wanted to be in the business, they had to follow the actions of other studios. They had to take writers off the market if they wanted to be a real production company. This created an atmosphere where every deal was the result of an auction and every auction resulted in an all-out bidding war. The prices just kept getting higher and higher. As soon as it seemed that a ceiling had been reached and the major players had an implicit understanding that they would not bid the price of talent any higher, a hungry and well-funded new upstart would join the battle and drive the prices up again.

As one might imagine, the aggressive new business school–savvy agents had a field day. In 1998, TV writers collectively earned $355 million, 47 percent more than they had in 1994. Writers were becoming just as hot as the dot-com stocks that were also coming into favor. And our representatives just played these companies that wanted us against each other, driving up our prices to levels that the original WGA members—hell, members even ten years earlier—would never have dreamed. Trying to put a value on a new writer who might come up with a hit show really was like trying to put a price on a pint of Bochco's blood.

In the eighties, a writer might be paid five figures, usually low to mid five figures to develop a pilot. But now, brand-new writers—I mean, right out of school—were being paid hundreds of thousands of dollars to develop and write a single script. Many of these new writers remained untrained throughout their careers, even if the script they were writing went into production, because the writers with experience who could actually mentor them were so outnumbered by all the new talent. Anyway, those that did actually have some experience in the business were busy—thinking up their own ideas. *Their* compensation ran well into the seven and eight figures. Take a look at the kinds of deals that were being reported in the trades:

- Alexa Junge, writer-producer, *Friends*, two years, $2 million.
- Paul Manning, supervising producer, *ER*, three years, $2 million to $3 million.
- Charlie Craig, executive producer, *Prey*, two to three years, $2 million to $3 million.
- Tom Hertz, coexecutive producer, *Spin City*, two years, $3 million.
- Mark Driscoll, executive producer, *Ellen*, two years, $4 million.
- Brannon Braga, coexecutive producer, *Star Trek: Voyager*, three years, $5 million.
- Pam Brady, writer-producer, *Just Shoot Me!*, three years, $6 million.
- Jay Scherick and David Ronn, writer-producers, *Spin City*, three years, $6 million.
- Rene Balcer, executive producer, *Law & Order*, three years, $6 million.
- Josh Goldsmith and Cathy Yuspa, executive producers, *The King of Queens*, three years, $7.5 million.
- Warren Bell, executive producer, *Ellen*, three years, $9 million.
- Chris Keyser and Amy Lippman, executive producers, *Party of Five*, three years, $12 million.
- David Milch, executive producer, *NYPD Blue*, four years, $15 million.
- Brad Hall, executive producer, *The Single Guy*, four years, $15 million.

- Mike Judge, executive producer, *King of the Hill*, four years, $16 million.

- Steven Levitan, executive producer, *Just Shoot Me!*, four years, $16 million.

- J. J. Abrams, executive producer, *Felicity*, four years, $16 million.

- Tim Doyle, Ric Swartzlander, and Matt Berry, writer-producers, *Sports Night*, three years, $18 million.

- Bruce Helford, executive producer, *The Drew Carey Show*, four years, $20 million.

- Chuck Lorre, cocreator, *Dharma & Greg*, four years, $20 to 32 million.

- Phil Rosenthal, executive producer, *Everybody Loves Raymond*, four years, $50 million.

Remember, these numbers are strictly for developing and producing services. Again, writers were often paid these sums just to think up new ideas. These figures do not include the additional compensation such as script fees, assorted payments, residuals, or, most significantly, back-end participation in syndication revenues, which typically ran well into the tens of millions during this time.

In short, the demand for new shows was so high that anyone in any way affiliated with a working show for a season or two was offered additional money to develop a new one. Nearly all coexecutive producers were offered at least a million dollars to develop new shows, and nearly all executive producers were offered at least an extra few million, for starters. According to the *Los Angeles Times*, 20th Century alone handed out more than $100 million in development deals to just a handful of writers in the several years leading up to 1997.

That was when, in 1997, I went back on the staffing market. It felt different than it had just a few years earlier. During the years that I spent freelancing and working at Disney, the entire industry had gone through a great sea change driven by enormous sums of money and the promise of even more. The whole town was filled with a sense of breathlessness—you felt it in meetings, talking to colleagues, heard it in your agent's voice—it was somewhere between exultation and panic.

When I was a kid there was a game show that I used to watch that featured a phone boothlike glass box filled with cash. A contestant would step inside and a fan would blow that cash all around the box. The idea was for the contestant to grab as much cash as he or she could before the machine was turned off. This is what it felt like to be working in television in Hollywood at this time. Except none of us knew that the machine would soon be turned off.

TEN

The Seasons of L.A.

"We have no obligation to make history. We have no obligation to make art. We have no obligation to make a statement. To make money is our only objective."

—MICHAEL EISNER, IN AN INTERNAL MEMO

The 1997–98 staffing season was a record one for television writers. More writers were employed that season and earned more money than ever before. During that season, 2,968 television writers were employed, with about half of them, 1,557 writers, in prime-time broadcast network television (as opposed to cable and first-run syndication). And the vast majority of those jobs were full-time staff positions. Yet despite the records and the mad rush for writers, there were still 7,883 active WGA-West members, out of which about 6,000 were in the TV category. And many, if not most, of those TV writers who got jobs those years already had jobs when staffing season began. That is, they had spent the previous season working on shows that had gotten picked up, and when those shows got picked up they got picked up. Everyone else that season played the staffing game, competing for approximately 500 open staff positions on prime-time network shows. I was one of those competing.

Now, this was a bit disorienting for me. I needed to get, as it were, back in the game. I needed to get back in the *rhythm* of the game. You see, if you work in TV, your life is subject to a cadence that is driven by the business. Let me explain.

While the rest of the country has winter, spring, summer, and fall, in L.A., the weather is always pretty much the same. Yeah, sure, it rains for a few weeks around February—such a rarity that it's always a top news story and causes drivers to behave as though flaming meteorites were falling from the heavens—and the Santa Anas blow the hot Mojave winds into the city for weeks in late fall, causing a sort of nuclear winter feel for the holidays. But for the most part, the weather in L.A. is famously consistent: seventy-twoish and sunny, disconcertingly perfect. Still, L.A. has its seasons, though unlike the rest of the country, these seasons refer to phases of the television business. There is pilot-development season, pilot production season, pickup season, and staffing season. And trust me, as powerful as Mother Nature can be, the influence of the industry's seasonal ebbs and flows are even more so.

Traditionally running from July 4th to Thanksgiving, pilot-development season is when the studios and networks make decisions about which projects to green-light for development. On any given day during this time, an executive will read five or six scripts and hear at least a dozen different pitches. Likewise, writers, often with agents and attached executives in tow, schlep their dog-and-pony show pitches to all the various studios and networks.

One of the truly quirky aspects of the TV business is that

writers have a much harder time selling a script for a new show that has been conceived, developed, and entirely written, than a fifteen-minute verbal pitch. Yes, it's counterintuitive, but this is the process. You'd think, particularly given not only the expense but also the fact that writers really do like to write, that the studios would be more interested in purchasing something tangible, but they are not. The "million-dollar spec" phenomenon that exists in the movie industry has no parallel in television. Studios do not bid against each other for the right to acquire a hot TV pilot spec the way they will for the right to acquire a writer. The reality is that most pilots are purchased for their *potential*. This is partially a function of the fact that when an executive purchases a pitch from a writer, as opposed to a written script, this gives the executive the opportunity to be part of something, to substantiate his salary. He wasn't just the guy that bought a script. He was the guy who *developed* such and such hit show.

As I continued to work in television, I also started to develop another theory. Scripts are hard. That is, they require reading, evaluation, consideration. In the middle of pilot season, when on any given day an executive has fifteen meetings at the office as well as meetings over breakfast, lunch, dinner, and drinks, as well as dozens of phone calls to return, as well as dozens of memos and e-mails to weigh-in on from colleagues' meetings—a fifteen-minute pitch often gets much more attention than sixty-nine bound pages, unless the first of those pages has J. J. Abrams written on it. Moreover, if an executive buys a completed script and green-lights it for production and it fails, unless the lead actor was truly psychopathic, or the director had a serious crack problem, the green-lighter's tastes are much more accountable than if he or she simply hired a writer to start from scratch. Everyone knows how invariable the development process can be and, thus, it is much more forgiving—a safer, as well as easier, way to go.

Consequently, most TV pilots are sold in pitch meetings during pilot-development season. The prevailing wisdom on this process is to bring in a concept that is generally familiar but a little bigger than the biggest concept presently on TV. It should be immediately identifiable but somehow cooler, pumped up a notch. For example, series are often pitched as: "Think [insert hot familiar TV show of choice] meets [insert another hot familiar TV show of choice] on acid." Or "It's [insert hip familiar movie of choice] meets [insert another hip familiar movie of choice] on steroids." Or "The series is basically [insert hot familiar TV show of choice] meets [insert hip familiar movie of choice] but with lesbians." Or "dope-smoking priests." Or "lesbians who sleep with priests, do acid, take steroids, and smoke dope." The general idea is to walk in and say, "This one's just like the others that have worked, but 'this one goes to eleven.' " And then you're given a quarter of a million dollars or so to go home and figure out what the hell you've sold them.

No matter how passionate a network may be about a pitch, the reality is that they have no idea what they're actually buying. If you pitch to five different executives in the room, they all have different mental images of what you're talking about, and that is assuming that they are actually listening to you as opposed to thinking about the previous pitch or the subsequent lunch meeting. Most TV shows are born and manufactured on nothing short of a giant leap of faith. Networks rarely really know what they are going to get when they write a check, and so they often do not know how to judge what they do get on its own merits. This begins to explain how Fox let *Dawson's Creek* slip through its fingers.

In 1995, Paul Stupin had recently left a position as a network exec at Fox and taken an overall deal to develop projects for Columbia TriStar Television, Sony's major television production arm. It surprised very few people who met Paul to learn that he was a former executive. A collector of trendy gadgetry and a consumer of all things pop, Paul was Sports Club/L.A. fit, the kind of guy whose shirt was always tucked in, even at midnight, standing in line in Westwood for the latest *Harry Potter* release. Paul's major claim to fame for his time at Fox was his involvement in the development of Darren Starr's *Beverly Hills, 90210,* the series that pretty much put Fox on the map in the nineties. So the executives at Columbia TriStar listened to Paul when he championed Kevin Williamson—who had just sold his spec screenplay, *Scream*—for the development of a new youth-oriented series. Since this was a market in which all nets were becoming increasingly interested, the idea of Kevin was very appealing to Columbia. Paul and Kevin talked for quite a while about developing a TV show. Numerous ideas were kicked around. Kevin really did not have anything concrete. Eventually, he just started talking about his life, where he grew up, experiences in high school. Paul thought there could be a show in all that somewhere. Kevin went home and outlined a series about a boy who lives on a creek, always dreamed of being

Steven Spielberg, and shares his bed with a girl he's known since early childhood.

At the beginning of the pilot season, Paul then took Kevin to his former employers at Fox. Kevin pitched the idea and Fox essentially bought it right there in the room. Kevin was hired to write a pilot script. Later, as pilot-production season was just gearing up around the holidays, Fox passed on the show. They weren't thrilled about the script and thus were not going to produce it. A Fox executive said that the script seemed odd, old-fashioned. He felt that Kevin's dialogue was stilted and archaic.

Pilot-production season, which usually occurs between Thanksgiving and March, is the time of year when a handful of pilots are given the green light for production. (This, by the way, is "staffing season" for actors. Every actor in town jockeys for a spot on a pilot that he or she hopes will become a series-regular role and make them a household name.) This is when a network has to make a real substantive decision about how much they believe in a project. A script is sixty pieces of paper, a couple of brads, and a few hundred grand. A pilot episode is millions of dollars and a major undertaking. Dozens of writers wait by the phones, wondering if they will be future showrunners, or back on the market. About fifteen to twenty scripts per network are green-lighted for production.

But Paul refused to give up. He took the script to a brand-new network that was struggling to find its way. They decided to give it a shot. The new WB network did not commit the resources to a full produced pilot for *Dawson's*. Rather, a thirty-eight-minute "pilot presentation" was produced. A pilot presentation is made by producing just parts of a pilot script, as opposed to the whole thing. An order for a pilot presentation, used by executives to judge a show's potential merits, essentially means "We *love* the project. We are BIG fans. Just not big enough to commit $5 million."

I first saw the *Dawson's* pilot presentation tape in the spring of 1997. Everyone in the entertainment business heard about it and wanted to take a look. It quickly became the "it" show of the new season. You just knew the WB had something really special on their hands. Whether or not they would know what to do with it was another issue. It was only two years earlier that ABC had dropped the ball with *My So-Called Life*, another "it" show. When I saw the *Dawson's* presentation, I felt the same way as when I first saw *The Wonder Years*. I knew I wanted to work on that show.

⁓

Visitors to Los Angeles often remark how beautiful the city is year-round. It is true that lavatera and hibiscus, even some bougainvillea varieties, adorn the L.A. basin throughout the year. Still, there is nothing as far as I am concerned that compares to the jacaranda tree bloom in late April. For me, and I believe (on some level), for most TV writers, this is like a billion little purple flags being run up thousands of flagpoles from Burbank to Santa Monica, signaling the official commencement of television staffing season. No matter where you live or what you do, if you are an Angeleno, you can't miss it. When I saw the purple flowers all over the city that spring in 1997, I knew that the meetings were about to start.

Staffing season, which traditionally takes place between late April and the beginning of June, is best described as a game of musical chairs. Here's how it works. Writers who know they are going to be on the market during staffing season begin their preparations as early as possible. Often series get canceled after the initial order of a pilot plus twelve, so the show's writers know around late November that they'll be available. Sometimes the network waits until the very last minute in late May after a full season of twenty episodes have been made to announce that a show is not coming back. Even if you are the most beloved staff member on a top-ten show that is definitely coming back, sometimes your showrunner gets fired, followed by everyone on the writing staff. Sometimes a showrunner takes a huge development deal, leaves the baby he created, and a new showrunner is hired who brings in a new writing staff. Sometimes the network and/or the studio decide the show needs a change in direction and thus new writers. Sometimes a showrunner or another key staff member will cannibalize the writing budget of the show, double or triple their own salaries, and let other staff writers go. When Beth Uffner said, "You want security, go sell insurance," she wasn't joking. The truth is, even in the best of years, part of the job in a television writing career is writing and part of the job is getting your next job. Since you never really know for sure how long your current job will last, one way or another, even in the best of years, you are always working on the next.

Writers do several things to prepare for staffing season. First, they get their spec material in order. That season my agency sent out my five-year-old *Northern Exposure* script because Dan felt it was sort of charmed by the success we had with it at Disney. He also really liked the teaser, which opened with a man bleeding from the wrists and collapsing in the center of town. Dan liked these sorts of things. He got quite worked up when he pitched them to executives. Listening to Dan pitch the opening of my *Northern Exposure* to an executive over the phone one day, *I* got worked up. He made me sound thrilling. I felt like I'd written *Marathon Man*.

But he strongly believed that we needed something else that season, too, something darker. That was a word you heard a lot from agents about this time, partially, I think, because of the influence of Chris Carter's work on the one-hour market. Dark became the new cool. And then edgy became the new dark. Naturally, like most writers, I never quite new what the hell any of these terms meant any more than I knew what "soft" meant. Although I did know that in the days of *Millennium* and *The X Files* agents told us that people did not respond if you were too soft, but they were big fans if you were dark, and *really* big fans if you were edgy.

I told Dan about how *Simon & Simon* loved my *Molly Dodd*. He told me not to ever mention *Simon & Simon* again. "You want people to think you're like fifty?" Dan rasped. He took the show off my credit list that the agency sent around with my specs, and he also advised me to talk a lot about how I had earned my brown belt in karate, presumably so that people would know that I was not soft.

Now determined to approach television as work rather than full-time play, I professionally acquiesced and specced that laugh-riot *Profiler*, about an FBI criminologist on the trail of a brutal pathological serial killer. And as it turned out, Dan was absolutely right. That script ended up being the absolute perfect piece of material for the show I would get that season. This was because, as my agent pointed out, he was a genius.

And also, as we have repeatedly seen now, in TV, you just never know.

In addition to writing, TV writers also prepare for staffing by engaging in intelligence-gathering ops. This begins by following which new shows might get on schedules. During pilot-production season, most agencies generate a list that meticulously tracks all available information about each and every show in development. Every piece of data is collected: who has been cast, who is directing, which writers are attached, and how the studio and network like the project so far. Mind you, this information is not collected through official channels or some formal process. It is all simply word of mouth. Agents talk to executives who leak tidbits of information. Writers tell their agents what they have heard. Agency assistants talk to their assistant pals at the networks and studios. All this rumor and hearsay and speculation is compiled. Finally, the assistants in charge of the list at each agency will often tactfully share intelligence with each other the way kids trade marbles. At any given day during pilot-production season a good lit agency can fairly accurately lay pickup odds for most pilots. My agency sent me the List every few days as it was updated.

A similar process also tracks which positions might be available on returning shows. Agencies try to figure out which shows will definitely come back and which one are "on the bubble." Information is collected about which showrunners and writers on these series might be going into development or moving on to better shows. Information is also collected about which showrunners and writers might not be having their options exercised. It is not uncommon for this knowledge to be on the information market before it is known to these showrunners and writers themselves.

And along with intelligence, pilot scripts and tapes are furtively passed around in the TV writing community. Starting in the fall, when the pilots are green-lighted for production, agencies begin sending their clients pilot scripts. In later years when I knew I would be on the market, Dan sent me as many as fifty scripts a season. My friends and I would loan and trade these scripts with each other.

In order to stay abreast of what was going on in the market, you had to read these scripts. Even more valuable are tapes of produced-pilot episodes, like that *Dawson's* presentation tape I got. By the end of pilot-production season, around late March to early April, these tapes start appearing all over town. No showrunner, studio, or network wants rough cuts of their pilots to get out into the community. So sometimes it can take as long as a week or two before they do. A veritable black market exists for these shaky bootleg tapes. It's an odd feeling you have when you start one of those tapes, somewhere between fear and excitement. For this rough approximation of a potential TV series may turn out to be a living hell to which you get yourself contractually tied, or it may be the show where you spend the next seven wonderful years, the show that forever on appears in parentheses after your name.

All of this, the intelligence, the scripts, and the tapes, creates— that's right—buzz. And you hear it everywhere. I always made appointments to see my dentist during this time. Partially because I knew I was gonna get busy and partially because not only did he work on actor-producers like Mel Gibson but also several A-list showrunners, so he always had good info about what was hot. I also found that the waitresses at Art's Deli seemed to be in the know. As pilot-production season segues into staffing season, during April, the whole town goes as mad as bees making the season's first honey.

Then the meetings start, first with the execs. There are essentially two varieties of television executive, development and current. The studios and the networks usually have both. Not surprisingly, the idea is that development execs *develop* TV shows and current execs oversee shows *currently* on schedules. There are also usually executives who specifically develop or oversee drama, and others who develop or oversee comedy. Those highest up on the food chain (presidents, senior vice presidents, etc.) manage both genres in both stages. The way this all operates is no big surprise, either. When you pitch a pilot, it's to the development folks. When you meet for a show that has been picked up, it's with current. If a show *might* get picked up, you might meet both.

By the end of April to the beginning of May, the entire town is engaged in a whirlwind of these meetings. My agency would call me several times a day during this period to schedule meetings, sometimes three at a time. They would often call back an hour later to cancel and reschedule meetings. During this time writers are never away from their phones. Just as writers and their agents track shows during this time, executives track writers. Just as writers compete for a limited amount of good jobs, the networks and studios all compete for the best talent. It's a feeding frenzy.

The purpose of these staffing meet 'n' greets is not to sell any work, pitch any ideas, or present any potential TV shows, it is simply to let those in charge at the networks and studios

get a look at you so they can give their blessing. Ideally, executives and writers get to know each other a bit, get a sense of
each other. But when an executive has a dozen of these meetings before lunch, simply putting a name with a face, a script
with a person, is often the main result. I had meetings during
this time that lasted maybe ten minutes. And I'd have several
in any given day. To make a comparison to dating, or better
yet speed-dating, is not wholly inaccurate, although I would
actually liken television executives more to the watchful parents of the potential date. Because at the end of the day, although they do have the contractual right to put down their
foot and dig in their heels and say "over my dead body is he
coming to work here!" it is, in reality, the showrunning
writer's decision. As important as it is to have "network approval" and "studio approval," the bottom line is that if a
showrunner wants you, everything else is pretty much mean-
ingless. That's not to say that good executives can't help their
busy and totally overwhelmed showrunners make good
staffing decisions. But from what I was seeing, I started to
think of TV executives, in the best cases, mainly as trusted advisors, as wartime consiglieri.

When I first came to Hollywood it was my impression that
the development executives were just a little hipper than their
counterparts in current. They dressed a bit more fashionably.
Had slightly trendier haircuts. Meet 'n' greets featured discussions about favorite TV shows (of course) but also included
lengthy riffs on the latest subtitled film at the Laemmle or the
one-man play at the Zephyr, and impassioned conversations
about travel, particularly to retro-hip locales that were decid-
edly anti-L.A. These meetings were shameless improvs that

wove Brand Falsey, Mamet, and grits into a tapestry of cool, leaving the participants assured that they belonged to the same club.

Current executives, on the other hand, seemed to talk the talk of research departments. Conversations included Nielsen numbers, up-front ad sales, and the benefits of working for the particular studio. Meetings felt more like legitimate interviews than jazz sessions. And the current executives looked . . . not just a bit older physically, but older soulfully. They knew how to manage an unmanageable showrunner. They were accustomed to keeping stars in line. They knew how to put out fires, and frankly, they didn't take a lot of shit.

By the time staffing season 1997 rolled around, things seemed different to me among the electric door–closer set. In short, the lines between development and current, between the cultures of those departments and those worlds, blurred. Most of the mid-level current managers and directors that I met started looking a lot like the development managers and directors. They got a tad hipper. A bit cooler. There was a sudden preponderance of goatees and so-called flavor-savers. More of those bookishly trendy glasses began to appear. I suppose this was partially an effect of the demise of Fin-Syn that allowed networks and studios to be owned by the same company, creating a sort of homogenization of the business. It was partially due to the even younger people joining the ranks. And partially because there was no need for the buttoned-down current executive who effectively managed a studio's stalwart series for a decade, because the studio, as we once knew it, was gone, as were most of those blue-chip 30-share shows. That kind of programming was being usurped by upstart little shows on upstart little networks, and no one knew for sure the future of either. In short, everything, including current programming, started to be more speculative, more high-flying, more pie-in-the-sky. That was the nature of making TV during the age of what people would call media consolidation.

I had a staffing meeting with the director of creative affairs in the Team Disney Building (Eisner's new monument that Roy Disney despised) on May 18, 1998. I'm still not clear if this particular hipster-suit was in current or development, studio or network. I think he was a representative of them all. Throughout the meeting, while I waxed poetic and did my best to give good meeting, he watched the stock ticker scroll across his muted television set, which was tuned to CNBC. He did this throughout the entire meeting, glancing back and forth between me and the ticker. Though I'd had seven or eight meetings in the past few days, I'm sure he'd had at least that many before I came in. I couldn't help wondering if he was monitoring his DIS options, perhaps to see the market's response to the fall schedule announcements. For me, this was a sign of the times, the state of the TV business during this era.

The real meetings, the showrunner meetings, start as soon as there is something substantive to discuss, when a show has been picked up or when it looks like such an event is imminent. This is the climax of the entire process, pickup season.

This happens during the two middle weeks of May, when "upfronts" take place in New York. Upfronts are an event, a sort of TV convention if you will, where television programming executives unveil their fall schedules to media buyers in order to presell ad time "up front" on those shows. This is when the official announcements of network schedules take place. In an average season, networks pre-sell about 80 percent of their advertising time during upfronts.

During this time, much of the L.A. television community heads to New York. Agencies and studios take over entire sections of hotels. Actors and showrunners are flown in. Held in fancy hotel ballrooms and theaters like Radio City Music Hall, the presentations feel like a cross between the Emmys and a pharmaceutical sales conference. The network's celebrities are trotted out. Network presidents make flashy presentations. Executives lobby media buyers at extravagant studio-sponsored cocktail parties.

And in the middle of all this, TV lit agents are hard at work positioning their clients for staff gigs. Frequent and frenetic calls to the skeletal staffs at L.A. offices are made. Cryptic text messages are sent out to anxious clients all over the L.A. basin. It is a time of high, high drama.

During the last week of May writers rush around town taking meetings at a moment's notice. I got an urgent call from Dan early on Monday, May 26, 1997, saying that despite how charming I was at my recent breakfast with writer Scott Shepard at the Riviera Country Club, *Justice League of America* was not getting picked up and he was sending me on meetings, starting tomorrow at 1:00 with a new show called *Three*, about three hip con artists all forced to work together. He then snapped at his assistant who was listening in—as assistants always do—to courier the script and a tape to me ASAP. The assistant said they didn't have the tape yet. Dan said "get it" and hung up.

So after spending the entire afternoon reading and rereading the script, and thinking of story ideas, and the entire evening watching and rewatching the bootleg tape when it finally arrived, I drove to Paramount the next day, clean-shaven, nervous, focused. Throughout my entire fifteen-minute meeting with Evan Katz (the future EP of *24*), the pilot's writer, he sat behind a desk and quite literally shoved a foot-long meat sandwich into his mouth while going through the motions of asking me what I thought of his script. To me, he was a guy who might hold the key to my future. To him, I was another thing he was forced by the studio to look at. I remained professional, reminded myself that this fellow writer was probably just too swamped to find time to eat, and told him that I thought *Three* was "brilliant—dark, edgy, without ever losing its sense of humor." He thanked me for my time and did not bother getting up from his lunch at the desk. On my way out, passing the next clean-shaven, nervous, and focused writer waiting to see Evan, I did not consider this to be the pinnacle of a career in television.

I called Dan from the car before I'd even pulled off the lot. He wasn't available but his assistant had another meeting for me with another new show that had just gotten a go in New York—*C:16* it was called, an FBI thing. My agency called me back moments later with a time and place: tomorrow, Brillstein-Grey's offices on Wilshire. The script and tape were already at my house, sitting on the front doorstep, by the time I got back.

However, as I reached down to pick them up, the phone rang from inside. Grabbing the phone, tearing open the material for tomorrow's meeting, I was told that I now had another meeting the day after tomorrow, with Paul Stupin for *Dawson's Creek*.

So after another night of cramming and prepping—and trying to keep my mind on the FBI and off angst-ridden teens—I arrived the next day for my 4:30 meeting with Michael Duggan (former co-EP of *Law & Order*), *C:16*'s creator. Moody and charismatic, Duggan was described to me by a well-known writer as her "elevator man": Meaning, he was the one person with whom, if she was ever stuck in an elevator with him, she could have sex and her husband would understand. The truth is, I hadn't heard much buzz about *C:16* that season; no one had. It was a show that nearly everyone had discounted. So when I saw the pilot, frankly, I was a little blown away by how great it was. Liking the show as much as I did made the meeting a pleasure. The meeting lasted for more than an hour, which in the climate of staffing season is a very good sign.

The next day, Thursday, May 29, I met Paul Stupin in his office on the Culver Studios lot. Paul was gregarious and animated from the minute I walked in the door. Part of this, as I would eventually come to learn, was simply his personality. (Even with his office door closed while he had highly sensitive conversations about the writers on his staff, the writers on his staff in the story room next door often heard every word he said.) But part of this can also be chalked up to a special kind of effusiveness that only comes from knowing that you have the hottest show in town and *everybody* wants to work on it. For a producer, especially a nonwriting producer, this is as close to stardom as one comes. This is "fuck-you" time, as in, "Fuck anyone who's ever fired me, fuck anyone who's ever not returned my call, fuck anyone who's ever shoved a sandwich down his throat while in a meeting with me, fuck anyone who's ever refused to fuck me, fuck you all—I have the hottest *fucking* show in town, so kiss my ass, and do it nicely."

That said, I liked Paul a lot. I liked how totally excited he was about *Dawson's*, and not just the response it was getting, but the show itself. We shared that in common and, in TV staffing, unabashed unambiguous love of a show goes a long way when it comes to getting a job on that show.

As always, I called Dan from the car on the way off the lot and told him I'd had a great meeting. I think I was even a bit giddy because I told him I thought I was going to get an offer. Dan did not seem even remotely convinced.

Most shows, I knew, started the first week of June, which was Monday. On that preceding Friday, to say I waited by the phone would be like saying that a mother hen waits by her egg-filled nest. It was a long day. Dan did not call. At 5:55 P.M., I called him. Nothing. "Try to relax," he whisper-said, his voice nearly gone by now. "Enjoy your weekend." Even for a man who never stopped speaking during a month of eighteen-hour days, this was much easier said than done.

⌒

The first day of the first week of June is a special demarcation point for TV writers. It is a day of celebration, or a day of grief. To have your staff gig lined up by this day means that your season is set. You know what you will be working on. You know that your mortgage will be paid. You know what your life will be like for at least the next few months, which is the most a TV writer realistically hopes for. But if you don't have a position by this day, then you join all the other writers still competing for a handful of errant positions still left during the first week or two of June. After that, the music has stopped. The jacaranda blooms fade, and the city is covered in a silent shower of purple. Like tattered confetti, they line the gutters along Hollywood Way and cover windshields of newly leased cars on backlots from Culver City to Century City. The party is now over. What passes for L.A.'s spring gives way to June gloom, a marine layer of thick clouds that settles over the city until mid-July, when the dry heat burns them off and TV production begins. Until that time, the thrilling buzz has been replaced by the quiet sounds of writers off working long hours behind closed doors. Sure, there will be a few shows that hire during the off-season, some cable series and first-run syndies. There will be a handful of shows that have some needs as a few writers wig out and walk out of contracts when they discover what they signed up for, and perhaps a few more as some shows decide they need different voices in the Room. And of course there will be the possibility of freelance scripts, which can be staff auditions, at some point. But by the second week of June, it's pretty much a done deal. Like accountants on April 16, TV lit agents all go on vacation. And before they leave for the Ritz in Maui or the Four Seasons in Bali or a Viking cruise with the kids, they always tell their clients and colleagues and the trades the same thing, that this was by far "the most brutal staffing season yet" but that they "still staffed almost all of their writers." This gives little solace to those writers who were not staffed. But those writers left without a chair will move on. They will start thinking about next season. Because development season begins again in earnest on July 4th, and the whole cycle starts anew. No matter what kind of staffing season you had, no matter how "brutal" this year really was, no matter how good or bad the entire business is, just as sure as the sun will rise again tomorrow, there will always be another TV season. It's part of the natural rhythm of life in L.A.

"Enjoy your weekend," rang in my ears. While many friends who had their gigs lined up headed off for one final quick jaunt to Cabo or Palm Springs, I got a large motorized tiller from Aaron Rents and, to the dismay of my wife, spent most of the next forty-eight hours digging up the backyard and replanting the garden. It was not a pretty sight, but I had to do something.

On Monday morning, still unable to get the mud out from under my filthy fingernails, I heard that I would not be receiving an offer for *Dawson's*. My heart dropped. Had my carefully measured levels of deference and awe been too carefully measured? Or did I gush? Did I not reference his past work enough? Or did I know too much and come off as creepy?

Dan explained to me that I wasn't hired because nobody was hired. He said that Paul was not in a position to take on a writing staff just then. As much as the WB made it known that they loved the show, they only gave Sony a pickup for eleven episodes, an atypically small order. Because of the odd size, the staffing needs were minimal and because of the odd premiere date, January, the writing staff would not start until August. This did not make me feel much better.

However, as I was beginning to think I would spend much of the next year writing another project for Yakov, ninety minutes later Dan called back with an offer from *C:16*. Evidently, my *Profiler* worked. After a little negotiation we accepted, and I went to work at 9:30 A.M. the next day, exhausted, relieved, and excited.

~*~

After the initial couple weeks in temporary offices at Sunset Gower Studios, the writers moved to our permanent space in an old office building off National in Venice. The building was pretty decrepit and bland, and the other tenants always thought we were up to something suspicious, seeing as how we didn't seem to be dressed for a proper day's work, but I loved the place. Aside from the fact that the office was just minutes from my home in Santa Monica, we were right over the See's Candies customer-service department, so the story room often smelled of chocolate, particularly on hot days, which was most.

Produced by Brillstein-Grey for ABC, the new series was extremely promising. It was about the FBI's major case squad. It was fast-paced, pulled no punches, and was very smartly written. The pilot looked awesome. It was the only show on television to be "letterboxed," giving it a cool, movielike look. Those black bars you see above and below the picture when you watch a movie in its original wide-screen format on a television set is letterboxing. Michael Robbins, who was credited with giving *NYPD Blue* its distinguishing look, directed and was on board as a producer. The cast was great—Angie Harmon, Morris Chestnut, Christine Tucci (Stanley's sister), D.B. Sweeney, and a bearded Eric Roberts. Even the critics, for the most part, were extremely enthusiastic. And the writing

staff—Bonnie Mark (*NYPD Blue*), Anne Lewis Hamilton
(*thirtysomething*), Patrick Harbinson (*Law & Order: SVU*),
Marjorie David (*Chicago Hope*)—read like a who's who of
Hollywood's best one-hour drama writers. However, the show
did not work.

And this was not simply due to the simple winds of chance
that end so many TV shows. No, *C:16* is a textbook example
of controllable reasons for why a show fails. For starters, anyone who saw Duggan's pilot would have understood that *C:16*
was a 10:00 show. The tone was mature, the characters sophisticated. But ABC plugged us in at 8:00, which immediately clipped the show's wings, significantly limiting the stories
we could tell and the way we could tell them. In addition, they
plugged us in on Saturday night, a graveyard for television unless you were a babysitter sitcom or maybe a movie, and we
were most certainly neither. (In fact, the last time the American Broadcasting Company had had even a modicum of success with original programming at 8:00 on a Saturday night
was in 1991, when they moved *Who's the Boss?* there from
Tuesdays. The series died the season it was moved there.) The
C:16 pilot was shot in letterbox, as were the first four
episodes, but in later episodes the format was changed upon
directive from the network. This not only fundamentally
changed the surveillance-like look and voyeuristic sensibility
of the show, it also made production days longer and more
expensive. When the network began promoting us, the ads
made us look like the next *NYPD Blue*. And we wrote
episodes accordingly, quick, procedural investigative story
lines. But somewhere around September, the ads started featuring Angie in a short skirt with her gun. And we started to

focus more on the personal stories. Not that any of that mattered by this point, though. By then it was clear, at least to me, that the show was a goner.

The network messed with us for all the expected reasons networks do these things: executives with an agenda, the politics of programming, simple inexplicable blundering. But at ABC, at this time, there was more than the usual share of this sort of thing. You see, the main reason we could never quite figure out who we were was that our network couldn't quite figure out who it was.

At the 1997 upfronts, ABC tried to reinvent itself with the slogan "TV is Good." This was the brainchild of ABC's new head of network television, Jamie Tarses, whose struggles with the network and senior management are well documented. Most people I knew made fun of the slogan—which you could understand since it pretty much begged for satirization—but honestly, I liked it. I thought it was hip, self-referential. The trouble was the network's shows were not. Well, some were, but the rest, like our show, were all over the place. Rather than specifically positioning themselves, focusing on a specific demographic of the audience, ABC was pretty much trying to target everyone: the heartland base that loved *Roseanne*, urban men who watched *NYPD Blue*, young working white girls who showed up for *Dharma*. Hell, on *C:16* we had full-on A-stories that featured black actors like Morris Chestnut involved in actual stories with other black actors, this on the same network that featured Ellen, TV's first lesbian. And all of this, by the way, was ultimately managed by the network's new owner, Disney, which was pushing for ABC to be "the family network."

Despite some of the less than charitable comments that made their way through the rumor mill at the time, I actually thought Jamie had the right impulse. Trouble was, she could not have been at a more wrong place at a more wrong time. For in the mid to late nineties, being the new head of network entertainment was less about creating entertainment and more about creating a network. The fact is, in the 1997–98 season, whether they wanted to be or not, ABC was a network of true diversity, and this no longer worked in broadcast television.

By our second week, we were actually *trailing Total Security* at 9:00 in the ratings. This was the last series Bochco developed for ABC as part of his original 1988 ten-show commitment, and the show for which we were supposed to be the lead-in. By the end of October, we were the second-lowest-rated series on the network. We were barely getting 8-shares.

It's an odd thing, working on a lame-duck show. There comes a point where no matter what kind of happy talk the network publicity department is pumping on the skewed ratings propaganda you find in your in-box—*Congrats goes out to C16! Best in Males over 80 in the entire Metro Wichita market!*—you know it's time to start working on another spec. There's also the odd phenomenon of having to write and produce several episodes that you know will never see the light of day in an English-speaking market. Stories previously deemed too weird are dug out. Assistants are given shots. People start casting spouses and significant others. There's a lot of gallows humor. "Friday afternoon martinis" become simply "afternoon martinis," and then it's just a matter of time until a blender is running nonstop in the break room. It is a noise that ominously starts to bring to mind the sound coming from a heart monitor when the patient flatlines.

C:16 was mercifully laid to rest in November after just seven episodes, although due to fans writing in, ABC aired the remaining six in the summer of 1998 on Thursday nights. Several of the writers became extremely close friends, some of whom spent a great deal of time dining outside in our garden after the show was canceled, since much of what I planted that weekend back in staffing season had sprouted and grown like mad by the late fall. And over the next few months, as we waited for the coming season, we had plenty of time to kick back and enjoy it, which we did.

Three premiered in February 1998 and was summarily canceled in March 1998. *Dawson's Creek* premiered on January 20, 1998, and was a huge hit, even bigger than we all imagined. Making it part of our appointment viewing, my wife and I watched every single episode.

ELEVEN

Vertical Integration
and Segregation

*"Everybody comes from a dysfunctional family—it's the nineties.
The only happy families are in TV syndication."*
—Pacey Witter

"We become what we behold."
—Marshall McLuhan

The 1998–99 season was also another record one for writers, the peak of nearly a decade of sharp and steady increases. That year, 3,137 writers worked in all forms of television, about half full-time on staffs. I was one of them.

This season I had even more meetings, of all sorts. There were silly meetings, like one in a Wilshire Boulevard penthouse with Laker Rick Fox, who thought he might want to make a TV show. There were humbling meetings, like one I had with showrunner Joanne Waters, who just a few years earlier had been a student at Carnegie Mellon in a seminar that I went back there to teach. Her show *To Have & to Hold* was one of the hottest new series on the schedule that season. And there were meetings where everything just clicked, like the one

I had with Joe Dougherty at Warner Brothers on May 26, 1998.

A writer with whom I cowrote a script on *C:16*, Anne Lewis Hamilton, had worked closely with Joe on *thirtysomething*. They remained friends even after the show was canceled, partially due to their curious shared interest in kitschy disaster memorabilia. When it looked like his new series for the WB, *Hyperion Bay*, was gonna go, Anne called Joe and recommended me. This is, by the way, how nearly all writers eventually end up on staff, through recommendations made to showrunners by their friends and colleagues. By this point in my career, I was able to see a clear chain of recommendations, starting with Wells. Even with jobs where I had the right specs, recommendations still came into play. For *C:16*, Piller had called Duggan on my behalf. By this point I had figured out that while screenwriters have the luxury of being monsters if they are so inclined, playing nice with others is a key attribute of a writing career in episodic television. Perhaps this is why there are lots of books written by insiders about the movie business, but no one wants to do the same about TV.

I was hired as a coproducer and started pretty much immediately. I couldn't have been happier. My first day of work the first week of June was a one-on-one story breakfast with Joe at DuPars on Ventura. A former playwright who was initially hired and trained by Marshall Herskovitz and Ed Zwick (creators of *thirtysomething*), Joe was a gifted and highly respected television writer. Possessed of a Michael Moore–like zeal, Joe loved working with individual writers, and he especially loved teaching younger ones. I felt honored, lucky to be working so closely with someone like this. Not only had Joe won the Humanitas, he had been nominated for three Emmys and won one. Still, even after a single breakfast, one had the distinct impression that if there was no television business, Joe would either be a professor at a junior college or sitting on a bus bench somewhere screaming at a stranger about Howard Hawks.

Hyperion Bay was created to be the WB's answer to *thirtysomething*. People around town sort of nicknamed it "twentysomething." Like my previous gig, this series showed tremendous promise. Mark-Paul Gosselaar led an outstanding cast. Joe handpicked a talented and atypically small eclectic staff, along with the two of us, Bernie Lechowick (*Home Front*), Marlene Meyer (*Law & Order: CI*), and Wendy Goldman (*Room for Two*). After the first couple weeks we moved into our permanent offices in an old double-wide trailer next to the Warner Brothers wood shop on the ass-end of the lot. If you ever wonder just how valuable your show is to the studio, you can always tell by where they put you. For example, if you worked on *Friends*, you spent your time in the plush high-rise digs of Bright/Kauffman/Crane's offices with an awesome view of the Warners lot and all the double-wide trailers below.

Nevertheless, we all took great pride in what we were doing, and you could see this in the show. It was meticulously, even lovingly, developed. Every detail, no matter how minute, was considered and reflected upon. One day Joe marched into the story room and made a big announcement to us. After several weeks it had finally crystallized in his mind that Marjorie (the protagonist's mother, played by Cindy Pickett) did not wear a watch. This was a big deal. Watching Joe reflect on and develop character and story reminded me very much of the sorts of things we did in drama school.

Bernie Lechowick and I went to the summer TCA tour with Joe that year. This is the Television Critics Association tour, when about two hundred journalists who cover television from around the United States and Canada meet with the producers of TV shows in L.A. to get the scoop on the new fall season. Well, standing by Joe's side at the Ritz-Carlton in Pasadena, I don't think I ever felt so proud of a TV show. Our characters were all thoughtfully conceived. Our story lines had resonance and irony and poetic poignancy. The quality of the show made everyone involved with it proud. Unfortunately, the ratings did not.

After fairly respectable promotion, we premiered on Monday, September 21, 1998, in the 9:00 to 10:00 slot with a 3.7/5-share. Not too shabby for a new network, but from there it was pretty much downhill. By the time the fourth episode aired toward the end of October, it was fairly clear that the show was not working. It was a valiant effort, it really was. As Wells would say, we fought the good fight. But in the end, the show was not prevailing. It happens in TV. It happens a lot. This was not a case where the show needed more time to find itself. It knew what it was. That network at that time simply did not have the audience for the show we were making.

Now, when *C:16* hit this point, the drinks started flowing, we finished up our commitment to the network, and that was the end of it. And if *Hyperion Bay* had been made in any previous season, that too would have been the end of it. We would have eventually met with a dignified and noble end. We would have died a natural death.

But this was not a season like any other that had come be-

fore and this was not a show like any other that had come before. *Hyperion Bay* was the very first television series that was
made by Warner Brothers (the studio) and broadcast on the
WB (the network)—both owned by the same parent company,
TimeWarner. We were not gonna just go quietly into the night.

Even before the ratings started coming in, the notes arrived
from the network. And they were radical and substantive. The
network seemed to be asking for something that was in many
ways antithetical to what their own studio had sold them.
They kept saying "Melrose" to their *thirtysomething*-trained
showrunner, who was told in no uncertain terms to find hipper stories and pick up the pace. Directives like "It's not Ibsen!
It's television!" were not well received. By episode #3, to say
that our showrunner's relationship with the network had become contentious would be, well, courteous.

In the third week of October, Joe was fired and Frank South,
the former executive producer of *Melrose Place*, was hired. Suddenly, our carefully and lovingly developed series was Spelling-
ized. We burned down our set. Relit the whole show in bright,
vivid colors. Played campy music under all the scenes throughout the entire show. Gave the actors great hair, put them in
skimpy clothes, and wrote them stories where they were running around sleeping with each other. Oh, and we hired Carmen
Electra, an artist who ruffled more than a few feathers for our
costumers, lighting designers, and several cast members when it
was discovered that she refused to wear underwear.

It wasn't long before we had a fairly fleshed out character
for Carmen—we called her Sarah and made her a Harvard
MBA. At that point, one of the writers literally broke down
crying to me as we walked from the parking lot, saying she

just couldn't do this. She was able to get out of her contract. Another writer had already quit. In the end, Bernie and I (and one more young staff writer who joined us) helped Frank make "The New *Hyperion Bay*." In a heartbeat, we went from being associated with Emmys and the Humanitas to being "Hyperion Baywatch" or "Hyperion Place." As silly as it was, though, I have to admit, I thought it was actually fun. Writing lines where Carmen Electra talks like a brilliant, Ivy League–educated, razor-sharp CEO is an experience very few TV writers ever get to have.

After Joe's departure and Frank's arrival, the network effectively took over. I don't know how much of this was simply the sheer force of personalities at the WB and how much was due to their clear and unambiguous focus on their mission, but it seemed as though the studio threw up their hands and said to their network, "Do whatever you want. You're owners of this thing now too." The voices that I heard now on speakerphones were network voices. The notes I was given I was told came directly from the network. Most of what I heard and was given came from the WB's head of current television, John Litvack, a man who obviously had great authority and yet, curiously, could not have been more different than his associates. Although those above him were about my age, John was just about old enough to be our dad. Replete with pallid white beard and nicotine-yellowed teeth, one was reminded much more of a Civil War officer than a creative executive on the hippest network in town.

To fully appreciate this point you have to understand that television—and the WB in particular—was thought to be so age-conscious in its hiring practices that thirty-two-year-old writer Riley Weston felt she had to lie about her age, claiming she was *nineteen*, in order to get hired onto *Felicity*. Everyone believed her story: the producers who put her on the show, her agents at UTA, even the executives at Touchstone, who so felt she was an authentic teenage voice that they gave her an additional $300,000 development deal to create new shows. *Entertainment Weekly* listed her as one of Hollywood's 100 Most Creative People before she was found out. How could all these people fall for this? Partially because Riley, a divorced professional actress whose real name is Kimberlee Kramer, was so young-looking. And partially because the premium for delivering young audiences was so significant, and the need for new writing talent that could speak to those audiences lagged so far behind the proliferation of new programs being created for them, that producers, agents, and executives did not want to ask too many unnecessary questions when they found someone who seemingly fit the bill. Nevertheless, despite the downright obsession with youth, Mr. Litvack seemed to have absolute authority. In addition, it was impossible for a writer not to note his devotion to what he was doing.

Though everyone in and out of town naturally assumed that the "new" *Hyperion Bay* sprung full-born from the mind of *Melrose*'s Frank South, this was in truth not the case. Shortly after being hired, Frank realized that he was there to give the network precisely what they wanted, something his predecessor refused to do. John Litvack insisted that there be a "Heather" (à la *Melrose*) on the show leading to the hiring of Carmen. He literally demanded that our young ingenue, played by Cassidy Rae, take off her shirt as soon as possible on the show. In fact, he was so steadfastly committed to seeing this particular actress engage in a story line that would culminate in such an action that the objections of the actress were met with outright disdain.

Though the impulses for these kinds of salacious characters and stunts may have been to pump up ratings on what was perceived to be a floundering series, they actually ended up doing much more damage than good to the show. In retrospect this is very easy to see. But at the time, there was virtually no recourse for the show. Joe's treatment at the hands of the network and the studio was a clear and present cautionary tale for the cast, crew, and staff, as well as for other TV writers around town.

In the days when MTM produced television shows, the studio's executives actively participated in the creative discourse that determined the overall direction of a series. Since the studio was concerned not with provisional stunts that would just keep a show going week to week but with its overall quality—which translated into better syndication sales—a studio supported the writer and the integrity of his or her vision. With the studio now out of the equation, this checks-and-balances system between studio and network were gone. The network now had free and unadulterated run of all aspects of a series, from marketing to casting to story. Television was now, quite literally, at the mercy of an individual network executive's personal predilections.

Network executives, who had previously been a gear in a complex and balanced system, became autocratic heads of the entire operation almost overnight—and they were charged with running everything. It was a creative coup d'état financed by the world's biggest media giants, and while the global business possibilities were very exciting, to say the least, the effects this had on the actual product were detrimental. Removing the studio from the mix was like taking Congress away from the president. There were no advisors, no forum for debate, no creative due process. Dissent was disallowed and dealt with harshly.

In the thirties the studio system rose to prominence. In the fifties and sixties, this was usurped by the rise of the star and their agents. By the eighties, the true golden era of television was born, ushered in by the supremacy of the writer and the competitive spirit of the independent production companies. In the late nineties now, TV had entered a new era: the age of the conglomerate.

When I was in college in the eighties, there were about thirty major media companies. As of this writing there are six: GE, Viacom, Bertelsmann, TimeWarner, Disney, and News Corp. One way or another, through coproductions with each other, a stake in a formerly independent subsidiary, or complete vertical ownership—meaning the studio that makes the show is owned by the same company as the network that airs it—nearly all TV today is made and broadcast by just these six companies.

By the time Joe Dougherty was let go and John Litvack took over, much had changed in the ten years during which networks like ABC loved writers so much that they not only insured their lives, they valued their souls—so much, in fact, that they left them alone. In the 1998–99 season this change was most readily apparent on shows like *Hyperion Bay*, but it would soon become apparent on many other shows as well.

Although from a purely business perspective, the consolidation of media made a great deal of sense, the conglomerates did something that did not. As they drove the price of writing talent to irrational levels, they simultaneously disempowered the talent that they so desperately sought.

In many ways the entertainment business came full circle in the late nineties. Once again, just like in the early thirties, writers were increasingly perceived as replaceable labor, simple properties of the studio to be used or not used as executives saw fit. The big difference, of course, was that now there was a rock-solid union. There were contracts and powerful, moneyed representatives who lived to enforce them. So while the companies could move writers on and off projects, as they so frequently did in the early days, there was now a cost for doing so. You see, when a TV writer is "fired" or someone is brought in over him (which I think is technically what happened on *Hyperion*), what this essentially means is that he or she is told to stop providing the originally agreed-upon services for a show. It does not mean that he or she stops getting paid. Unless a settlement is negotiated, writers continue to collect their paychecks from the company that "fired" them while they begin working on something else and often for someone else. Although Joe went home, he continued to collect his massive executive producer salary from Warner Brothers, a burden the production had to carry. More and more, as executives became creative participants, this became a common scenario throughout the writing community.

Even after firing the unrepentant Emmy winner, John Litvack continued to be nothing short of outraged at Joe Dougherty, infuriated that Joe still had to be paid from the show's budget, hampering the network's creative options. Even though writers were being paid more and more money, it was with greater and greater derision. Given the tremendous amount of work that network executives were now putting into the TV shows they covered, especially creative work that was once done strictly by writers, it is easy to understand their growing frustration with talent whose jobs they were essentially doing. It was as though John saw *Hyperion Bay* not as a failed TV series created by writer Joseph Dougherty. John saw it as his network's property, as *his* show. He talked about it in first-person terms. I would soon see these same kinds of attitudes about authorship represented again on *Dawson's*.

Honestly—and I recognize I must sound quite naive here—Joe's dismissal was very disconcerting to me, as well. By this point in my career, I'd seen plenty of writers get fired. I'd known of showrunners in whom the studios had lost faith. But I'd never seen such a swift and forceful turnaround during my time in Hollywood. Just a few months earlier Tony Jonas, the head of Warner Brothers Television, came into our story room (which was a very big deal), threw his arm around Joe in front of the writing staff, and declared how much the studio loved him. I think there was even a hug of some sort. I remember thinking, "Man, I am lucky to be on a show that is so loved and protected by the studio. This baby is gonna run forever."

But I was also upset because the very day that Joe had been let go was the same day that my second episode of the show started production. Episode #9, entitled "The Rope," featured an A-story in which the protagonist, Dennis, donates money to his old school only to find out that his gift will be used to build a new gym named after his nemesis, the gym teacher who tormented him throughout high school. The B-story was a love story that culminated in two of our characters kissing for the first time. People seemed to love the script. Mark-Paul, the show's star, called me at home the night my script was published and thanked me. He was extremely complimentary, saying that he had spoken to all the actors and this was their favorite episode of the series. I'd never gotten a phone call like that before. I beamed, until I found out that my episode would not be shot as written. This was the beginning of the overhaul by the network. Several scenes were to be cut, and I was instructed to write one full day's shooting worth of new material. Most of the A-story was thankfully left intact. The primary change was to be the removal of the penultimate moment of the entire episode, the kiss.

The kiss I wrote was between our blond ingenue, Trudy, played by Cassidy Rae, and our dark, handsome, new series regular, Marcus, played by Chaka Forman. Cassidy was white. Chaka was black.

African Americans were not exactly a new phenomenon on the WB. It must be remembered that the network began by exclusively programming black sitcoms. On Wednesday, January 11, 1995, the network offered its first night of television shows, with *The Wayans Bros.*, *The Parent 'Hood*, *Unhappily Ever After*, and *Muscle*. WB CEO Jamie Kellner had previously worked with many of the actors and producers associated with these first shows when he was an executive at Fox, and he knew he could use this talent to find a niche market for the new netlet. But it wasn't long before the network began branching out from its original audience. In August 1996 the network started programming Monday nights with *7th Heaven*. But the real success would come a few months later on March 10, 1997, with *Buffy*. Although the network had captured a strong African American market with its ethnic sitcoms, and despite the relatively strong ratings (especially with families) for *7th Heaven*, it would be *Buffy* that would define the network. After *Buffy*, the network's identity came into clear focus. After *Buffy*, development would no longer be like the broadly targeted, diverse, hit-or-miss strategies over at ABC. The WB now knew exactly who it was, and it programmed accordingly. So when *Dawson's* came its way during this pivotal time, the decision to pick it up was an easy one. When *Dawson's* premiered, more than 6.8 million people watched, the network's largest numbers yet, and the vast majority of them were the lucrative teen audience. Nine months later, in October 1998, *Felicity* aired and it was the same story, 7.1 million viewers. Although ABC won the night in overall viewers, *Felicity* ranked number one in its time period among teens 12 to 17, with a 20-share, and was through the roof among teenage girls, with a 33-share. By this point, the network's brand image was a done deal. While Kellner's former employers at Fox tried to expand their base beyond the *90210* and *Melrose* audiences with shows like *Ally McBeal*, the WB consolidated the teenage audience and by 1998 became the number-one network with that valuable hard-to-reach market.

Although ABC and the other big nets continued to beat the WB in overall ratings, because the network was able to deliver the young audience most desired by marketers, the reality was that advertising rates on the WB were often higher than top-rated but older-skewing shows, like CBS's *60 Minutes*. The teen audience, along with the 18- to 34-year-old audience—the 12 to 34s—is prized by advertisers because they have disposable income and they try new products—actually, they *want* to try new products. They eat fast food, go to the movies, listen to music, consume soft drinks, and focus on the latest fashion. This is who most television is made for, quite simply because this is who most advertisers want. So even though *60 Minutes* may have gotten great numbers, they were numbers of people who were spending the bulk of their money on gas bills, a mortgage, and expenses not paid for by Medicare—not a particularly useful group for most marketers. In 1999, during *Dawson's* third season, NBC lost 16 percent of its female 18 to 34 audience, whereas the WB was up almost 20 percent in that same demographic. In 1996, the netlet took in about $100 million at upfronts. By 1999, it took in well over half a billion dollars, about $600 million, in ad revenues. Clearly, the network was on to something.

Anyone surfing their TV at this time knew without a doubt when they landed on the WB. You could watch a WB show and know within seconds what network was broadcasting it. No other broadcast network had been able to create such a strong brand. Unlike ABC, WB shows had a very specific look, sound, and sensibility. While the big three all went for images that emphasized their broad appeal to the American public at large, Kellner chose a frog as the network's logo. Based on the 1955 Warner Brothers cartoon, Michigan J. Frog, it was fun, lighthearted, and most important, youthful. And unlike ABC, which was unable to live up to the promise of its hip image, the "Frog" shows did. Unlike the major networks who were clumsily defined by the shows they picked up, the WB exclusively picked up shows that fit its own definition. Unlike the big nets that really were nothing more than the sum of their parts, the WB had a rock-solid brand that actually meant something to its audience. You see, the WB had really become very much like what MTM once was, a producer with a clear vision for its own unique brand of programming—only the WB was a network, not a production company.

By this time, all the networks were growing increasingly involved not just in programming but in the hands-on production of the shows in which they now had an interest. But the WB was often even more involved. And as the network became clearer about their brand, they became even more proactive in making sure their products conformed. By the time *Hyperion* rolled around, the WB was very clear about this. From music to story to casting, the WB made sure their flagship shows all had a consistent image. From vampires on *Angel* to aliens on *Roswell* to the nerds on *Popular*, everyone was young, fashionable, and hot. Even extras had to have a "WB-brand look." Computer geek day-players on *Hyperion* who looked too authentically geeky or "too cool for the room" (the politically correct way to say "not good-looking enough") were let go and replaced with WB-brand geeks, models wearing glasses and ill-fitting clothing. And attractiveness was not the only desirable trait of the brand look. Race was a significant factor as well.

Although the actual slices of audience shares were much smaller than the major nets, the demographics on nearly all the WB shows were among those most sought by ad buyers. Mind you, I'm not talking about individual shows produced by a specialty shop like MTM, I'm talking about all the shows on an entire network. If there was one thing that was crystal clear about the entertainment and media industry at the start of the millennium, it was that diverse mass-appeal broadcasting was dead and "narrowcasting" was the wave of the future. The new model for television that the WB mastered became not just creating a good show that everyone will like, but creating a certain kind of show for a certain kind of audience and then letting that audience know precisely where they can find that show and others just like it.

Probably the best way to fully understand how this manifests itself in TV is to look at the people who were hired to write it. If there is a dirty little secret in the TV business, this is it. It may not surprise most people to learn that TV writers are young, white males. But let me spell it out. According to the *Hollywood Writers Report*, the season right after *Hyperion*, 1998–99, the people who wrote television were 93 percent white, 74 percent male, and (in 1996–97) 83 percent younger than fifty.

This has remained a stunningly consistent story since then. In the 2004–2005 season, the small group of people who created most of the content that drives the global media machine were 91 percent white, 73 percent male, and 82 percent younger than fifty. Of the 3,015 writers who worked in television that season, only 822 were women and only 287 were minorities, 5 percent African American, 2 percent Latino, 2 percent Asian.

But to really understand the true story, you have to look even deeper. Of those women and minorities who do work, most work at the bottom of the ladder. Of the 288 showrunners, only 17 percent were women and only 9 percent were minorities. The vast majority are staff writers and story editors.

And if you dig even deeper, you will see that many, if not most, of these women and minorities who are working are not working on major broadcast network shows, but cable shows. They are not working on popular mainstream shows, but specialty programs placed in certain segregated timeslots. Women worked on female-themed shows with small audiences like *Strong Medicine* on Lifetime or *Eve* on UPN.

The minorities who worked did so almost exclusively on minority-themed UPN shows like *One on One*, *Second Time Around*, and *Cuts*. In fact, seven of the top ten shows that employed the most minorities were UPN minority-themed sitcoms. Nearly half of all TV shows, 44.2 percent, did not employ any minority writers.

How many black, Latino, or Asian writers were employed on WB shows during the 2004–2005 season?

• *Charmed*	0
• *Everwood*	0
• *Gilmore Girls*	0
• *Jack and Bobby*	0
• *Living with Fran*	0
• *One Tree Hill*	0
• *Reba*	0
• *Smallville*	0
• *Summerland*	0
• *What I Like About You*	0
• *7th Heaven*	1

By 2004, after the WB's original African American sitcoms were canceled, as far as I can tell, the network employed just one minority writer.

And if you look at the 1999 season, when the minority-themed sitcoms were still on the air, *Buffy*; *Angel*; *Felicity*; *Roswell*; *Popular*; *Jack and Jill*; *Zoe, Duncan, Jack & Jane*; *Young Americans*; and *Dawson's Creek*—the shows that the network vigilantly made sure conformed to their brand—employed exactly zero minority writers. The entire writing staffs on all of those shows were white.

But the few remaining minority-themed sitcoms that were consolidated and programmed in blocks on Friday nights that season—*The Steve Harvey Show*, *For Your Love*, and *The Jamie Foxx Show*, employed twenty-two minorities. The staff of the latter was 100 percent minorities.

When I was in high school, on several occasions, my friends and I drove from Atlanta to Charleston, South Carolina. There is a stretch of I-20 before you get to Augusta that takes you through some rural sections of Georgia where time pretty much stands still. I will never forget the experience of eating lunch in some of the establishments one finds along this corridor. Although racial segregation in public places was legally abolished in Georgia in 1964, the white folks and the black folks still sat in completely different sections of the restaurants in these places. I do not know why. My best guess is simply habit. As a customer, coming into one of these places, it was as clear as the color of your skin where you were to sit. For me, the image of those two groups, eating together but separately under the same roof, reminds me very much of the television business since the end of Fin-Syn. Women write women's shows. Blacks write black shows. Broadcasters place these products where their targeted customers will find them, branding their shelf space accordingly.

⌒∦⌒

The more I worked in Hollywood the more I saw that the disparity between the general population and the people I worked with was nothing short of stunning. Fifty-one percent of Americans are female, but only 27 percent of TV writers are female. More than 30 percent of Americans are nonwhite, but only 9 percent of TV writers are nonwhite. Spanish is the second most popular language in this country. The number-one network evening news program in America—often ahead of ABC, CBS, and NBC—is *Noticiero Univision,* which is on the fifth-largest American network, Univision. More than 12 percent of Americans speak Spanish, yet only 2 percent of the people who write TV are Latinos. Although small L.A. communities, like Brentwood and Westwood and Malibu, which are heavily populated by above-the-line entertainment industry professionals, may look pretty white, the reality is that L.A.'s population is nearly half Hispanic. Even if you are riding in the back of a limo, you can't get from Santa Monica Canyon to any of the major studios without noticing this. Yet the stories we tell are white stories written by white people and cast with white people.

Now, while it's tempting to accuse Hollywood of racism, in the generally agreed-upon sense of the word, this just isn't the case. In fact, from my experience, nothing could be further from the truth.

Despite the ongoing prevalence of white boys on staffs, the

TV writers and executives I met, as a rule, are fervently liberal. Despite being in the top 1 percent of this country's income bracket, these people militantly support the democratic agenda, including tax increases on the wealthy and especially expanded social programs. TV writers in particular are extremely vocal about their liberal causes. In fact, in one story room, I happen to know for a fact that one of the writers was actually a registered Republican. Gasp! Actually, this writer was a closet Republican who was nothing short of paranoid about keeping it that way. And I have to tell you, from what I saw, this was not a bad career decision. Perhaps with the notable exception of Donald Bellisario's staffs, the Fox News–watching gentlemen who wrote *JAG* and such, nearly every TV writer and executive that I met was on mailing lists from Move On to Farm Aid, Greenpeace to the American Black Film Festival Awards. I can't tell you how many times I agreed to sponsor someone running ten kilometers in support of something involving the breast. No, the more I worked on TV staffs the more it became perfectly clear to me that racism has nothing to do with how TV gets made. Quite simply, it's all about money.

No one likes to talk openly about this in Hollywood. But privately, they do. I participated in heated conversations about this topic around the story table, in commissaries, at dinner parties. I heard it discussed with great conviction, season after season, but nothing changes. The audience blames the networks. The networks blame the advertisers. The advertisers blame the audience. And in the middle of this endless cycle, writers just try to write shows that will get picked up and stay on the air.

One of the reasons no one likes to talk about it openly is because it is such an emotionally charged topic. At a seminar for TV writers in 1994, David Milch explained that he felt it was hard for African Americans to write TV dramas because "when they wrote out of the complexities of their own experience . . . the result might be powerful and compelling as art but not commercially successful." Although he was strictly trying to give an honest assessment of the situation for purely instructive purposes, *The Washington Post* ran an article, essentially accusing him of racism.

Here's the deal. The distasteful truth is that white audiences are worth more money than black audiences to advertisers. Even though racial minorities are clearly growing in size and affluence in this country, they are still not as desired by mainstream television networks. The average white person is believed to earn more money than the average black person (the NAACP supports this statistic), so the white person is more desired by an advertiser in the same way that a young person is more desired than an old person. Thus, a network that can deliver the more affluent viewer can charge a higher rate for his or her attention.

"Market segmentation," "narrowcasting," and "branding" are all fashionable buzz words that essentially mean "find the money." Thirty seconds of a seventeen-year-old white girl's attention is worth more money than her mother's, her father's, her grandmother's, her grandfather's, and nearly all African Americans'. If a shampoo company can get that girl to try their product, they could very well have a customer for life. She is gold to them, and they will pay accordingly for access to her. For the corporations that control our media to put

anything—social consciousness, public interest, producing quality TV simply for quality's sake—above the pursuit of profit, would run counter to their clearly mandated, even *legally required*, charter.

But here's where it gets more complicated. Despite the fact that blacks earn less money as a rule and so therefore are worth less money to Madison Avenue, they also watch a lot more television. This means that they should be easier to entice to other types of programs, more diverse shows on more diverse networks. This would lead one to believe that more shows would be developed that would be inclusive to these loyal viewers. But instead, the opposite occurs. Blacks are directed to the handful of black shows. They are herded to black blocks of programming. The same is done with older audiences, to a certain extent with women, and with other subsets of the market as well. And as television is no longer experienced in familial groups or watched with friends but increasingly downloaded onto a very personal two-inch screen, TV shows are increasingly being tailor-made for the highly specific audiences that buy it and the specialized hardware on which it can be watched. Ironically, in the post-McLuhan world, television seems to be destroying the very "global village" it not so long ago created. Instead of a "retribalization," we are experiencing a *de*tribalization.

Whether it is the nature of human beings to huddle together with their own kind to hear stories exclusively about their own experiences, or whether network programmers are culpable for the phenomenon, I don't know. But one thing's for sure. As offensive as executives may find the situation on a personal, moral, and even creative level, it is not in the interest of an entertainment conglomerate to desegregate television. Knowing precisely where a certain audience is located is the defining principle, the defining achievement, really, of modern media buying. Programming effectively branded entertainment is the machinery that accomplishes this.

When I was growing up in the seventies, blacks and whites watched the same shows. Programs like *The Jeffersons*, *Diff'rent Strokes*, *Good Times*, and *Amen* were not only popular hits, they were broadly popular. When black kids and white kids talked about last night's TV shows at school, we had a shared experience. Not so long ago, we all drank from the same water cooler. A decade or so ago, black sitcoms written by black writers and airing strictly with other black sitcoms on a single night on an otherwise white network did not exist. Instead, we had shows like *Cosby* and *A Different World*, which were lead-ins for *Cheers*, the anchors of TV's most popular night of programming. Where did these shows come from? Independent producers. In 2004–2005, 18 percent of the writers employed by Carsey-Werner, producer of *Cosby* and *A Different World*, as well as *Roseanne*, *3rd Rock from the Sun*, *Cybill*, *Grace Under Fire*, *Grounded for Life*, and *That '70s Show*, were minorities. Carsey-Werner was the last fully independent production company, squeezed out of the business in July 2005. Scott Collins of the *Los Angeles Times* said it perfectly: "Carsey-Werner basically became the equivalent of a mom-and-pop grocer in a Wal-Mart world."

If money is the heart of the problem, consolidation is the force that is squeezing the heart. In what has to be one of the great paradoxes of our time, the FCC ultimately got rid of Fin-

Syn and deregulated media so that the unfettered marketplace would encourage all voices and interests to join in and compete. You know, laissez-faire free-market capitalism and all that sort of thing. The theory being that the best would rise to the top. But here's the rub. Who's to say what's best in television? We can easily say what's most watched, but unlike other industries, popularity does not necessarily correlate with value. As we have seen, TV's appeal is purely subjective and absolutely unpredictable. We are all touched, moved, and tickled in entirely different ways. We all like different kinds of TV. There are millions of different strongly held beliefs about what is the best television, and they are all valid. Deregulating the mechanisms that produce and distribute entertainment and expecting the best TV shows to then rise to the top is like putting a few hundred random paintings up for auction and assuming that the ones that fetch the most money are the best. The deregulation of the media has created a market where those with the most money get the best TV shows made for them. And those with the most money control access to the production and distribution mechanisms, thereby creating barriers to entry that are virtually impenetrable. If you are a wealthy white kid, yeah, TV is good.

Forget about the implications that media deregulation and the consequent consolidation has for our press and our political system should GE, owner of NBC, a company that was the third-largest producer of nuclear weapons and still sells military hardware to the Pentagon, really be reporting the news?; combining the producers and distributors of nearly all television into a small handful of entities is the greatest obstruction to diversity in entertainment. This plays out in all aspects of television, from what is broadcast, to how new shows are pitched, to how existing shows are run.

Those with the authority to green-light would like nothing better than to pick up the next big drama from a minority writer with a minority lead. But when shows like Bochco's acclaimed *City of Angels*, made in 2000 with African American writers and African American actors for CBS, struggles to find ratings, then is given a pickup anyway but still fails, executives think twice about such a move. Who knows why it failed? Maybe it was the behind-the-scenes problems with some of the original producers and actors. Maybe African Americans didn't like the show. Maybe they didn't know where to find it. Maybe the show would have eventually found an audience. CBS claimed it was doing everything possible to support the show, but in the end, after a season and a half, *City of Angels* never achieved the ratings necessary to justify the expense of production. The cancellation was just business, nothing more or less. But after these kinds of attempts, a major studio-network simply cannot responsibly explain to its shareholders that it is developing similar programming because maybe next time or the time after an important show will find traction and become profitable. When networks are under pressure from their corporate parents and stockholders to attain rapid and demonstrative success, those with the authority to green-light are under great pressure to pay attention to the business model of the WB.

Likewise, why would a writer, black or white, male or female, bring a pitch for a cool new show with a diverse point of view to one of the big studio-networks, where it would have little chance of getting picked up and little chance of getting support? If a writer did have such a concept, his or her representation would bring the writer to the appropriate cable channel or specialty network. On several occasions I presented ideas for a new show to Dan, who took me specifically to Lifetime or specifically to Fox. When you add this to the void left by the disappearance of the independents, the major networks aren't even presented with many good options for broadly targeted shows.

And likewise, remember how those recommendations come into play when staffing a show? What this really means is that showrunners are staffing their shows almost entirely with their friends and friends of friends. Friends tend to run in the same circles and, as we all know, these circles tend to be defined by age, sex, and race. However, in Los Angeles, these circles are tighter and smaller than in perhaps any other city in this country. Once again, this is a function of money more than anything else. There are many cities and communities in America where an individual can live just fine on $36,000 a year and a family of four can live just fine on $60,000 a year. This is hard to do in Los Angeles. To be blunt, there is no middle class in L.A., not in the way there is in the rest of America.

Particularly in the entertainment community, people have either great abundance or they live hand to mouth. The more I worked in the business the more I saw that those who work regularly tend to live a lifestyle predicated on the former, and consequently they become removed from the greater society. Usually, it happens slowly at first. A nicer car. Then a house in a hip part of Venice. Then a gardener, a personal trainer, and the next thing you know you're living behind gates. Suddenly and seemingly without warning, you know much more about

Lutron light switches and automated curtains than you do about the people who install them. Your real and direct connection with the greater culture is severed, supplanted strictly by what you talk to other working writers about, hear on certain radio stations, read on certain blogs, and especially by what you see on TV. It is a strange and ironically self-perpetuating pseudo-reality where what is important is decided by hearsay rather than by direct experience. Many white writers in L.A. will tell you quite openly that they just don't know a lot of black people. They don't know stories they feel they can tell with real authenticity beyond their own experiences, and the longer they live in L.A. and the more successful they become, the narrower those experiences become.

Every showrunner I ever worked with wants to make strictly meritocratic, color-blind decisions when reading through a pile of scripts. In fact, I watched many try hard to do this. But when push comes to shove, especially on a new series or a series that isn't a keeper yet—which is most shows—staff hiring decisions are made in the comfort zone. It's understandable. With the support writers used to get from studios gone, replaced by creative mandates from meddling executives and the fear of a fate like Joe Dougherty's if they are not met, showrunners are under fire from all sides. The fact is, in the wake of the consolidation that began in the nineties, Hollywood became more insular and closed than anytime in its history.

So you see, there are a lot of reasons why there were no black people having A-stories on the A-shows on the WB network. But at the end of the day, here's the main one. It has been twenty-eight years since the first interracial TV kiss, between Nichelle Nichols and William Shatner on *Star Trek*. It is hard to imagine that the *Hyperion Bay* kiss was deleted because the network feared controversy. A few months after the kiss was removed, the writing staff on *Dawson's*, of which I was a part, dreamed up a female African American character who would befriend our lead, Dawson. Her name was Nikki. We cast her with a young actress named Bianca Lawson. We pitched the idea of a romantic relationship between her and Dawson to the network, but that never got very far. Nikki appeared in four episodes before we stopped writing her.

The interracial kiss on *Hyperion* was not deleted because anyone was afraid it would cause a stir. It was removed because it did not fit the brand.

TWELVE

Kissing Katie Holmes

"Art may imitate life, but life imitates TV."
—Ani DiFranco

A t the end of October 1998, the same week that Joe Dougherty was fired and Frank South and John Litvack took over, we got the double blue lines: my wife was pregnant. I'll be honest. As all-consuming to the point of shameless narcissism that a life in TV can be, this news had a way of putting *everything* into a new perspective. I have no doubt this is one of the main reasons I not only stayed with *Hyperion*, worked my ass off, and wrote five scripts, but also did these things with a smile on my face.

To be sure, getting pregnant immediately causes you to reevaluate everything in your life, from where you live to how you spend your time to who you spend it with. As all who have had children can surely attest, there is nothing more life-altering. However, when you live and work at the center of popular culture, impending babyhood causes a special kind of assessment. For as anyone who grew up watching Kevin Bacon in *She's Having a Baby* knows, having a baby is historically proven to take a toll on one's cool quotient.

Now, that's not to say that TV writers don't have kids. As they become elderly and approach their midthirties, many do. And many find a way to temper the loss of cool by joining the Hollywood baby culture. It's an odd culture. Your Lamaze class is filled with celebrities who adorn the cover of *Fit Pregnancy*, women who are swapping names of the best night nannies because they sure as hell aren't gonna be getting up at three A.M. to comfort a colicky kid. The militant La Leche League ladies who stop by to instruct you on how to breast-feed are out-of-work sitcom actresses who leave their headshots on the way out. We had friends in other parts of the country who were giving their kids hip throwback names like Max and Hannah and Maddie, while the people we hung out with were going for unheard of things like Zoe and Eliana and Sydney (which, as of this writing, I think, are now broadly popular).

On the advice of several high-profile female writers we knew, my wife and I got the name of one of the best ob-gyns in town, a woman who we were told delivered *everybody's* baby. We had a hell of a time finding this physician's office because her door was unmarked, which we later discovered was to keep the paparazzi from staking out the place. While we met with her, trying to decide if we wanted her to deliver our child, the woman made a point of not only referencing her traditional credentials, but of repeatedly name-dropping as well as providing a few spicy details. She *had* delivered everybody's baby, and she wanted us to know about it.

It is a common practice among all business owners in L.A. to let you know who their customers are. Every single dry cleaner you go into has that wall of headshots. Auto repair places have them. Insurance sales offices. While you wait to be seated in nearly any restaurant in town, you read signed 8 x 10s by people like Farrah Fawcett and Dom DeLuise and Ellen DeGeneres declaring their special affection for a particular course and expressing their gratitude for "Not only the best baklava but the best service in town, too!"

However, my wife and I felt that gynecological care is where we had to draw the line. Not only did we go with a highly experienced and significantly more discreet ob-gyn (we didn't find out until after our daughter was born that he had recently delivered Maria Shriver's baby), we also began to wonder if we really wanted this kind of baby-makes-three life in Hollywood.

My wife had a very successful career in print modeling. You know when you go to buy a picture frame there's that temporary picture of a woman in the frame? That's my wife. You've seen her on digital camera boxes, Fortune 500 shareholder reports, the IHOP menu. She's the woman on the Pizza Hut point-of-purchase display biting into that cheese in the crust pizza. Often hired as "the young mom," she spent a lot of time working with Hollywood kids, and this had a strong effect on her attitudes about child-rearing. Eight weeks pregnant, after finishing up a fourteen-hour shoot for a GMC Safari ad on the Santa Monica Pier where she posed as a mother with a young boy, the young boy model refused to release her. He literally would not stop clutching on to her. Evidently, this kid, who had missed school all day, was so lacking in parental

attention and so burned out from being dragged around to auditions that he just wanted to go home with her. That experience put my wife over the edge, making her determined to find
a way for *us* to keep working in Hollywood, but to raise our
kid as far out of it as possible.

A few days later, while I was working at Warners, my wife
went looking at houses. She called me late in the afternoon.

> *Wife* (over happy noise in the background):
> Hi, honey!
>
> *Me:* Hi. Where are you?
>
> *Wife:* Mimi's Cafe.
>
> *Me:* Where's that?
>
> *Wife:* It's the most adorable little restaurant filled
> with moms and kids and . . .
>
> *Me:* (suspicious): *Where are you?*
>
> *Wife:* Valencia.
>
> *Me:* Not gonna happen.
>
> *Wife:* I love it up here.
>
> *Me:* Honey, there is no way in hell that I am mov-
> ing to the suburbs. Trust me, it's not gonna
> happen.
>
> *Cut to:* Three months later, the moving truck
> unloads our belongings in our new house in
> Valencia.

Valencia is a rapidly developing planned city thirty miles north
of Los Angeles. It has good schools, paseos (pathways) that wind
behind the houses, and a plentiful and convenient assortment

of brand-spanking-new Super Targets and Olive Gardens. When Realtors in Valencia hear that you are "in the business" they are quick to point out that a lot of industry people live there. I soon discovered that this was true, although the "industry people" were the so-called below the line (referring to where one's name falls on a TV show's call sheet) employees, meaning truck drivers, grips, cameramen, teamsters. This began to change right after we moved up, but I'll get to that.

Many of our friends thought we were crazy. Hilary and Chad literally did an "intervention," confronting us and finally trying to talk us into Westlake Village, an "above the line" suburb down the 101 just past Calabasas. But my wife was determined, and after I got used to the idea and realized that I could, in fact, still be a writer, I started to love it.

We bought a big, brand-new, 3,500-square-foot box, on a tiny 5,700-square-foot lot, for $437,500. It was ugly as hell, cheaply constructed, and the property line was precisely sixty inches from the house—all the property lines were like this— so if I reached out my bedroom window and my neighbor reached out his, one of us could hand the other a cold Bud. In fact, the houses were so close that we used to pick up our neighbor's children crying on *our* baby monitor, as well as other things that it would not be gentlemanly to go into.

But the neighbors were all very nice. They had wonderfully boring jobs and fascinatingly regular lives and couldn't have cared less about what I did. The house had all the modern appliances and conveniences they stuck in these big boxes. Getting a gallon of milk from the just-built Super Ralphs with all the special "Expectant Mommy" parking at anytime, night or day, was not only easy, it was safe. We held hands and took long walks with Maggie on the paseos at night. Looking, I'm sure, like the treacly sweet couple on the cover of the "Welcome to Valencia" brochures, we were about to have a baby, and life was great, no matter how uncool. In fact, I reveled in my uncoolness. And *that* was somehow kind of cool.

We moved into our new house the exact same week that *Hyperion Bay* met an unnatural death and was finally canceled on March 8, 1999. Not surprisingly, the Carmen Electra version of our show did not do any better in the ratings than the original version. It was now time to prepare for staffing season again. So you see, even though we were living in the suburbs, we were still very much living an industry life. I think it's fair to say that we were the only people on our street who had just moved into a brand-new house, started furnishing it, were expecting a baby in a few months, and had no job. That's a life in TV.

I think it's also fair to say that I was the only man on my street sitting around his house in sweatpants all day during April 1999 writing a spec *Felicity*.

After staying up all night on Thursday, April 15, I sent my *Felicity* to Dan on Friday, and on Monday got word that he wanted to use my *Northern Exposure* and *Profiler* again that season. He did not respond to my new spec. I was bummed. Not just because of all the recent effort I'd put into it, but because I knew in my bones the thing worked. On the first couple pages, Felicity, about to have sex for the first time, ends up having to do the Heimlich on her boyfriend Noel, who chokes on the condom wrapper. By this point in my career I'd realized that the first few pages of a spec were by far the most important, and at the very least the teaser in my new script, this first scene, worked. I asked him to give it to his assistant, which of course he did. In a town where your assistant can literally be running a TV network a few years after she's answering your phone, Dan knew to trust her taste. She loved it. He sent it out, and, sure enough, readers responded. Within days I had a batch of fresh meetings. Some of the more exciting ones were at DreamWorks for *Freaks and Geeks*, Granada for a new series, *Cold Feet*, and with a screenwriter, Les Bohem, for his new Spielberg-produced miniseries, *Taken*. But I still kept thinking about *Dawson's*. Despite some inexplicably peculiar episodes in the second season, I remained a huge fan.

Whenever you go to these staffing meetings during this time of the year, you always see stacks of TV scripts in executive and showrunner offices. These are scripts from all the other writers who are also in consideration for a job on the staff. Some of these stacks are five feet high. Most have fancy, powerful covers on them from the likes of CAA and UTA and ICM. And you often know whose scripts they are because some poor assistant with an MBA has just spent many late nights writing the writer's name in black Sharpie on the spines of the scripts. So as you sit there, waxing on about how blown away you were by the show on which you are meeting, you realize just how many other highly qualified writers, many who you know, are also in consideration. You also know just how hot a show is by the height of the piles.

Although the *Freaks and Geeks* piles nearly covered the windows at DreamWorks, I knew that in May 1999, Paul Stupin's were probably among the highest in town. And I knew that if I had any hope of getting to the top of one of his piles, I would have to do something. So I called my friend Rita Hsiao, who had recently written a pilot for Paul. She was delighted to call Paul on my behalf. Paul told her he had just hired a new EP and would talk to her about me. The new EP was Tammy Ader, another Beth client and a very dear friend of mine during my first five years in town. She read my *Felicity* and liked it. I met Paul and Tammy on May 5 at the *Dawson's* offices, and a good time was had by all.

That night, as I sat in our Valencia Lamaze class with the other excited dads and noncelebrity moms-to-be, I felt good. I knew something was in the works. It's a sensation that most TV writers tune in to at some point. Yes, at the end of the day, an insistent showrunner is the main reason you get on a staff. But more often, especially in the post–Fin-Syn world, staffing is a more complex and often even diplomatic process. Often, getting a staff job, particularly on a great show, requires a tremendous amount of enthusiasm from many different fronts. Sometimes it requires so much buzz, in fact, that you can just about feel the stars being pushed into alignment. You know that your senses are correct and that the alignment is occurring when they call your representation for your quotes (your last episodic rate, which, in 1999, had to be topped), and when you get called in for the official executive vetting.

Six days after my Paul-Tammy meeting, I was asked to appear for the vetting. Driving onto the Culver Studios lot where Columbia TriStar Television was located, I passed a huge billboard of my wife. Though she looked quite happy in her Air New Zealand flight attendant uniform, I knew all too well that behind the girl-next-door smile she was really thinking,

"Get something good this season. *Please* don't bring Carmen Electra into our lives again."

The management offices were in The Mansion, a massive grand colonial mansion used in the opening of *Gone with the Wind*, a perfect replica of Mount Vernon replete with sweeping lawns, manicured hedges, and ever-blooming rosebushes. As I parked and walked across the historic old backlot, I put out of my mind the images that were filmed here of my hometown Atlanta burning to the ground.

The head of current programming at Columbia TriStar, Sony's TV arm, was an extremely nice lady named Jeanie Bradley. Her job was to represent the studio's interests in *Dawson's* and the other Sony shows currently in production. Having been involved in shows like *Who's the Boss?*, *Designing Women*, and *Mad About You*, Jeanie had been a television executive for many years, quite a feat for most who do this sort of work. It didn't take long after meeting her to understand how she had been such an integral part of Columbia TriStar's long legacy of success. She was graceful and understatedly able in a way you don't often see in a Hollywood executive suite. So much so that later I found myself wondering how she managed to tolerate what was happening to her studio. Let me explain.

In 1998, Columbia TriStar Television (CTTV) developed a new comedy called *The King of Queens*. However, right before giving it a pickup, CBS reportedly refused to put the show on their schedule unless CTTV agreed to share ownership of it. Realizing that they were being shaken down, the executives at CTTV debated it, looked at all their options, and came to the conclusion that they had none. Unlike Disney, which had

ABC, or Warner Brothers, which had the WB, or 20th Century, which had Fox, or CBS Productions, which had CBS—Columbia TriStar Television studio did not have its own network. So if CTTV wanted one of the shows it made to get on the air, it had to do whatever a network wanted, including sharing the back-end profits.

This was how business was now being done. CBS ordered seven new series that year. It co-owned six. NBC reportedly refused to renew *News Radio* unless Brillstein-Grey shared ownership. ABC extracted longer license fees from studios because, well, it could. According to *Variety*, ABC flat-out refused to pick up Columbia TriStar's *Cupid* unless CTTV lowered its already prenegotiated license fee by as much as a hundred grand an episode. The fact is, it took a lot more than grace and competence to run a successful TV studio at this time, it took a network, which Columbia TriStar most certainly did not have.

I liked Jeanie a lot. We had a terrific meeting. I called my agent before my car was even off the lot and told him how much I looked forward to working with her. Although I would hear Jeanie's name mentioned (always in a positive and upbeat light) over the coming years, the day I left The Mansion was the last time I saw her or spoke with her. I know that the *Dawson's* nonwriting executive producer sometimes spoke with her on the phone, and I saw her quoted in the trades a few times as the studio's representative of the show, but during the seventy-three episodes in which I was involved as a writer-producer, I had no further contact with her. My interactions with executives for the next three years, especially on creative matters, would be almost exclusively with those from the WB, the network. The notes and direction I received came mainly from John Litvack. The story pitches I delivered for episodes were to him. All major casting choices were run by him. He was the ultimate creative arbiter of the show. What I would come to see is that *Dawson's Creek* was run much more by the network that aired it than the company that made it. It was molded by the network's input. It conformed to their brand. The only nonnetwork person that I dealt with during my tenure was a low-level Columbia TriStar studio executive, an easygoing young woman named Melissa Kellner, whose father was Jaime Kellner, the head of the network.

As these things often go, right before I got an official offer from Sony I started to have second thoughts. On May 19 I met the writer of *Cold Feet*, Kerry Ehrin, at a Coffee Bean at Fashion Square Mall in the Valley. As much as I liked her pilot, I really liked her. On Friday, May 21, Dan was fielding offers for both shows.

When you work on a new series, ratings become a major part of your life. The first time the pilot episode airs, the entire staff is fixated on the numbers. You call before the sun rises on the West Coast to get the "overnights," the ratings of the major markets. Then you wait breathlessly throughout the day for the rest of the markets to report in. Everything is considered. Do you hold your lead-in? Do you drop off? How'd you do in the half-hour—did people leave or stay or join in? And how were those demos?! This scenario is repeated every week, every time an episode airs. You just pray you don't drop too far down from your splashy pilot numbers. You just pray the network is happy and picks up "the back nine" (the rest of the season order) in October. For TV writers, our lives are led by those numbers. Sometimes, like Bernie Lechowick was fond of saying, this is "a rich man's problem," meaning you have no idea whether or not you can plan to attend a big family vacation that is six months away. But sometimes the overnights quite simply determine whether or not you can pay your mortgage.

As I was starting to figure out, the trick to the whole thing—where you earn $50,000 a month but have no idea how long that will last—was to get a mortgage far below the ones the bank excitedly told you they would fall all over themselves to give you when they see your 1040s.

My wife agreed that *Cold Feet* was awesome, as was any executive producer down-to-earth enough to meet at a Coffee Bean. But after several years of living Nielsens-to-Nielsens, and with a just about overdue baby constantly kicking at her bladder, let's just say that I was strongly encouraged to go to *Dawson's*, which, aside from being a show that I also loved, had a pickup for a full season and was as close to a slam dunk as you get in TV to run for several more. (My wife, as always, was right, by the way. *Cold Feet* was canceled after just four episodes.)

Dawson's Creek was a one-hour drama focusing on the lives of four teens, all close friends, growing up together in a small seaside town in Massachusetts. It is best described as a quintessential coming-of-age show, only there had never really been anything quite like it before.

I arrived for my first day on the show the first week of June 1999. My credit was producer. The writers' offices were off

Olympic, less than a mile from where I had just moved in Santa Monica. My new house was only thirty-eight miles away, but in order to make a ten A.M. meeting, I had to leave my house before eight. There is an entire culture that I became a part of on the 405 every morning. Driving up the hill from the Valley, crawling inch by inch, I watched people eat complete meals, read the *Los Angeles Times*, read scripts. I watched men shave. I watched women spend well over an hour applying their makeup. I watched people tend to all sorts of personal and private matters. It was fascinating—well, for a while.

By this point in my career, even on a show that had a multi-season guarantee and gave me a rock-solid contact, I had learned never to show up for work with more than one box of belongings. I had learned to think of myself as a perpetual freelancer, or more precisely, as a migrant worker. When a very well-respected playwright I had befriended quit a show we were both working on, she came into my office the day she left and gave me a big black Jolly Roger flag that she always hung on her door when she started staff television jobs. "Remember," she said to me, "when we do TV, we're pirates." While I agreed with her, I opted not to hang the pirate flag on my first day of work at *Dawson's*.

Usually when you join a successful show—that is, a show that is returning—you're the new guy. But this was not the case with *Dawson's*. Groups of veteran *Dawson's* writers were not hanging out in the hallways swapping stories about last season. The assistants were, but except for Greg Berlanti (returning for his second year in the business), all the other writers were new to *Dawson's*. Furthermore, except for me and Tammy, the other writers were essentially new to television staff work: Tom Kapinos, Gina Fattore, and a writing team, Hadley Davis and Bonnie Schneider. Everything felt fresh, fun, promising. We all knew we were dealing with a tabula rasa, and if anyone had any doubt, all he or she had to do was look at those big white dry-erase boards hanging all over the story room with nothing written on them yet but "Season Three!"

The first few weeks on a writing staff are like the first few weeks in a new relationship. You are on best behavior. Great effort goes into hiding all potentially offensive or embarrassing habits. You not only keep your true feelings about important things to yourself, but you are pathologically agreeable. In fact, everything that you hear not only sounds like a good idea, you also want to talk about it, explore it, roll around in it. There's a glorious "Kumbaya" quality to it all because you are so lucky to be together. This, of course, does not last.

During the first two weeks, with Tammy at the helm, the seven writers and Paul all piled into the story room and pitched all sorts of ridiculous things that we got ourselves all excited about. Tammy quickly started leading us down a *Risky Business* story where Pacey gets Dawson a hooker. She stood at a dry-erase board scribbling down all kinds of possible ideas for the story. Sounding as good an idea to me as any, I joined in, pitching possible moments that came to mind that might help create the episode. As the only one in the room who really knew the characters, Greg probably felt we were high, but being the first two weeks, he lent his support too. Whenever a new idea would be pitched and the story would grow, Paul scanned the faces in the room, looking for one that would tell him if this thing would make a kick-ass season opener, inevitably covered in a front-page story in *Entertainment Weekly*, or whether it would be a humiliating disaster, ultimately resulting in another entire new staff of writers. At one point, someone, Bonnie, I think, was concerned that the story was no longer simply being *inspired* by the movie but that it was sounding *exactly* like *Risky Business*. This immediately worried Paul. But right before he threw cold water on the whole thing—and revisited a curious idea he had for constructing a story around a satellite that was circling the planet—someone, Hadley, I think, suggested making Dawson *aware* that it was just like the movie. "That's right," I confidently shouted. "We'll claim it!"

"Claim it" was among my favorite story-room buzz words. To claim something in a script means to have a character consciously reference the material you are stealing. That way you looked smart and cool because you *meant* to do it, instead of looking like you were just incapable of developing your own original story.

I loved story-room buzz words. "Resonate" was another one of my favorites, as in "The A-story really works because it *resonates* off the B-story." I loved "dramatize" too, as in "Great idea, but how do you *dramatize* that in sixteen beats or less?" And "intimacy," as in "Yes! There can be so much *intimacy* in that one moment, it makes the entire story work for me." These words, of course, are essentially bullshit, and the more they are in use the more you can be certain that your stories are pretty much bullshit too. But hey, you have to start somewhere, and that is precisely what those first two weeks are for.

So that was pretty much the pattern for the beginning of

the season. Throughout much of it, Gina Fattore said very little of substance. She just feverishly jotted down notes and twirled her hair with ever-increasing nervousness. And Tom Kapinos not only said little of substance, he said nothing. Although he periodically grinned like Billy Bob Thornton in *Sling Blade*—causing me to wonder *What the hell was going through this guy's mind!?*—he just quietly observed, leading some of the staff to quickly discount him. This would later prove to be a mistake, as would much of what went on at the beginning of Season Three.

As we continued developing our stories those first weeks, we hit several bumps in the road. Some of these came out of left field, like the day James Van Der Beek, who played the cerebral and self-effacing protagonist Dawson, walked into the story room looking like a linebacker. He looked this way because when he finished the football movie *Varsity Blues*, he didn't stop working out. So we had to write in that Dawson had been strangely "lifting" all summer.

But some of the bumps were built into the show. These were story problems that we inherited, and as we got further and further along it was becoming more and more apparent that the show was in fact not such a blank slate after all. Many of the stories we wanted to do were hindered by the backstory of the previous season. In fact, we soon realized that while those storyboards may have been blank on our first days of work, they might as well have been halfway filled in because Kevin Williamson and what had remained of the previous year's staff had painted us into quite a corner.

No matter what kind of spin *Entertainment Tonight* might put on things, let me assure you, television shows do not turn over their creators and entire staffs because the writers got bored and needed "a new challenge." What I eventually learned while working on the show was that the path *Dawson's Creek* had taken since the first time I had seen that brilliant pilot was indeed a bumpy one, to say the least. No doubt, all new TV shows have a rocky road to travel, but by most measures *Dawson's* had been especially rough.

Most fans of the series always use the first twelve episodes of its first season (half a season, really) as a sort of revered touchstone. Famous Season One stories include tomboy Joey (Katie Holmes) appearing in a beauty pageant; her sister Bessie having her baby in Dawson's (James Van Der Beek's) house; and all the characters surviving a detention together, à la *The Breakfast Club*. There were groundbreaking stories like fifteen-year-old Pacey (Josh Jackson) dating his teacher. There were extensive and explicit conversations about penis size, masturbation, and sex. Lines like Jen's (Michelle Williams's) "Well, I guess I'm no longer the Virgin Queen of Dawson Leery's handheld fantasies" had never been heard before on network television. The show was an instant hit from the very first episode. The young, previously unknown actors became overnight sensations. A series of collectible *TV Guide* covers featuring the four stars followed soon after the premiere. An *Entertainment Weekly* cover came out as well.

Dawson's was also a sociological phenomenon, referenced in wide-ranging and diverse places, talked about as the defining show of a new generation. It was hot. The way the characters spoke, with verbose, self-referential language filled with sophisticated allusions drawn from politics to pop culture, had never been heard before on television, certainly not coming from the mouths of angst-ridden teenagers. And real-life teenagers related to it.

The show was also immediately surrounded in controversy for what critics perceived to be a preoccupation with sex. While Kevin Williamson always maintained that this was not his intent and that the show was not about sex-starved teenagers but rather about romance—"weak knees and sweaty palms"—many parents and watchdog groups saw it otherwise. L. Brent Bozell and the Parents Television Council declared that *Dawson's* was the absolute worst show of the year—the best thing he could do for the series, of course. The controversy only helped the ratings.

However, after the Season Two opener, which featured Dawson and Joey in bed yakking after their first kiss while the new Fastball song played loudly, the show went south. The writers tried to find what they had in Season One, but it just wasn't there. I knew they were trying too hard when I saw the episode where Dawson's dad wants an open marriage and befriends a wife-swapper. The show suddenly had an "ick" factor. Season Two had its moments—like "The All-Nighter" episode in which all the characters study all night for an exam—but as the season wore on, those kinds of episodes became few and far between. What had been a cool, provocative series suddenly became a simple soap. Pacey's girlfriend, Andie, went crazy. His former lover and teacher inexplicably returned to "unload some real estate." Dawson went on the requisite drinking binge. And my personal favorite: Joey wore a wire to entrap her father for the Feds and send him back to jail on drug charges, something to which every teenager can relate. And, just as we had been instructed to do with the *Hyperion* makeover, Season Two culminated with a primary set (The Ice House) being burned to the ground. So you can see, as the other new writers and I faced those boards at the beginning of Season Three, we had a hell of a lot of history to deal with.

In addition, when Season One began, *Dawson's Creek* was not only a happy set on which to work, my understanding is that it basked in what I have heard repeatedly described as a kind of magical glow. The cast and crew were all hunkered down, filming and living, in Wilmington, North Carolina, far removed from smog, traffic, and the standard trials and tribulations of show business. James Van Der Beek and Josh Jackson were roommates and great friends. The cast was bonded. However, by the middle of Season Two, the personal relationships of the actors, as well as their personal feelings about the scripts they were given, became a factor in how the show was written and produced.

Now, it's not uncommon for actors to have problems, particularly when they become celebrity actors. When I was working at Universal, Gerald McRaney had some very big and emotional "story issues" very early on when *Major Dad* was trying to find its way. However, I watched Universal's studio executives rectify those problems in a swift and unambiguous manner, which was beneficial not only to the show and the studio but to the actor as well. But by the time *Dawson's Creek* was born, powerful autonomous studio executives had gone the way of the powerful autonomous studio. The actors often called the network and the network often placated situations. But the only true protection the actors had came from their creative leader, their showrunner. And by the middle of Season Two the *Dawson's Creek* showrunner, according to sources associated with the show, was holed up, writing scripts piecemeal and trying to hold it all together.

By the middle of Season Two, barely a year into the life of the show, the coexecutive producer had "left" (though of course he was paid for the whole season), stories were not being developed on time, production deadlines were missed, and scripts stopped showing up when they were supposed to. This meant that sets could not be built. Directors could not prepare. Roles could not be cast. Actors could not understand their character arcs. They couldn't even learn their lines. Scenes, not scripts but individual scenes, written out of context would simply appear on set in the morning, moments before they were to shoot. It's no wonder that *Dawson's Creek* was going south. One former writer on the show during this time characterized it as "the Nixon White House."

"It will definitely return to a first-season sensibility," promised the WB's Jordan Levin in an interview with *Entertainment Weekly* about the time I was hired. "Dawson will have something to say, instead of the cast reacting to bigger-than-life plots."

How did a promising and important show get like this?

⌒⅍⌒

One of the first things you have to understand is that *Dawson's Creek* was not just a television show. It was a launching pad. When I worked at Ogilvy & Mather, we made commercials and placed them on TV shows. A decade and a half later, TV shows like *Dawson's were* the commercials.

This played out in many ways. The most obvious was in advertiser-bought product placement. By no means was the WB the first entertainment outlet to use product placement. Forrest Gump chugged Dr Pepper. E.T. loved Reese's Pieces. The Teenage Mutant Ninja Turtles were big fans of Domino's. But *Dawson's* was one of the first TV shows to accomplish the seamless amalgamation of entertainment and merchandising. Before the series debut, our actors appeared in J.Crew catalogs. All four of them. Once on the air, they wore J.Crew clothes on the show. In Season Three American Eagle became the "official *Dawson's Creek*" clothing provider. Our characters drove Ford automobiles that were provided by Ford for this purpose. Boxes of footwear from a variety of companies cluttered actors' trailers. And it wasn't long before actual story lines were written around the products. Now called "product integration," TV writers performed duties that were identical to the ones done by copywriters at Ogilvy & Mather, making it clear that *The Truman Show* was in no way just an impossible spoof.

One of the best ways to understand what happened is to look at how music was used on the show. The WB, a TV network, did more for the failing music industry than Columbia or Epic or any of Sony Music's brands ever could have. *Dawson's* featured pop music prominently throughout all episodes. Songs were often earmarked during story sessions at exactly the same time that stories were being conceived.

This was a great setup for the studio. A band would give Sony a discount or just waive the license fees for their songs, allowing *Dawson's* to play a hot band's music fairly cheaply under scenes. In return, at the end of an episode, the show would replay five seconds of the band's music while showing a shot of the band's CD cover.

Of course, Sony was actually advertising for itself, as much of this music ended up on the million-selling *Songs of Dawson's Creek* compilation CDs. In fact, though the show sometimes featured new indie-label artists, the vast majority of the music came from the Sony label. Shawn Colvin, Wood, Shooter, Shawn Mullins, Adam Cohen, Lara Fabian, Train, Five For Fighting, Nine Days, the Jayhawks, Pete Yorn, Splender, Wheatus, Evan and Jaron, Heather Nova, Jessica Simpson, all featured on the series, all featured on the compilation CDs, all on the Sony label. Many of these artists also performed at events like the *Dawson's Creek* and Ford Focus music concerts. Critically acclaimed but little-known artists became overnight sensations after their songs ran on *Dawson's Creek*. Paula Cole—not on our studio's label but on our *network's* label, WEA/Warner Brothers—became an international celebrity.

And music was just the beginning. When our characters watched a movie, or when something played on television, more often than not it was a Sony title. When they played a video game, it was *Crash Bandicoot*, a Sony title, on the Sony PlayStation. Sony put out all the expected *Dawson's Creek* paraphernalia, posters, calendars, T-shirts, and whatnot. Sony Consumer Products also aligned with WTAA International to manufacture a line of *Dawson's Creek* bottled water, and with 1-800-FLOWERS.COM to release a line of *Dawson's Creek* flower bouquets. Much of this stuff, as well as DVDs of the show, could be purchased at dawsonscreek.com, where fans could not only chat about the show, but tell us what they wanted to see next. The wishes of viewers had a very strong impact on the direction of the series. In fact, staff members were hired to interact regularly with fans online. There were *Dawson's Creek* books and magazines, and promotional feature articles placed in other magazines that were owned by the network's parent company, TimeWarner. New actors were planted on the show and given story lines in which they had relationships with the star actors, for the express purpose of spinning the new actors off onto their own WB shows. In the past, TV shows had their merchandising elements. I loved my *Partridge Family* lunchbox. But this was different. Commercialism was not simply a corollary of the show, it was the soul. We were not simply a pop TV series, we were a brand.

Even before it premiered, *Dawson's* was promoted like a major motion picture. One-sheets (movie posters) were all over bus stops. Movie-style billboards were all over town. There was a major radio campaign, a major television campaign, trailers shown to *movie* audiences in theaters. There are reports that the WB even hired a marketing unit of Procter & Gamble to leak an advance script of the show to teens in order to create word-of-mouth excitement. Never before in television history had there been so much advance buzz about a series. Forget about the kick-ass pilot ratings, *Dawson's Creek* was quite literally a hit *before* it aired.

So if you want to know what happened to *Dawson's Creek* in its second season, you have to understand that there were really two *Dawson's Creek*s. There was this whirlwind of synergistic merchandising and commercialism swirling around in a network-created vortex of buzz, fueled by controversy and press. And then there was the actual television show.

Likewise, there were really two Kevin Williamsons. At the center of all this tornadic hype and money, there was the overnight star, the artist on the billboard, the legend. And then there was Kevin Williamson, alone at his computer—Kevin Williamson the writer.

And Kevin Williamson the writer did the best he could do when confronted for the first time not with press interviews but with the realities of making a full season of twenty-two TV episodes. This was not *Buffy* creator Joss Whedon, who had a fully realized show on his hands and was fully prepared to take it somewhere else if the network screwed with him— which he eventually did by taking *Buffy* to UPN in 2001. This was the result of what post–Fin-Syn Hollywood was doing to gifted and promising young writers in the late nineties. It was a result of the downfall of training that was once a funda- mental part of the culture at places like MTM, and it played out in similar ways all over town during this time.

You see, once you cut through all the urban legend and all the PR releases, what you had in reality was a kid from the South with a cool personal story who had once sold a screen- play but who had never ever worked in network television be- fore. With no mentor to help him, no experienced writer to train him, no studio to back him, with a powerful network that had an agenda and the only creative consistency coming from a producer who did not write, Kevin was in a tough spot. He tried not to believe his own press. He tried to rely on writer's instinct and the passion that had got him here, but running a TV show takes a hell of a lot more than that, especially when you are on your own. As one high-level producer on the show put it, "Kevin started believing his own hype." In the end, Kevin's own words to *Entertainment Weekly* summed it up: "It's best I'm not part of it this year." And though there are various and differing accounts of under what terms he left, he left. The one-time "voice of a generation" moved on from his hit series to develop, write, and produce *Wasteland*, *Teaching Mrs. Tingle*, and *Glory Days*, a path with many more downs than ups that would ultimately lead him back to *Dawson's*, years later, to cowrite its final episode—when it was, in fact, a very different show from the one he had once created.

Two weeks to the day after we started *Dawson's Creek* Season Three with Tammy Ader at the helm, we were joined by Alex Gansa who, it was explained to us, would be a co-showrunner. Now, I will not recount the experiences where I had seen or heard of this sort of arrangement enacted before, because I think even the layman is savvy enough to understand that this was destined to be about as successful as putting two captains in charge of a nuclear submarine during wartime.

Here's the best and most succinct way I can explain the situation. During the very first hour of his very first day of work, Alex told all of us that not only was this show something he didn't really get, but that he was essentially doing it for the money and because next season he would get to develop full-time. He then proceeded to tell the entire room of writers and assistants a story about how his personal corporation, Cherry Pie Productions, got its name. It was a rather off-color story told with masterful detail about how when Alex was a little boy he came upon a man in the woods who was performing cunnilingus on a menstruating woman.

At that point, on his first day, the story room understood his assertion that his sensibilities were probably not quite in line with those of a coming-of-age teen soap.

How much of the decision to hire him was due to a lack of confidence in Tammy I cannot be entirely sure, but I don't think it was significant. I know that the intent was there well before Tammy began working in the story room, and I know Sony loved her and I know she had proven herself to be an excellent producer on shows like *Party of Five* and *Sisters*.

What you have to understand is that Columbia TriStar's corporate strategy was known throughout town as "throw everything at the wall and see what sticks." During the gold-rush years of the nineties, CTTV was always a leader in development and pilot production, but 1999 was a record year. That season I started on *Dawson's*, CTTV was producing more pilots than any other studio in Hollywood. They also rang up about $75 million in writer development deals, like Alex's. You see, with no network to guarantee access for their shows, and getting pushed around by pip-squeak little start-ups like the WB, the best CTTV could do was develop as many shows as possible and hope that something stuck.

And when something did stick, like *Dawson's Creek*, they applied this same thinking to staffing. I know it seems crazy, but CTTV wasn't the only company behaving this way. This was the corporate pathology throughout Hollywood at this time.

So, along with the corner we were painted into from the previous season, Alex now had to deal with the tracks that

Tammy had lain, and these were quite different from the ones that he would have set forth had he been in the room two weeks earlier. It was tense. Gina's hair-twirling increased with startling velocity. Tammy's knee began to shake for extended periods of time under the table. I pitched an ever-imaginative amount of bullshit. And Tom kept silently grinning. Alex, not to be outdone, I suppose, produced an odd device that he brought to work with him, a Batchler sheep castrator, which he would grip in his hands whenever he was forced to take a call from an increasingly freaking-out James Van Der Beek. Paul was on the verge of a heart attack.

And *on top* of all of this, the more we sat in that insane room, the more we realized that the damn show wasn't about anything. The network PR's little slogan sure was nifty: Can four friends grow up without growing apart? But try writing that every week. Try breaking that into acts and scenes and beats. *What does it mean?* The fact is, we had no doctors or lawyers or cops, nothing inherently driving the story every week. We had a theme, and a pretty place to shoot, but no *franchise*.

You can just imagine the kinds of absurd stories we came up with over the next few weeks. Bad girl Jen Lindley (Michelle Williams) somehow became the head of the cheerleading squad. Along with the world's most provocative cheerleading outfit, we had her in fishnet stockings and army boots. It was bizarre. The hooker in the *Risky Business* story (played by Brittany Daniel) somehow ended up in future story lines doing all sorts of weird, unexplained things, like breaking into Jen's grandmother's house. We had a bunch of drag queens show up as the entertainment for a formal homecoming party.

I wrote an episode, #304, where film geek Dawson gives a rousing speech to the entire school football team, of which his father is now suddenly the coach and just out-of-the-closet Jack suddenly the star player. In the original teaser of that episode—which I wrote days after my daughter, Sophie, was born on July 4th—I wrote a scene where the audience learns that one of the male characters is circumcised and one is not. While I was instructed not to use the terms "anteater" and "fireman's hat," the original draft was as follows:

> *Riffling through a closet, the guys come across Dawson's Baby Book. A PHOTOGRAPH falls out.*
>
> *Pacey:* Oh, look at this artifact, Dawson's first baby picture in his birthday suit.
>
> *Pacey picks it up and the guys stare at it. Pacey looks not only surprised, but a little startled.*
>
> *Pacey:* Wow.
>
> *Dawson:* What?
>
> *Pacey:* I've known you since birth, man, but I've never known *this* about you.
>
> *Dawson:* Hey, it's not like I was given a choice in whether or not it was done.
>
> *Pacey:* We never are. We never are.

Fortunately, Greg Berlanti, who was made squeamish by the idea of the scene from the moment I brought it up, had the good sense to suggest in strong terms that it be removed. I followed his suggestion.

As you can see, we were floundering, to say the least. And

it was right about this time that Greg pitched the Kiss. Frankly, it was very exciting. We knew we were on to something. Both Tammy and Alex immediately responded. Bonnie and Hadley made a lot of noise about it. There was a great deal of jumping up and down from seats, grabbing colored markers, and writing stuff on the boards. Paul was in heaven.

The fact is, at that moment, Greg had invented *Dawson's Creek*, the TV series. And we would soon learn that kissing Katie Holmes was the franchise. However, before we were able to put the idea into action and realize just what we had, the bottom kind of fell out on the show. This started when Tammy turned in her first draft.

The first script of the season did end up loosely and referentially following *Risky Business*. It featured Dawson on a powerboat about to have sex with a stripper named Eve (Brittany Daniel), and Joey (Katie Holmes) taking her shirt off à la *Hyperion Bay*. The response to Tammy's script was not one that she liked, and within a day or two of turning it in she was off the show. Whether she was fired or quit seemed to be a matter of opinion, just as it was with Joe Dougherty. And just like Joe, of course, she still collected her pay. None of this was relevant for long though, as she quickly developed *Strong Medicine* for Sony.

At this point, Alex took over entirely and the series really began to spin out of control. In a winding plot that we had written ourselves into, somehow Eve is revealed to be Jen's half-sister. Once we premiered, the fans were not only confused, they were getting angry. And the actors were nothing short of enraged with what we were sending to Wilmington. With no studio to back them, with no network presence on location, they called our offices constantly. I'd walk by Alex's office and see the poor guy in there, squeezing that sheep castrator, trying to assert authority even though he effectively had none. He just wanted to make a quick buck and develop his own ideas, not deal with this shit.

After the first few episodes aired, freelancers were brought in to write scripts. One of the freelancers was a young woman named Heidi Ferrer. Heidi worked for about a week with the writing staff and developed a story that featured Michelle Williams. We had felt that her character, Jen, was being underutilized that season, and we wanted to give her more screen time. After we helped Heidi create a story that we all liked, she went into a conference room to pitch it over the speakerphone to the studio and network. I was with her when she did this, and as far as I can remember only John Litvack responded to her story.

Heidi's pitch did not go very well. Presumably fed up with how the show was being managed, John had a great deal of notes for Heidi. He repeatedly interrupted her while she pitched to the triangular Polycom speakerphone. "What's the story! What's the story!" he yelled. He did not want to hear a story that featured Michelle Williams. But that's what Heidi had, so that's what she pitched, with growing anxiety, increasing her tempo and volume until, finally, John Litvack simply cut her off: "I don't care about that chipmunk-cheeked cunt!"

Right after the network's head of current programming made his creative and personal preferences clear, Heidi burst into tears, picked up her bag, ran out of the conference room, and left the *Dawson's Creek* offices. I never saw her again.

Production of our show was shut down shortly thereafter.

THIRTEEN

Adventures in Hair
& Makeup

*"If civilization survives . . . it will be possible
for each person to have his own TV channel."*
—ISAAC ASIMOV, "THE FUTURE OF TELEVISION," 1977

The production shutdown was another in a long line of unexpected costs for Sony. Although our sets were still up and our staffs still compensated, nothing was being made. At this same time, Alex Gansa was basically relieved of his duties, though not his multiyear, multimillion-dollar salary. Just like Tammy and all the others, he kept getting paid. Heidi Ferrer was paid too, of course, even though the work she provided was not used. It was the same story for another freelancer who had been brought in. These were just a couple of many *Dawson's Creek* scripts that Sony paid for but did not use. I had just finished writing one about a winter storm that traps the characters at school entitled "The Ice Storm." The assistants, my colleagues, my bosses, all loved it, but the script never made it out of our offices. Just like on *Hyperion Bay*, we were going to "revamp" the entire series, and that meant new

stories, new scripts, new overall direction, and new investment. For starters, we would need another new showrunner,
and that meant millions more.

But this kind of spending raised few eyebrows, certainly
not among Sony's senior management in Tokyo. From the
summer of 1999 to January of 2000, in less than nine months,
Sony's stock price rose more than 350 percent. This was the
story all over town. In 1999, Paramount went on what the
trades called a "spending spree." Along with Milch's $15 mil-
lion deal, the studio spent another $10 to 15 million on John
Sacret Young (*China Beach*) and Glenn Gordon Caron
(*Moonlighting*). Then the studio went on to spend another
$45 to $50 million on Bochco—even more than his landmark
deal with ABC back in 1988. That's $75 million on just four
writers in less than a month. Unprecedented demand for writers and speculation fever gripped the industry.

At exactly the same time, Mike Ovitz invested $100 million
of his own money in a new television company, Artists Television Group. Instead of following the traditional approach of
slowly starting up operations, Ovitz rushed headlong into the
business, quickly spending more than $60 million on talent
deals and outbidding all the major players for TV writers like
Darren Star, Adam Chase, Paul Haggis, and Tom Fontana.
Even though he had no revenue stream like the big studios,
Ovitz was convinced of the immediate value of speculative development deals.

The major money machine fueling all this was advertising
revenues. Starting in 1993, ad rates for television programming did nothing but rise sharply and steadily, year after year.
In 1999 the six broadcast networks raked in well over $7 *bil-*

lion in advertising revenues, an unprecedented amount. However, 1999 was also the first time every one of the major broadcast networks had single-digit composite Nielsen ratings for the season.

The inverse relationship was astonishing: As ad dollars rose to record levels, audiences shrunk to record levels. It was completely irrational. But the money kept coming in. By 2000, studios would take in more than $8 billion, much of which would get funneled back into writer deals, back into development, back into keeping shows like *Dawson's Creek* afloat. It was one big freewheeling party. If anyone was looking for a crescendo, a bubble that was about to burst, this was it.

By early fall of 1999, Greg Berlanti's lawyer renegotiated his contract with Sony. This multimillion-dollar, multiyear deal made Greg the showrunner for the rest of the season and the following season, and allowed him to go into development after that. As it turned out, unlike *Hyperion*, shutting us down was the best thing the WB could have done. While the Kiss created the series, these next weeks were when the series was birthed.

Greg made several trips to Wilmington, not only calming the actors but getting them excited about the new story line. Bonnie and Hadley did not have their options picked up. And Tom, Gina, and I began to spend a good deal of time in the story room.

Tom had begun to speak. He claimed that he said nothing the first few weeks because he didn't know you were supposed to. I never quite bought that. His first episode, #307, "Escape to Witch Mountain," which was very well received, was a stand-alone, meaning it was little affected by the weird winding plots that the rest of us were running through our episodes. I think he had been behaving just like his episode, wisely staying out of the mess.

Gina not only was speaking but she did so a lot and with increasing excitement and volume as her work began to make an impact on the series. She made it her mission to become the series historian, and she approached this task with nothing short of obsession. She knew absolutely every historical fact about absolutely every character on the series, to the point where she lived and breathed these characters and spoke of them like they were all cherished family members.

Tom and Gina were my colleagues and dear friends over the next few years. As we went through the war together, the more I got to know them the more I realized that they were nut-jobs, pretty much total nut-jobs, just like nearly every other TV writer I had worked with so far.

From Milch to Earl to Bob Brush, from Ron Cowen, who would lie on the sofa clutching a pillow while he broke story, to Joe Dougherty, who chewed out the network, to Alex with the sheep thing, I was working with a bunch of lunatics. And these were my bosses. My colleagues were even crazier. As my career progressed, I used to think that it was just TV fate that brought me to such oddballs. But by the time I was on *Dawson's Creek*, I was sure this could not be simple chance. There was a definite pattern here.

At Ogilvy & Mather there was a girl down the hall who collected Pez dispensers. Anne Hamilton, however, showed up for work on *C:16* with boxes of toys and kitschy decorative paraphernalia—things like a glow-in-the-dark St. Clare, the patron saint of television—and a Costco-sized collection of Tums, Maalox, and Pepto-Bismol. Once notes starting coming in from the network, Joe Dougherty passed out cans of Go-Away-Evil air freshener to his staff. By this point I knew that, quite simply, there is just no other group of professionals anywhere in the world that are like television writers. I once wrote a pilot with someone who refused to stop working for any reason once we got on a roll—even when his wife was in labor in the next room. *Hang in there, Linda! Jeffrey and I are almost finished with the second act!* I worked with a writer who had OCD so bad he couldn't punch-up a joke without tapping his hand in highly ritualized patterns—crazy, yes, but man, he was funny. I worked with a writer who moved his bowels frequently during the day and pitched his best jokes to me through the door while he sat on the toilet smoking a cigar. I worked with pencil-biters, nail-chewers, people who burst into tears. I worked with screamers and whisperers and those who say nearly nothing at all. The collection of tics and quirks and phobias and dysfunctions and downright paroxysms that I saw regularly displayed by a group of people in this country's top tax bracket must surely be without equal. The people I knew and worked with were so neurotic they made Larry David look tame. When my colleagues walked by my office and heard me in there mumbling to myself, no one thought twice about it . . . well, usually.

I know at least two television writers who talk about parents who took lithium. One is fond of saying "Growing up with the mentally ill was an excellent preparation for a career in television."

After giving away more than a million dollars to numerous women he didn't know in order to give them time to write, David Rosenthal quit his job at 20th—the studio that was paying him $2.5 million a year just to "think funny"—so he could pursue his life's passion wholeheartedly, having sex with supermodel Heidi Klum. I read in the *The New York Observer* that his father had two guards and a psychologist pick him up and take him to UCLA Medical Center.

Why are TV writers like this? By Season Three on *Dawson's Creek*, I had developed a theory. First, like so much in TV, I think money has a lot to do with it. I think it messes with writers' heads. In most businesses you work your way up, earning more and more each year, expanding your lifestyle and expenses accordingly. Even in industries where young people can make a ton of money, like Wall Street, there is a training period of some kind. Even seven-figure-a-year brain surgeons start out living like monks during their many years of residency. Even Mike Ovitz and Barry Diller and Bernie Brillstein started in the mailroom. But none of this applies to the new TV writer who presently starts at an absolute minimum of $3,581 a week but usually makes much, much more.

Professional sports is perhaps the only useful comparison. But even athletes don't all of a sudden one day discover that the entire world thinks they have talent and is willing to throw money at them. A kid who's drafted into the NBA has had a pretty good idea for quite some time that professional success was a real possibility. But in television, one day you're cranking out a spec in the Starbucks on Third Street wondering how much longer you can keep writing all day without having to start working behind the counter, and the next day you're putting a Warner Brothers parking sticker on the windshield of your new Saab and talking to Realtors in Marina del Rey.

And because of this, the sudden success and the seemingly arbitrary nature of it, the sense in TV writing that your success is all a big mistake never really goes away: *How did I do it? This time they will find out I'm a fraud!* In basketball, you make the shots, you get the stats, you validate the pay. You validate it for all to see, including yourself. In TV, there is no such clear measurement of success, so no one ever really takes comfort in his or her laurels, no matter how grand they may be, no matter how much money they may have generated. Most TV writers will tell you—I sure as hell will—that there is almost always a pervading sense when facing the blank page that up until now it has all been One Great Fluke, and that this time *I will be found out!* Living like this tends to make one a bit wacky.

In addition, there is the pressure of regular regimented inspiration that is so unique to television writing. Sure, all kinds of writing and all kinds of creative endeavors require good ideas and innovation, but try coming up with twenty-two TV episodes every single season, year after year. It simply is not the same as writing a book or writing a play. Not even close. TV writers under this kind of pressure do all kinds of nutty stuff. I have heard of sitcom writers who won't work during the day because they think they can only be truly funny after nine o'clock at night. I heard about a one-hour drama writer who gets much of her writing done naked. I know another who conceives entire stories in the bathtub. I know an Emmy Award winner who likes to take transcontinental plane trips just so he can write. I keep a pen and small notepads in my car, my bathroom, my kitchen, my nightstand, and in a pocket of my bathrobe. On more than one occasion, I have pulled off the road and written whole outlines with my hazard lights on.

And finally, I think TV writers are nut-jobs because TV writers are nut-jobs. I think a lot of them come into the world wired this way and somehow find their way to Hollywood. Everyone has a good story to tell and many people actually work on them. And history has been very clear about the personalities of writers; everything from alcoholism to opium addiction to clinical insanity is well documented. But imagine the mind of someone who can sit in absolute solitude behind a computer day after day, night after night, year after year, making up imaginary stories. Imagine the kind of person that can sit in a closed room sixteen hours a day making up stories with a bunch of other people. I'm talking about people who not only *want* to do this, but have a *need* that compels them to.

Tom and Gina, along with Greg, achieved rapid success on *Dawson's Creek*. While I had worked with many good TV writers by now, most of them had fairly established careers when I met them. Writers like Dougherty and Anne Hamilton had an ability to turn a phrase, construct a story—you could tell them about something that happened on the way to work and they would look at it the way a sculptor looks at a fresh block of marble. They could just see something in there, something that many others did not. My three colleagues on *Dawson's* were cut from the same cloth.

It's hard to explain in succinct terms just what makes a good TV writer, and by association good TV, because of course you're dealing with something that is subjective. But by this time, just like I saw a pattern in the pathology of all my colleagues, I saw similarities among the most talented. Obviously, they all have good skills, a mastery—or, at least, an intuitive understanding—of craft. But with hard work and commitment that can be picked up. There's something else, too. The best way I can explain it is that they have a sensitivity to the world around them, a sort of sixth sense. They pay attention to the little things that others miss. Every outing to the bank, mall, or post office is a chance to people-watch. They listen for subtext instead of just what someone is simply stating. They watch body language, what someone is wearing, how someone is behaving. They always look for the inside joke. They examine and consider how everything tastes and smells, to the point where even a simple lunch from Baja Fresh is subjected to extended critical analysis. Everything is turned over, reflected upon. They look for connections in the chance. Meaning in the random. Metaphors in everything. Their interactions with the world become a process of looking for secrets and clues that will unlock the Great Truths, so that these things can be examined and written about for the ever-approaching next episode.

Now imagine most of your friends and colleagues, the people you eat with, go to the movies with, share your life with, all having not only unique, but dare I say neurotic personalities, but also a degree of this intense awareness. That was my life.

At times, frankly, this life can be downright exhausting, when every little thing from the shoes you chose to wear to the haircut that's overdue to the entirely unintended double entendre that slips out in a story session all become subject to notice, analysis, and lengthy discussion. However, to be a TV writer, to hang out with TV writers, is one of the most fascinating and interesting ways of life imaginable. Simply put, TV writers are original and whacked-out people. And by the time I got to Season Three on *Dawson's Creek*, I knew for certain that they were my kind of people.

During Thanksgiving week of 1999, Greg, Tom, Gina, and I, along with temporary consultant Doug Steinberg—a writer whose ability to bring adult diaper humor into the story room was a welcome respite—all wrote episode #312 together. Culminating in a moment where Pacey watches Joey sleep, this would be the episode that first introduced Pacey's affections for Joey. On December 2, I flew to Wilmington to produce the episode.

This trip, which would become a major part of my life during my time on the show, always began with a crack-of-dawn limo pickup. Because of the time difference and the required transfer through Charlotte, the first-class trip was an all-day affair. While I was in the air, the first production draft of the script, called the "Full White," was simultaneously e-mailed to the Wilmington production offices, then published and distributed to cast and crew by nightfall, right about the same time I arrived.

The very first thing you see when you pull out of the tiny Wilmington International Airport is a prison. If this does not give a writer pause, the very first thing you see moments later upon pulling into Screen Gems Studio does: a sign at the front gate that reads: CHECK ALL HANDGUNS AT THE GATE. If you had any doubt that you are in the deep South, it is now gone.

Not having any handguns on my person, I was swiftly whisked through the front gate and led to see Greg Prange, the ranking producer on location. A director who had been living in Wilmington since the beginning of the series, Prange was affectionately called "Kurtz" by the writers, because he had been upstream so long.

Indeed, to really know what it was like to make *Dawson's Creek*, you have to understand the profound disconnect between L.A. and Wilmington, between the writer-producers and the cast and crew. There is a clash of these two cultures that always exists to some degree on television shows. Part of it is simply a matter of such fundamental differences in working styles. Life on a set follows precise, to-the-minute scheduling. Actors must be ready and must know their lines at a certain time. No matter how many magazines are featuring them on the cover that week, they are subject to the production schedule, even if that requires a three A.M. pickup for hair and makeup and a blocking rehearsal at five A.M. Job descriptions for the entire crew are likewise clear and regimented. A grip or a boom operator or a director can work on *ER* one day and *Law & Order* the next with virtually no learning curve. They often do. But life in the story room is nothing like this, because with writers, every series is different because every Room is run differently, and because every showrunner has his or her unique way of somehow coming up with a season's worth of shows.

On most TV shows, which are shot in L.A., the two worlds are bridged by the showrunner, who at any given moment can take a call from the set, march out of the story room on a lot, zip down to the set in a golf cart, talk to the actors about a scene, tell the director to make sure certain shots are covered, make the entire cast and crew feel that they are being looked out for, and head back to the story room.

But this didn't happen on *Dawson's*, of course, because the story room was on the other coast. Now sometimes showrunners would spend time in Wilmington, but between the end of Season Two and the middle of Season Three, *four* showrunners—Kevin, Tammy, Alex, and Greg—had cycled through, and soon, Tom would take the reins. Let me put it to you like this. One of the showrunners characterized working on *Dawson's Creek* as "Every man for himself!" That this had more to do with factors surrounding the nature of making TV at this time, rather than simply the goals of those in charge, mattered little to the cast and crew.

I liked Greg Prange a lot, not only because he always welcomed me to his creek, but because I felt that he was doing a necessary and virtually impossible job bridging the gap between both coasts. Whenever I arrived I always went straight to his office for the update. With the weather channel constantly running silently in the background—Wilmington is a tropical-storm magnet and production is a slave to weather—Prange would fill me in on everything from how the prep with the director was going, to the general mood of the crew, to why the episode I was there to produce was absolutely unproducible. (Whether it meant borrowing money from the budgets of other episodes or slyly talking me into cutting entire scenes, he would, of course, always somehow find a way to make them producible.)

My second stop after that was to the shoot. Even if it was very late and I was completely jet-lagged, I always made sure

I did this. Sometimes this meant a quick walk over to the soundstage. But more often it meant hopping in my rented Taurus and driving out to a location. Along with the exterior work at Dawson's and Jen's houses out on the creek, we shot interiors and exteriors throughout Wilmington, especially in the downtown area. These were easy to find. You just looked for all the trucks and the teamsters that drive them, who would invariably be standing around smoking cigars and barbecuing chicken wings.

When a TV crew works on location, they basically set up an entire mini-city in a matter of hours. Our location shoots included a large 30' x 30' tent where meals were eaten, as many as ten trucks for lighting, properties, costumes, cameras, and such, and five huge trailers, some for the actors, some that served as bathrooms, and one that was the Hair & Makeup trailer. After Prange's office, this was where I always went next upon arrival in Wilmington, as I quickly learned that Hair & Makeup was where the true power of a TV series resided.

Walking into the Hair & Makeup trailer on location at one in the morning was always a bracing experience. You would step out of the humid, chigger-filled darkness into a world of bright lights, happy music, and every kind of stage makeup imaginable. It feels like a high school musical crammed into a mobile home. Hairdressers skirt about actors, washing them, rinsing them, blow-drying them to perfection. Makeup artists, tool belts strapped around their waists laden with cosmetics, create faces. Ordinary pretty faces that would go virtually unnoticed at the grocery store are transformed into worldwide franchises. The whole thing, the whole place, is rather astounding.

This was where I often found actors so I could greet them and get a sense of what they thought of the just-published script. Often they had it in their hands and had just started reading it, so they were politely positive but still developing an opinion. I did a great deal of this preliminary work with people who were lying back with their heads in sinks. But the most valuable work I did was talking to the Hair & Makeup artists once the actors left the trailer, because the Hair & Makeup artists knew everything.

I had discovered that the people the actors trusted with applying their makeup and doing their hair were people they trusted with a lot, especially in the middle of North Carolina, especially on *Dawson's Creek*. They were confidants. I learned that of all the people to befriend in television these were the most important; for not only did Julie the hairdresser know exactly how a particular actor really felt about a potentially sensitive story line, but a positive comment from her into an actress's ear suddenly put the "Good Script" stamp on what I was down there to produce. It was my understanding that one of the caterers, the people who owned the company hired by Sony to feed the entire cast and crew, did not treat a hairdresser the way she wanted to be treated. We had a new caterer within days.

My next task was always to track down James so that I could get his notes and do what the writers referred to as "the James Pass." Now, on every other show I had worked on, and for that matter heard about, writers did not perform this service for particular actors. On some shows actors have zero input. They are expected to adhere to their contracts, show up on time, and say the damn lines exactly as they are written. On more shows, at least the ones I worked on, showrunners' doors are open. Specifically, this means that if an actor has a problem with a story line, a scene, or a bit of dialogue, he or she can politely call the EP or request a quick meeting and express a concern. Most showrunners will make occasional adjustments, and some might even reconsider an entire story line. But on *Dawson's* I would literally do an entire pass through the script, for James. Sometimes, especially in later seasons, he would love a script, and this was really minor stuff. But sometimes, especially in Season Three, I spent much of my first few days and nights in Wilmington writing.

As extraordinary as this was, and as much as this tended to piss off the writing staff, you have to understand that this December trip to make episode #312 was my second trip to Wilmington. Just a few months earlier I watched this guy try to perform a speech to all the football players on his father's team, which was nothing short of ridiculous, and he was well aware that he came off the same way. And when I say he, I don't just mean the character.

You see, for a writer to work on a troubled show, your career is not on the line. For one thing, everyone around town knows it's a troubled show, and for another your agent is already working on getting you another. The most important thing for a writer's career is not the show, not the credit, it is to work hard, contribute to the Room, write scripts that satisfy the showrunner—basically to get along. If you do these things you get good recommendations, your showrunner and your colleagues want to hire you again, and good buzz follows you, no matter how stupid the show.

However, if you are an actor on a stupid show, it is *your*

face saying those stupid words. You become forever associated with them. Actors' businesses are the characters they are associated with, and if the characters on the TV show they are doing are not being cared for, they get tense. This is pretty much how I would characterize the overall mood of the actors when I started on *Dawson's Creek*. Writers did not want to come to Wilmington, certainly not for any extended period of time.

I also met with the other actors and received their notes, which, though never as comprehensive, could sometimes be considerable. One way or another, they were all addressed. Whether or not this improved the quality of episodes is a matter for debate, and it was certainly debated around the story table. But it made the actors feel like they were being tended to, which they were, and I believe it kept them doing the show.

Once I was finished in Hair & Makeup and on set, I headed for the Inn at St. Thomas, the "quaint" inn the writers stayed at because downtown Wilmington didn't have a Hyatt. It wasn't too bad, I suppose. I always stayed in the same room, the Santa Fe suite, named for the Southwestern theme to which the furnishings adhered. It was comfortable, a good place to write and watch the occasional hurricane swing through, though I could have done without the skull of some sort of horned animal that hung on the wall in the living room.

On the #312 trip, I headed back to the offices at Screen Gems the next day for the meetings that always preceded production. At 11:00, there was casting. Most of the major casting was done out of L.A. So this meant sitting with Lisa or Craig Fincannon, the easygoing local casting directors, for two hours and watching scores and scores of people who drove hundreds and hundreds of miles from Florida and Georgia and Virginia so that they could read five lines in the hopes of being cast in a day-player role. It was generally mind-numbing and heart-wrenching, but when someone walked in who had what you were looking for and then some, it could be thrilling.

At 1:15, there was the tone meeting. Prange, the director, and I would sit in Prange's office and have a speakerphone meeting with Paul and, occasionally, the showrunner, back in L.A. The idea was to go through the script page by page so that Paul could essentially explain to the director his vision, or the story room's vision, for each scene. If there was ever any doubt that TV is not a director's medium, as it is in film, that can be laid to rest right here. At 2:30, there was a tech scout. At this time I piled into a Suburban with department heads so that everyone could see the locations where we would be shooting and prepare accordingly. At many of these locations, I often found myself on my cell phone with Los Angeles, assuring somebody that the director did in fact understand everything he was being told in the tone meeting and that the locations we were scouting could indeed by made to look semi-nice by stringing up a bunch of "twinkle lights." At 5:30 there was a production meeting. This was when we went over the entire script again, page by page, with heads from the entire production team, from properties to lighting to transportation. At 7:00, over something inevitably chickenlike that was brought from the catering truck, I then sat down with the director, got his notes, and went over the script again, page by page. By this point, I knew the episode so well I could have performed all the parts without a script. And the day wasn't even close to being over, because in L.A., it was three hours earlier.

At 9:00 EST, I took a call from Paul, who relayed the network's notes. Since the WB was in the loop on this episode, they were fairly minor. But on some episodes, entire story lines would have to be reworked. While I was on the phone, Paul faxed the network's Standards and Practices comments to me as well. Jet-lagged from the time difference, lacking sleep, swamped with actors' notes, the director's notes, the production notes, the network's notes, the nervousness of my non-writing executive producer, comments from Standards and Practices, the network's censors, this all seemed nothing short of surreal.

On most television shows, each episode is more often than not a negotiation of some sort with Standards and Practices. On *Dawson's*, we had caught on that the best way to get what we wanted approved was to leave material in drafts of scripts that we knew very well would never fly, simply to strengthen our negotiating position. The memos from the network censors were remarkable. The number of potentially objectionable words, phrases, and situations are tabulated, and many are required to be removed from the scripts. They sounded like this:

"Please reduce the number of 'crap's by half in this script and consider spreading the remaining ones over the next few episodes."

"Please replace the disparaging term 'stanky ho-bag' with 'prostitute.'"

"Does the axe murderer have to use an axe? Please strongly consider less violent means for him to accomplish his task. If axe is used, unless it is a paid product placement sponsorship, 'Axe Company of America' is cleared with legal."

"Make sure that in Act Three when the characters 'have passionate sex on the kitchen floor' that they remain *fully clothed* throughout. Likewise, make sure that when the character takes a shower afterward he is not naked from the waist down. Can we do both of these scenes offscreen and simply reference them in subsequent scenes?"

"If characters drink excessively they must get sick. Please make sure such sickness is dramatized tastefully."

"You may have 'ass' but not 'ass-hole.' 'A-hole' will be accepted if you remove all of the 'crap's and 'butt-breath.' "

" 'Screw you' is an improvement from 'Go fuck yourself,' but it is still deemed inappropriate."

"If you remove two 'damn's and a 'hell' you may have the keg party."

Many writers even make up words and phrases that the censors allow but are ultimately more objectionable than the more commonly known references they are replacing. On *Dawson's*, these new terms quickly joined the American lexicon of popular slang.

And at the end of this day, Friday, December 3, my most important task was only just beginning: the rewrite. Somewhere around eleven P.M. or so, I drove back to the Santa Fe suite at the Inn at St. Thomas. While in the car, I took a cellphone meeting with my new boss, new showrunner Greg Berlanti, and made sure that we were on the same page about everything that needed to be done. Then, to the sounds of drunk UNC-Wilmington students and even drunker folks from every small town in North Carolina within a hundred-mile radius, all partying in the street outside the inn, I stayed up all night and wrote. Sometimes other writers would help with the rewrite too, and I think with this script, which was initially written by the whole staff, some may have.

Late on Sunday, I brought a disk of the rewrite to the Screen Gems production offices where the script, now called the "Full Blue," was printed, published, and sent out to cast and crew all over town. It is called a Full Blue because the pages of this version are blue. The previous version was white. And now whenever a rewrite is done, even for a few lines in a scene, the pages are printed on a different color in the following order: white (original), blue, pink, green, yellow, orange, buff, tan, goldenrod, lavender, white (again, and so on). These colored pages are then inserted into the blue script (unless you've done *another* entire page-one rewrite, in which case you've got a "Full Pink"). You know when your script is fairly monochromatic, you've had a good week. You know when you've got a rainbow in your hands, it's been a bear.

Monday morning, December 6, call time was at seven A.M. and the first shot was at eight. I arrived on set sometime before the first shot, and for the next five days, about twelve hours a day, unless I was back at the inn rewriting or working in the production offices or talking to L.A. on my cell, I sat in a chair next to the director, headphones on, listening to the performances, and produced.

This was my life throughout Season Four and Season Five as well. During my three years on the show, I received written-by credit on nine episodes, story on one, and entirely rewrote or contributed writing to a lot more. I made ten trips to North Carolina. Initially my trips would be a week or two while I produced an episode I wrote, but later they lasted a month or longer as I helped oversee additional episodes. I found that producing television required almost every experience I had in my life, from what I learned about story in playwriting school to what I learned about management in advertising. With the exception of some nearly page-one revisions, I loved almost every minute of it. For me, writing and producing TV was the culmination of everything I had wanted to do with my life since I started writing those plays back in high school.

When I wasn't producing on location, I was either at work in the writer's room or at home writing a script. Someone asked me a rather New Age-y question about TV writing: Is there a work/life balance? By 2001, Season Five, when I became a coexecutive producer, when my wife gave birth to our second daughter, it was clear to me that there was a work/life balance to TV writing, as long as everything in your life is about work. This was a problem.

FOURTEEN

The New Reality

"People cannot stand too much reality."

—CARL JUNG

Episode #312 was a turning point for *Dawson's Creek*. Called "Weekend in the Country," much of the episode was about the characters working together to help open Joey's bed and breakfast, so much of the episode was filmed in a small cottage on the creek. Just as writing the episode brought the writers together, filming it brought the cast and crew together. From what I saw, things were different in L.A. and North Carolina after that show. Some of this I'm sure was due to Greg's leadership and some of it due to the show having a direction. As much as I loved writing all the characters, I especially loved writing Grams. I found that she didn't sound like anyone else, except perhaps my wife's Baptist grandmother in Toccoa, Georgia. Lines like "Love is the hardest of woods," from episode #312, could only be pulled off by Broadway-trained actress Mary Beth Peil, who played the character. Over the coming seasons, Gina and Tom wrote episodes that became famous among fans of the series, like "The Longest Day" and "Downtown Crossing." In the spring of 2001, Greg effectively left the show to create and run *Everwood*, and Tom took over.

On May 1, 2001, my wife and I had our second daughter, who we named Charlotte. This was partially because when my wife was pregnant, I would often talk to her on the phone during layovers in the Charlotte airport on the way to or from Wilmington.

On May 5, we signed the paperwork to purchase a gorgeous new house. I'd learned a few things over the last two years in Valencia. First, while I originally thought that my neighbors had boring and regular lives, I later realized that nothing was further from the truth. In fact, I began to wonder if those who defined themselves almost entirely by their work were not only the ones who were truly boring, but were also missing out on things, larger things, beyond their diminutive scope.

Among other reasons, this made me want to stay in the suburbs. However, we had discovered two flaws in the house in which we were living. The first was that it was on a major cut-through street, which became instantly relevant when our oldest started walking. And the other was that we had unknowingly purchased a home on "the Christmas Street." You know how every city has that one street? Everyone goes overboard during the holidays, the local news always covers it, and people always drive by to look at the lights. That was our street. Only our street was legendary. We had tour buses filled with elderly people from all over the San Fernando Valley. We had traffic jams that were so bad I couldn't pull out of the driveway. The massive lit-up Nativity scenes and electric blinking reindeer and flashing dancing Santas were so bright that we had to put black-out curtains in our daughter's bedroom. And while I respect all religious traditions, this was not one of mine. There were a few monolithic menorahs on lawns, and one house had a six-foot dreidel, but as I wrote on everpresent deadline, I couldn't quite find the same holiday spirit. So while we loved Valencia, we decided to look for another street.

Like so much of Southern Cal, Valencia was exploding around 2001 and beautiful new homes were being built. We found one on a near traffic-free cul-de-sac. It was a Taylor Woodrow, Woodlands community, Presidio subdivision, Phase Seven, Plan Four, on Lot Twenty-five. The Plan Fours were the most desirable of the five models, I felt, because of the kitchen that opened to the massive family room. Ours had Richard-Marshall maple flooring in four-inch planks, which stretched generously all the way into the foyer. The hardware throughout was oil-rubbed Baldwin, the appliances all stainless Viking, except of course for the requisite forty-eight-inch Sub-Zero. The cavernous master bath was covered in hand-cut mosaic tile, and the master closet was about the same size as my first apartment in West Hollywood. Along with the kitchen, morning room, and family room, the house had a library overlooking the dining room, a living room, six bedrooms, and five and a half baths. The Old Santa Barbara–style structure was built around an outdoor courtyard to which many of the numerous French doors opened. It was, quite simply, the most beautiful house I had ever seen in my life, even more beautiful than the house of the writer who took that huge development deal back in 1990. It was my dream home, and just like my life, it was perfect. Or so I thought.

You see, despite the new house, the new baby, and the new promotion, things were much more tenuous than it all appeared—or more to the point, more than *I* really understood at the time.

For starters, the reason we signed the papers for the house on May 5, 2001, is because the day before, on May 4, the WGA signed another collective bargaining agreement. These agreements are signed every three years or so and guarantee labor peace. And since 1988, there had been labor peace—up until about 1999. That was when, in September, John Wells was elected president of the WGA on a "get tough" platform. In his campaign statement he demanded "respect for the writer as author and as the central force" in entertainment, and basically promised that if the union's upcoming demands were not met, "we will be on strike."

By the spring of 2001, what looked like the biggest strike in Hollywood history—one that would have made 1988 look like a walk in the park—was just barely averted. And although it was averted, the repercussions of the almost-strike of 2001 ripped through the coming TV seasons. In fact, we still feel the effects today. Here's what happened.

Back up about two years. On August 16, 1999, a month before Wells was elected, a few months before episode #312 was filmed, during the worst year yet for network television ratings, in the summer, a time when very few people watch TV, and right at the same time *Dawson's Creek* was struggling to reinvent itself and Sony and every other studio in town was spending record sums on development and production, a funny thing happened. A new show aired. A game show. It was in prime time on ABC. And not only did people watch it, a lot of people watched it, about ten million of them. In fact, it was the highest-rated program of the week not only in total viewers but also in the 18 to 49 demographic. It was called *Who Wants to Be a Millionaire?*

But you see, I was too busy in the craziness of the *Dawson's Creek* story room to pay attention, and my friends in Hollywood that did figured the show was obviously just an aberration. But in fact it wasn't. ABC stripped *Millionaire*, meaning they stuck it into four different nights on its schedule that summer, and every single night it worked in a big way. The week following its premiere, the show's audience grew 60 percent. On Sunday night, it built on its lead-in, *The Wonderful World of Disney*, by 100 percent. Suffice to say, it was quite present in ABC's 1999 to 2000 fall schedule. *Millionaire* led ABC to first place among the broadcast networks for the first time since 1994. And the truly amazing thing about it, particularly in the climate of bidding wars and eight-figure development deals, it cost nothing to make, barely half a million bucks an episode. A lot of the reason it was so cheap to make was because there were no union writers involved.

On Friday, April 14, 2000, I was driving home from the new *Dawson's Creek* writers' offices on Sunset Boulevard, happy that they would be a closer drive for me, happy about my sweeping view of the city, and happy that my option had been picked up for the next entire season. So I paid little attention to the news of the day, which was that the stock market had fallen off a cliff. The Dow Jones Industrial Average dropped 618 points that day, its biggest point decline in history. And the NASDAQ dropped 355 points, losing 10 percent of its value. Those who had ridden the markets up for so long with no regard for the fundamentals panicked. The studios and networks, all now under the umbrella of publicly traded corporations, immediately felt the pain. In the preceding two-week trading period, Disney lost 6 percent of its value, Viacom lost 7 percent, GE lost 7 percent, Seagram (parent of Universal) lost 9 percent, TimeWarner lost 19 percent, and News Corp. lost more than 20 percent.

At about the same time, oblivious to the carnage on Wall Street, a ragtag group of contestants were hanging out on an island in Borneo, competing against each other for a million dollars. Inspired by the success of the unscripted *Millionaire*, CBS programmed *Survivor* a few weeks later on May 31, 2000, and it was an instant smash. Sixteen million people watched, but best of all for graying CBS, the show garnered a 20-share with 18- to 49-year-olds. This was the official beginning of a new era for the Columbia Broadcasting System.

Survivor not only proved that successful content could be made without writers, it was the first series to demonstrate the true power of making television in a vertically integrated conglomerate. Viacom, CBS's parent company, filled its radio stations and TV networks with spots for the new series. From MTV and VH1 through several Infinity-owned radio stations, Viacom went after younger viewers that CBS never could have attracted if it had been on its own. Along with the WB's model, this prompted a new age in entertainment promotion and programming.

On July 5, 2000, CBS aired another reality show, *Big Brother*, a show which stuck a group of people in a house in Studio City lined with hidden cameras. It was another instant hit and solidified CBS's new place as a leader with young audiences. So powerful were these new unscripted shows that this was the first season since 1994 that did not have network audience erosion.

While studios like Sony all over town were throwing money at anyone who knew how to use scriptwriting software, unscripted TV shows soared to the top of the ratings. *Millionaire* was earning *38-shares*, meaning that two out of every five people watching television were watching a show that did not use TV writers.

Actually, it's important to clarify here: It's not that these shows didn't use writers, it's that they didn't use WGA writers. You see, "reality" was a bit of a misnomer for these programs. While early antecedents of the genre were entirely unscripted, like Allen Funt's 1948 *Candid Camera*, which filmed pranks played on ordinary people, many of these new shows were carefully conceived, staged, and edited. They were, in fact, very much scripted. The people who did these tasks—these *storytelling* tasks—were called editors or associate producers, but they were essentially doing the exact same things that my colleagues and I were doing. They put in long hours in a story room, brainstormed story ideas, arced out long-term character progression, cast "actors" based on specific story needs, and created a cohesive and compelling dramatic narrative by extensive editing in postproduction.

Although the "editors" on *Survivor* did not write the actual dialogue, they conceived and scripted scenes or scenarios. Although *The Real World* "associate producers" did not give the characters fully fleshed-out scripts, by the time they finished in the editing bay, they might as well have. The reality was that reality TV was about as "real" as professional wrestling.

And the studios, of course, loved it, because not only was it popular and cheap, but the studios took no lip from labor about how they wanted to make it. According to the WGA, one reality writer worked between twelve and twenty hours a day at least six days a week. Another worked nine A.M. to two A.M. seven days a week with no overtime. Another worked eighty-four-hour weeks for $7.41 an hour. With no minimum salaries and no requirement to pay health and pension benefits, conditions on reality TV productions were very much like those from the thirties and forties, or worse. Many productions were basically writer sweatshops.

Still, as cheap as reality shows were to make, they had some fundamental problems. First, they had no back-end value in syndication. Their DVD and aftermarket value was also limited. And many advertisers were apprehensive of being associated with some of them. In addition, as popular as they were, broadcast audiences didn't last very long. Unlike traditional scripted shows that often grew in audience share, the novelty of many of these early reality shows quickly faded. By 2001, *Millionaire* was not only fading, it was also rapidly graying, losing its young audience to other networks like the WB and leaving ABC with very few backup options.

But despite all this, despite the fact that reality shows did not look like they would ever be as lucrative as those billion-dollar syndicated blockbusters, the networks kept mindlessly cranking out more of them. You see, reality TV, in many ways, was more than just cheap programming. It was a threat to writers.

⁓

Now, throughout 2000, some part of my brain was aware that my union was pissed off and fighting with the studios. In September of 2000, I got a letter from Wells urging me to join him "in refusing to write extra scripts for stockpiling during a possible WGA strike." Evidently, remembering 1988, many of the studios around town had been trying to get extra scripts written for their series in case of a walkout by writers. But we weren't doing this on *Dawson's*. We were barely able to write what we needed for our current production, so I didn't give this much thought at the time.

But on December 12, 2000, Michael Mahern, the WGA's treasurer, took the staff of *Dawson's Creek* to lunch to discuss the guild's concerns. That was the first time I realized just how serious my union was about going out on strike when our contract expired on May 1, 2001. In short, the WGA was demanding an end to the vanity credits on movies—those "a film by" credits that are given to directors that completely overshadow a writer's contribution—as well as full fees for scripts from Fox, and a bigger piece of foreign TV sales, Internet downloads, and video-on-demand services. And the real sticking point was the demand for more residuals from the mushrooming DVD market.

In order to understand why writers, who were making money hand over fist, wanted more, you once again have to appreciate the mind-set of the Hollywood writer. This was not so much about amounts of money, or working conditions, as much as it was about treating the writer equitably, in this case with the overall revenue stream generated by what he or she created. Once again, it was about respect. However, management was resolute in their position that there just wasn't any more money to give, and writers were equally resolved. Essentially, it was 1988 all over again, only this one would be worse—way worse.

For one thing, the threat of a shutdown could not have come at a worse time. The day we had that lunch meeting, the NASDAQ had lost more than *half its value* in nine months. My studio's stock, Sony, lost over half its value as well.

According to a report commissioned by L.A. mayor Richard Riordan, a walkout by writers (and actors whose contracts were also up) would take at least $500 million a week from the L.A. economy. If the damage was anything like 1988, a strike would cost L.A. more than *$7 billion.* And this did not even begin to address what a strike at this time would do to television.

But no one I worked with really seemed all that concerned. Although we knew the studios did not necessarily have our best interests in mind, we felt they couldn't get by without us. Despite what a bunch of well-fed guys in suits were threatening in the trades, we saw the look in the executives' eyes when we pitched, and we heard the glee in our agents' voices when they fought over us. They built their empires on us. Sure they were making a quick buck with this reality goof, but that was bound to go away soon. You couldn't syndicate that stuff. They were, after all, television networks, and if they wanted to make TV, real TV, they needed us. So we weren't about to give in to their demands, no matter how many reality shows they threatened to stockpile.

Very few writers I worked with really knew much about 1988. The vast majority of the people in TV at this time had joined the industry in the last decade. The studios, on the other hand, had long memories. They recalled 1988 all too well, and they were not wasting any time getting ready for a coming war. Indeed, they had *planned* for such an eventuality, and it was here. To paraphrase Dick Wolf, the bottled water had been bought, the plywood stockpiled.

Reality TV departments now sprung up all over town. No longer were there simply drama and comedy divisions. Entire staffs were now devoted to developing and programming reality shows at the networks and studios. "Vice Presidents of Alternative Series Development" took pitches from game-show creators. Mark Burnett (creator of *Survivor*, *The Apprentice*, *The Contender*) and guys like him became very hot commodities. It wasn't long before William Morris was representing the creators of *Who Wants to Be a Millionaire?*, *Big Brother*, and *Survivor*. Soon all the major agencies opened entire reality TV departments. Eventually, even the small literary boutiques followed suit. Even Broder-Webb-Chervin-Silbermann opened a reality department.

On March 1, 2001, about $100 million apart, talks between writers and the studios collapsed. Wells proposed meeting halfway, but DreamWorks' Jeffrey Katzenberg said that that would "bankrupt" the studios. On April 27, the WGA started asking us about our availability for picketing. It really looked like this was gonna happen. In fact, at this point, most people I knew thought a strike was inevitable.

However, through determination, outside intervention, and mainly, I think, fear, a strike was finally averted in the eleventh hour. On May 4, 2001, three days after the deadline, a new contract was put into place, with both parties making concessions.

But a tipping point had been reached, and there was no going back. Reality TV was now not only an accepted genre in viewers' minds, it was deeply entrenched in the network-studio system.

Because of all the reality shows the networks and studios put into development as a potential backup to the strike, the 2001–2002 fall season was flooded with them. Not that I really noticed, because I was way too busy making TV to watch much of it. There was a small television in the Santa Fe suite at the Inn at St. Thomas on which I watched some new quality HBO fare during my occasional spare time in the 2000–2001 season. But during the 2001–2002 season, I had no spare time, because along with my writing and producing responsibilities, I was writing a pilot for Fox as part of a development deal I had made with 20th Century.

To give you a snapshot of what this entailed, in October 2001, during production of *Dawson's* episode #511, when the cast and crew broke for lunch, instead of eating I took a cell-phone call to discuss the pilot, with ten other people on the line: two executives from the studio; three executives from Fox, the sister network; one executive from the book company in New York that had a deal with the studio's parent company and was involved in the project; two executives from the

L.A. branch of the book company; one executive from the coproduction company that had brought in the initial writer on the project; and the initial writer on the project, whose overall deal the studio and the coproduction company shared. "Synergy" was the word I constantly heard used to describe this new way of making television. I heard other words for it as well. Suffice to say, I was busy.

And I wasn't the only one. On the other side of the continent, my wife was walking around, her footsteps echoing off those wood floors in the partially furnished gigantic house, managing teams of contractors while trying to provide loving care to a toddler and a breast-feeding infant. Even when I was physically home from location, I was of little use to anyone but those who were employing me. It wasn't long before my wife and I employed great quantities of help. Nearly overnight, along with Shelly the Chef, who cooked for us, and our regular cleaning help and lawn and household maintenance, we also hired Isidra, Mayra, and Diana, three nannies who worked various shifts throughout the week. Suddenly, we were living in this home—well, my wife was; if I was there I was in the attached "casita," which was my separate office—where the residents were significantly outnumbered by those keeping the place going. We knew there was something crazy about it all. But in the pace of working, and living, in television, it put a plug in the dam.

Right about that time, however, the dam that was keeping the television business afloat burst wide open. As my wife and I were both hard at work, the TV business went through what I can only concisely describe as an upheaval.

Throughout the gold-rush years of the nineties, much of the TV industry had been run on rising advertising revenues. This was coming from all the freewheeling money generated by the rising stock values of companies that were buying ads for themselves. Well, when the stocks of those companies suddenly dropped, their available resources dropped. And, as always, one of the first items that gets cut when corporations tighten their belts is advertising. Suddenly, companies took a good hard look at their promotional budgets and started questioning the rationale of paying more and more for television ads that fewer and fewer people were watching. Media buyers started playing hardball.

Up-front ad sales for the 2001–2002 season were basically a fire sale. When the smoke cleared and all the spots finally sold off, advertising revenues had dropped for the first time in eight seasons, down 16 percent from the previous year, a loss of more than a billion dollars.

When the advertising spigot got turned down, all of the expenses of producing scripted television almost instantly became as clear as daylight. From 1998 through 2001, programming costs alone rose over 20 percent. So the networks and the studios, now accountable to shareholders, did what all the other publicly traded corporations were doing in America at this time: They looked for ways to cut costs.

And what was most glaringly obvious to anyone looking at the books is that all those millions and millions being thrown at writers to develop actually resulted in very little. The next *Friends*, *ER*, and *Seinfeld* never did materialize from the laptops of kids sitting around the pool in Palm Springs. The companies never really got the grand success they sought from the many writers who took work simply because the "studio backed up the Brink's truck and started dumping money until they just couldn't say no." The studios and networks suddenly and simultaneously realized that the business model did not work and they had had enough.

In August 2001, Mike Ovitz's much celebrated Artists Television Group went belly up. Barely two years after pouring more than $60 million into writer development deals, the company abruptly passed out pink slips and shut its doors, wanting nothing further to do with the television business.

Studios immediately ordered their producers to trim budgets on all current shows. The studios opened new divisions dedicated strictly to producing scripted programming on the cheap. The nets slashed license fees across the board. They started ordering presentation tapes instead of paying for pilots. Rush messenger service, first-class airfare, holiday parties, business gifts, and employee lunches were among the line items quickly cut. Hiring freezes were implemented. Agencies let staff go. Law firms started downsizing.

And as the changes were picking up pace, terrorists flew airplanes into the World Trade Center and the Pentagon on September 11. The shock waves this sent through the overall economy were received like a tidal wave in Hollywood.

In October 2001, Fox laid off its in-house TV movie division. In December 2001, ABC told William Morris flat out that it was finished with these exorbitant packaging fees and simply would not pay a premium for Morris clients anymore. ABC said 3 percent tops, but refused the 5 percent that Morris had been receiving since the seventies. Other networks followed suit, and some started pushing to get rid of the fee altogether. With ad revenues way off, networks courted merchandising sponsorships, methodically sticking more and more product placements into scripted shows. And of course, many more reality programs went into development and production. Even the WB started making reality. Whatever the price of Bochco's blood, Burnett's was a hell of a lot cheaper.

When I was a kid I was intrigued with the movie *Network*, Paddy Chayefsky's far-fetched satire of network television. But what I saw now in no way seemed far-fetched. NBC's highly promoted *Fear Factor*, a reality show that featured models competing against each other in a series of stunts—such as dangling bikini-clad from helicopters and eating horse rectums—was becoming wildly popular. Similar types of programming destined for prime time were being cranked out all over town. Soon *Wife Swap* and *Are You Hot?*, *Being Bobby Brown* and *Breaking Bonaduce*, would become staples of the medium.

And left with few options, particularly in half-hours, audiences watched. And the more they watched, the less leery advertisers became about them. Soon, *Survivor* was taking in $425,000 for a thirty-second spot, close to a typical *Friends* episode. Merchandising and product-placement sponsorships quickly swamped the genre. And even if a reality show wasn't a hit right out of the gate—unlike outrageously expensive scripted shows—they were given plenty of time.

Suddenly, unless you were Kelly or Sorkin or Whedon, the overall development deal became a footnote in the history of television. Studios no longer saw the merits or value in taking masses of writers off the market to think up new ideas for shows. Writers who *were* hired to develop were given one-shot script deals. And the relatively few writers who were offered these script deals were usually highly experienced. Just as Wall Street investors sought safety in clear, carefully picked value-plays at this time, so did Hollywood. About 30 percent fewer pilot scripts were purchased in the 2001–2002 season.

Naturally, staffs on new shows started shrinking. New series were picked up with much smaller orders. Networks would hire only one highly experienced showrunner, give him a commitment for six episodes, and then he would write all or most of them himself, with no need for a writing staff. The days of fifteen writers sitting around the table disappeared.

As former employers like ATG dropped out and long-term, high-paying development deals evaporated, many experienced writers suddenly flooded the contracting staff market. Concurrently, for the first time in many agents' careers, they encountered something very strange: quotes were not being met. Studios had a set amount of money for a staff position. They would offer it to a writer they wanted, and if the agent turned it down, that was that. Agents weren't getting called back by business affairs an hour later. Many writers started taking the "consulting" title, even though they were in fact providing full-time services simply to protect their quotes. So instead of earning $3 million to develop a script for a season, high-level writers were now earning $35,000 an episode, plus scripts, fees, and residuals, to write and produce. Instead of earning $35,000 an episode, supervising producers were willing to work for $17,500 an episode. Scores of writers who had sterling prime-time credits began accepting offers from not only

Showtime, but also Spike TV and The Disney Channel. Many even started taking positions on nonunion productions—which meant reality shows. The aggregate effect of all of this put downward pressure on the entire writing market. Suddenly, all these relatively new writers who had recently poured into L.A. found themselves competing with much more experienced writers, in an atmosphere in which experience was now the truly valued commodity.

In a turn of the tables, where agents at the big firms once worked together synergistically to place their clients, they now worked against each other. During staffing season at this time, hundreds and hundreds of spec scripts flooded into *Dawson's Creek*, which maybe had a couple or three positions to fill. If an agent was called about an individual client, the agent would often send not just that client's scripts to the producers, but many writers on its roster. It was not uncommon for multiple agents at the same agency to submit multiple scripts from their own particular lists, competing with other agents at their own firm. Now it was the lit agencies, big and boutique, who were operating under the "throw it all against the wall and see what sticks" mentality. About this time I began to receive calls from writers with whom I had once worked, some who had trained me. They were looking for work.

In a matter of months, the TV writing market became a buyer's market. The situation was only made worse by the effects of consolidation. After more than a decade of getting squeezed, after years of little independents driving up the cost of writers, the conglomerates' entertainment executives were finally able to work together to drive down the cost of talent. And many on the receiving end of these take-it-or-leave-it offers felt that they detected something in business-affairs voices that could be characterized as glee. It was payback time.

However, even though the days of making deals for one writer to sit at home and think for more than a couple million dollars a year were gone, hundreds of writers were still doing this. That's because many studios had created their stables of writers by signing long-term contracts that had not yet expired, most notably Sony.

Nearly all the recent series that Sony had spent so much money on and fought tooth and nail to get into production had been canceled. *The Brian Benben Show*, *Maggie Winters*, *To Have & to Hold*, *L.A. Doctors*, *Martial Law*, *What About Joan*, *Pasadena*, and *The Tick* were all unsuccessful outings, abruptly cleared from network schedules partially to make room for cheap reality shows. Only *Dawson's Creek* and *The King of Queens* looked like they might have viable lives in syndication, but even if they did they would have a very hard time ever covering the studio's investments in all the canceled series, failed pilots, and unproductive writer deals. In the fall of 2001, rumors began to circulate that Sony was thinking about doing something drastic.

On October 25, 2001, right in the middle of a pilot season in which Columbia TriStar had more than twenty-five projects already in development around town, Sony confirmed several days of speculation and announced that it would fold its broadcast-TV production studio. "The numbers don't match up even when you do it right," Sony Pictures Entertainment president Mel Harris told *Variety*. "The mold we've broken is the large, roster-based, network prime-time deep-development, heavy-deficit, hoping-for-that-one-play-to-recoup-it-all mold."

Brian Lowry reported that according to insiders at Sony, what prompted the decision to shut down Columbia TriStar was an internal financial review of all studio operations known as the "21st Century Project." Top officials at Sony were said to be "chafed" at the amounts of money being spent by Columbia TriStar. Recent development deals, like the one with Danny DeVito's Jersey Films for nearly $10 million, especially rubbed top management the wrong way.

About seventy executives and employees were let go, including Columbia TriStar's president of television, Len Grossi, and the studio's president of production, recently hired Tom Mazza.

Sony shopped its stable of writers around town as a complete package, to no avail. That was the last thing studios wanted right now. Some deals, like a recent one with producer-manager Gavin Palone, Sony settled for cash. Others were sold, some bought out, but in the end, most writers were simply paid as their deals were allowed to lapse.

What little remained of the division that once produced *Bewitched*, *Mad About You*, and *Dawson's Creek* was folded into Columbia TriStar Television Distribution (CTTD), the studio's in-house syndication arm, which also produced programming like the Pamela Anderson vehicle *V.I.P.*, *Ripley's Believe It or Not!*, *The Ricki Lake Show*, and *Strong Medicine*. CTTD president Steve Mosko was charged with developing similar kinds of low-cost programming for a newly formed and strictly scaled-down TV department. This would be the directive at Sony for several years, until it figured out a new disciplined business model that would allow it to once again produce scripted shows for broadcast network television. CTTD continued to produce the remaining Sony products, *Dawson's*, *Family Law*, and *The King of Queens*, until those shows ran their courses a few years later.

On April 17, 2002, *Dawson's* aired its one hundredth episode, meaning we had enough episodes for syndication. I marched into Paul's office to congratulate him, but I was surprised at how reserved he was about the whole thing. On *The Wonder Years* this was huge. On most shows it's a very big deal. It means success for a show and its studio. But Paul felt that given how the existing syndication market, which was also racked by the changes in the business, was responding to serialized character dramas like *Dawson's*, it would have a very modest sale. He was right. The show eventually sold to TBS for about a couple hundred thousand dollars an episode. One hundred twenty-eight episodes were produced. Not exactly *Seinfeld* money, and given the costs, planned and unplanned, and the multitude of profit participants, it was hard to imagine that the series would ever be significantly profitable for Sony.

About this time, Tom and I had lunch at Hamburger Hamlet on Sunset. I confided that I was seriously thinking about talking to other shows for the coming season, what would absolutely be the last one for the series. As much as I liked working on *The Creek*, it was clearly time for a change. Tom thought this was a good idea. He also insisted that there was no way he would be coming back again as showrunner. I did not believe him. I'd learned a few things by this point, about both the industry and Tom. And I was right.

So I met with the usual suspects that 2002–2003 staffing season. The week of April 22 was ABC, Warner Brothers, CBS, and Touchstone. The next week was NBC, Spelling, and Touchstone. The next week was *American Dreams*, *That Was Then*, and *Ed*, and the meetings went on the next week, CBS again, and so forth. But nothing quite clicked, for the usual reasons and because of all the recent changes. Staffing needs were smaller. There were more writers on the market. And, most notably, there were far fewer scripted shows, let alone good scripted shows, being made. In early June, Dan tried to put me back on *Dawson's*, but that didn't work.

Thus for the first time in five years, I took another break from staffing. Dan did what agents do and tried to get me out there to pitch pilots. But all I wanted to do was take a deep breath and write. So over the next few months I wrote a pilot on spec, developed a couple more, and actually spent time around my house.

One night, I plopped down on my new giant leather sofa in my new giant family room and stayed up watching videos on my new giant big-screen TV. I watched birthday parties that I did not attend, first steps that I did not see, laughing and playing and crying, and my wife, in the middle of it all, a baby in arm, a nanny in tow, looking profoundly alone, like something was missing, which of course it was.

Determined to find a show that would be a bit more "family friendly," I went back on the 2003–2004 staffing market. Once again, I made the rounds: NBC, Universal, Paramount, CBS, Touchstone, NBCP, FBC, *Joan of Arcadia*, and so on. My buddy Bernie Lechowick was developing a show with his wife and sometimes producing partner, Lynn Latham. Actually, "buddy" wouldn't quite be the best way to characterize my relationship with Bernie. *Hyperion* writer-producer Wendy

Goldman often hummed the theme to *Courtship of Eddie's Father* whenever Bernie and I worked together.

A few years earlier, Bernie and Lynn asked for my notes on a pilot they had written, which I gave them, and which they found extremely helpful. So when it looked like their new show, *Wild Card*, might be a go, they asked for my help again. And when the show *was* picked up, they very aggressively worked to get me on it as their coexecutive producer. Because it was a cable show, I started very early, the first week of May.

However, by the middle of June, it was clear that they did not think I was a good fit, and by the second week of July I went home, just like Joe Dougherty and Tammy Ader had, continuing to collect my $25,000 an episode for the rest of the season. Several months later, the network decided that Bernie and Lynn were not a good fit, and while they continued to earn *their* massive salaries for another entire season, *Wild Card* came back with Doug Steinberg, the *Dawson's* consultant, as its showrunner. The show soon collapsed and was canceled.

Even though this was just business in the TV business—something a former Lifetime executive later smiled about and characterized as ridiculous—I wasn't able to shrug it off like that, partially because I genuinely liked the show—well, the pilot—a lot, and I felt that under different circumstances it could have been something really good. And partially because I felt that something *fundamental* was wrong here.

But the more I thought about it, and put it into context, the more I began to feel . . . hopeful. I know that on the face of it, everything that had happened in the business over the last couple years looked pretty disheartening. And believe me, a lot of people I knew certainly saw it that way. But I didn't. For one thing, I seemed to have found myself, really for the first time in my life, with real perspective. Since coming to Hollywood in 1988, I had not only seen TV go through cycle after cycle, but I had lived in it. From the sitcoms of the *Cosby* era to the one-hour character dramas during the *China Beach* period, from the dramedies of *The Wonder Years* to the teen soaps of *Dawson's Creek*, I had ridden the waves of television through its peaks of popularity and its valleys of flops. I had heard agents tell me that *this* kind of show was what everyone now wanted and *that* kind of show was now dead. And I had survived it all, and so had good TV.

While many writers around me felt that television was being destroyed for good, I was able to look beyond the last few seasons and see that the business runs in cycles, and we were simply in the middle of one. Just like the seasons of L.A., this was part of the rhythms of the business. How long this cycle would last, I did not know. How bad TV would be during it, I did not know. But every cycle I had seen over the course of my career always, inevitably, had the same endgame. Somehow, a writer with a good idea of what he or she was passionate about would ride or rise above the winds of fortune and start a new cycle. I watched that combination of talent, passion, and luck, which could not be bought, repeatedly find a way no matter what kinds of curves and constraints the business threw at it. And some had been pretty damn formidable. So my reason to believe that quality television would not in fact be killed off by anything, including the great conglomerates of our times, was not merely due to faith, but to direct and substantive firsthand experience.

You see, the more I considered what had happened to television between 1988 and the beginning of the new millennium, the more I actually felt that upheaval was not only what the business had coming, but what television itself needed. While my colleagues and I were all beneficiaries of one of the greatest run-ups in corporate America—what was essentially the leveraging of Hollywood—I came to believe that the overall effect this had on the business had ultimately hurt the product we all loved so much. What quality television needed was a break, a chance, if you will, to reinvent its creative soul. And so did I. By the spring of 2004, with good TV already well into its break, I had my chance, and I took it.

EPILOGUE

I n May 2004, partially because of the real estate market in Southern California, and partially because of those green envelopes, my wife and I left L.A. and moved into a lovely home on a magnolia-shaded cul-de-sac in a quiet suburban community in Georgia. Although that giant house in Valencia never actually made my father any more proud of me than he was the day he told me not to scab, it ended up being a blessing in many unexpected ways.

The same week that I moved my family east, the *Desperate Housewives* pilot tape started making its rounds through town. Hours after the movers had come, I sat by myself on the floor of my family room, surrounded by packing tape and empty boxes and the ruins left behind after a move, and watched the *Desperate Housewives* pilot on my television set, which had been enduringly built into the wall. In a world of reality shows and franchise dramas, Marc Cherry's character-driven serial—which he wrote *on spec*—had a phoenixlike quality. Just like David Chase and Linwood Boomer, who created important revolutionary shows (*The Sopranos* and *Malcolm in the Middle*) on their own, not when they were on a development deal, not when they were at the pinnacles of their careers, Cherry once again proved how important passion and singular vision is to the creation of a hit. His new show rose up out of the ashes left behind by the last few years of conglomerate-directed development. When I finished watching it, I removed the tape and packed it in my carry-on bag, smiling to myself as I headed for the door, knowing that this really was the harbinger of a new cycle, a new era, of writer-driven quality television.

As soon as we moved into our new home in the summer of 2004, the first thing I did was set up an office in the basement, plug in my computer, and, once again, start writing. I thought a lot about what exactly I wanted to write. I knew I had a chance, an opportunity, that very few writers ever got, and I was determined to make the most of it. After so many years of being compensated to lend my skills to tell other people's stories, I put great consideration into what was the first story I wanted to tell.

When we were working on *Hyperion*, and usually when we were directed by the network to do something that ran counter to common sense, Bernie Lechowick often said to me, "Every TV show, like every family, needs a historian." I took that to mean that remembering where you came from helps you know not only how you got where you are, but where to go next. This thinking led me to believe that the best story I had to tell was the one that I had been living.

During the time I have been writing this book, the television industry has seen some significant changes. Between 2004 and 2006, great writer-driven series were not only developed and made, but they were promoted and watched. When I pitched pilots during the 2001–2002 season, family shows, soaps, serialized character dramas of any kind were absolutely of no interest to the networks. As of this writing, entirely seri-

alized shows like *24* and *Lost* are among the strongest pro-
gramming on television, mainly because of the excellent writing. And series like *Grey's Anatomy*—which is run by Shonda
Rhimes, an African American woman—are at the top of the
Neilsens not so much because of their franchise, but because
of their complex characters and well-constructed storytelling.
There are several recent shows where this is the case. *Veronica
Mars, Big Love, Entourage, Studio 60*—all great writer-driven
TV, as good as anything that I was watching in 1988. Al-
though comedies are still struggling to reinvent themselves,
many have, including *Scrubs, The Office,* and *My Name Is
Earl.*

Despite the rebirth of quality television, reality still looks
like it is a fairly entrenched genre. *American Idol* is a phenomenon, pulling in *33-shares.* That's more than forty million
viewers, which in today's highly segmented viewing environment is nearly unfathomable. At a 2005 TV press tour, Amy
Sherman-Palladino, creator of *Gilmore Girls*—another show
that gives me hope—described *American Idol* as "like Nazis
marching through Poland. You gotta let them go and get out
of the way."

As of this writing, the Writers Guild is engaged in a major
and contentious battle to represent reality television writers.
The WGA estimates that currently there are as many as
twenty-five hundred nonunion writers, and many women and
minorities, working in reality television. One of the factors that
plays into this historic organization drive is that the strike war
drums are once again beating. Louder and louder each day as
this book goes to print, in fact. The primary issue is how to
compensate writers for digital downloads, Internet video on

demand, and other new and emerging technologies. Just as it was back in the thirties when writers realized they needed a real union, the early sixties when TV came into the picture, and the eighties when home video threatened to change the business, the industry is again facing uncertain and unprecedented times. Just how digital delivery will change the business is uncertain, though most think its effects on revenue streams, both established and developing, will be profound. The central issue is what formula the studios will use to pay writers when their work is viewed on iPods, cell phones, and the Web. The studios are currently using contracts that predate these new technologies. The writers want new pay formulas with higher rates. Once again, the studios seem to be dragging their feet while the WGA is holding its ground. The more the WGA demands a new formula, the more the studios threaten to program additional reality shows. Organizing reality writers is one way to offset this threat. The other issue that's on the table is writers' growing frustration with compensation for DVDs, which is based on old formulas developed when DVDs were expensive to produce. The current WGA contract expires in October 2007.

On September 17, 2006, the WB closed up shop. And on September 18, the CW network, composed of programming from the WB and UPN, launched. My last season on *Dawson's*, 2001–2002, was the peak of success for the WB. After that time, it struggled to create and launch new shows. From 2003 to 2005 only the modestly successful *One Tree Hill* survived. Part of this was due to its aging audience, and part of it to the almost predictable result of putting branding ahead of good writing, something the WB did not do when it first took on *Buffy* and *Dawson's*, before there *was* a brand. Jointly owned by CBS Corp. and TimeWarner, precisely how this will affect diversity on television remains to be seen, but early indications based on the network's 2006–2007 fall schedule are not especially promising.

Another notable change has been ICM's acquisition of the Broder-Webb-Chervin-Silbermann Agency for about $70 million. This only underscores the continuing significance and value of television, especially quality scripted television, in the overall entertainment industry. Although there are a handful of small competent players, Rothman-Brecher is the last major literary boutique in television.

As of this writing, Sony is back in the TV business. There are those who say that Sony's decision to fold Columbia Tri-Star was a bit of a ruse, nothing more than a short-term cleaning of the house. There are others who say it was the inevitable outcome of management's misunderstanding of the business, the company's missed opportunity to overcome foreign ownership hurdles and buy CBS or merge with NBC years ago when it had a chance. There is another school of thought that the corporation's senior management in Tokyo had just had enough of how its TV business was being run and simply wanted to purge the whole mess out of its system for good. Whatever its true reason for closing shop in 2001, as of this writing Sony has prudently produced a few excellent shows, such as *Rescue Me* and *Huff*.

Sony, along with most of the other studios, finally figured out that great scripted TV shows don't come from simply unloading the studio's coffers, but from identifying talent and passion. Watching writers like Marc Cherry, who many had written off, just show up one day with a hit on his hands has been a powerful lesson for Hollywood. Although the development deal has seen a bit of a reemergence recently, these deals are only being made after careful consideration of a writer's skills and interest in a project.

On the other hand, though there has been recognition of the importance of identifying talent and passion, empowering it is still another matter. The major conglomerates are still not only programming and promoting for ownership instead of quality, they are also still meddling. That's their nature, I suppose. But I firmly believe that if things don't change, these issues will ultimately prove to be the entertainment business's Achilles' heel.

Perhaps most promising, in 2004, the WGA and the entertainment companies agreed to create a Showrunner Training Program "to help promising writers develop effective showrunning skills." The first program ran in 2006, and it was a great success.

Today, Delbert lives on a farm in the pastoral Pennsylvania countryside. He has been sober for sixteen years. My ex-girlfriend is married, lives in Malibu, and surfs pretty much every day. David Rosenthal is running *Gilmore Girls.* Though the vast majority of TV writers have very short careers in television, an extraordinary number of my colleagues continue to sit in story rooms, walk in the shadows on sets, and plug away in solitude at their computers, quietly shaping and influencing the culture of the world. Joe Dougherty, Anne Hamilton, Gina Fattore, Tom Kapinos, and Greg Berlanti are among them. You'll probably see their names in your the living rooms sometime this week.

And finally, over the last couple years, I think I have truly figured out the balance between the writing and the living, the writing and the being a writer.

What TV has in store for me, I do not know. Television has always been a big part of me, and it always will be, not just because it was my first window on the world and not just because it has been my work for so long. When I think about TV—Kevin and Winnie's first kiss at the end of *The Wonder Years* pilot, Michael's father planting the tree on *thirtysomething*, Cosby having the funeral for the fish, Roselyn falling down the elevator shaft in *L.A Law*, that crazed Santa running around China Beach, Jerry and George pitching "a show about nothing" to NBC, the final moment of *Friends* as the cast walks off into the sunset, and of course that kiss, that Pacey-Joey kiss at the end of #317—these moments take their place along with all the other moments of my life.

I still love TV as much as I did in 1988, probably even more, though I've learned a few things since then. As of this writing, I get up every morning at dawn and head downstairs to spend the day writing, but not before giving my wife and daughters a kiss. You see, one of the most important things I learned in Hollywood is that some things are worth *more* than a billion dollars.

ACKNOWLEDGMENTS

One of the amazing things about being a writer is all the people in your life who take care of you, personally and professionally.

First, thank you to Jim Levine for responding to my work and introducing me to his partner, my agent, Daniel Greenberg. Not only did Daniel hone the vision for this book from the start, but he has been a hardworking advocate in every stage of its creation. Thank you also to my TV agent, Dan Brecher, whose insights and help with this project were, once again, boundless. And to Jamie Wolf at Pelosi, Wolf, Effron & Spates, I appreciate you looking out for me. And to Steve Sidman at Greenberg Traurig, thank you for some of the finest counsel and comradeship a writer ever had.

I want to express my appreciation to everyone at Gotham, especially Bill Shinker, Lisa Johnson, Beth Parker, Amanda Tobier, and Hilary Terrell. And special acknowledgment must be paid to my editor, Lauren Marino, whose enthusiasm and steadfast direction have been nothing short of a beacon throughout this project.

Thank you to all the executives and colleagues who spoke with me at length while I researched this book. Thank you to my friends and colleagues who have read various drafts, especially Aaron Levy. And thank you to my teachers and mentors, especially Arthur Giron and Michael Piller, who I am sure is drinking the La Tache every day now.

Finally, I want to acknowledge my family: my parents, Joel and Elaine; my creative brothers, Mike and Scott; my lawyer-cousin Mark Stepakoff; and my beautiful, talented daughters, Sophie and Charlotte. They have all played a part in my work. And my deepest gratitude to you, Elizabeth, for your humor, unyielding faith, and creative partnership, and for living a life very few people understand. Hopefully, they will now understand more.

A

ABC, 9, 12–14, 43, 45, 93, 109, 151, 156, 162, 176, 191–95, 208, 233, 279, 282, 289, 295
Abrams, J.J., 18, 168, 172
Academy Awards, 56, 152
actors, 36–40, 175, 266–69
Ader, Tammy, 3, 5, 6, 231, 237, 248–50, 252, 254, 265, 297
Adventures in the Screen Trade (Goldman), 75
advertising, 21, 73, 101–2, 144, 161–62, 184–85, 208–11, 216–17, 244–46, 255–56, 288, 290
AFI, 20, 22
African Americans, 207–8, 211–23, 216–18, 220, 222–23, 302
agents, 69; development deals and, 165–67; downturn and, 289–92; first meeting with, 33–36, 40–46; fortunes amassed by, 157; literary boutiques vs. big, 46–48; new breed of, 158–61, 163–64; packaging and, 38–41, 157–58; reality TV and, 285; rise of, 36–38; specs and, 76–77; staffing season and, 179–81, 185, 189; stealing from rival, 132–33; training programs and, 159
AGR (adjusted gross revenues), 39, 72, 157
Airwolf, 80

ALF, 119
Alice, 18
Allen, Fred, 123
Alliance of Motion Picture and Television Producers, 62
All in the Family, 102
Ally McBeal, 25, 105, 208
Almost Grown, 63
Amen, 119, 218
American Dreams, 296
American Eagle, 244
American Idol, ix, 302
America's Most Wanted, 73
Anderson, Maxwell, 97
Anderson, Pamela, 294
Andy Griffith Show, The, 39, 99
Angel, 213
animated films, 152–55
Annie Hall, 98
Anything But Love, 119
Apprentice, The, 285
Are You Hot?, ix, 290
Arnaz, Desi, 57, 100
Artists' Manager Basic Agreement (AMBA), 45
Artists Television Group (ATG), 255, 289, 291
Asimov, Isaac, 254
Astrof, Jeff, 165
A-Team, The, 80
audience: decline of, 73, 256; demographics of, 101–2, 105, 202, 208–12, 216–18
Austin, Steve, 17

Index

B

Bachelor, The, ix
"back-end" deals, 38, 47, 72, 109, 168, 233, 282
Back to the Future, 30
Baio, Scott, 50, 126
Balcer, Rene, 167
Ball, Lucille, 100
"barter" rights, 148–49
Baywatch, 148
Beauty and the Beast, 109, 152
Being Bobby Brown, 290
Bell, Warren, 167
Bellisario, Donald, 46, 215
Benson, 18
Berlanti, Greg, 6–7, 236–37, 251–52, 256, 261, 263, 265, 272, 275, 305
Berle, Milton, 56
Berry, Matt, 168
Bertelsmann, 204
Betty White Show, The, 102
Beverly Hillbillies, The, 99–101
Beverly Hills, 90210, 2, 174, 208
Bewitched, 294
Big Brother, 281, 285
Big Love, 302
B.J. and the Bear, 80
blacklisting, 55–56
Blinn, Bill, 66
Bloom, J. Michael, 46
Bochco, Steven, 10–15, 18–19, 23–24, 29, 64, 92, 94, 96, 105, 111, 141, 194, 220, 255
Bohem, Les, 230
Boomer, Linwood, 300
Borowitz, Andy, 18–19
Boston Common, 120
Boston Legal, 105
Boston Public, 105
Boys Don't Cry, 152
Bozell, L. Brent, 241
Bradley, Jeanie, 232–34
Brady, John, 57

Brady, Pam, 167
Braga, Brannon, 167
Brand, Joshua, 105
branding, 216
Breaking Bonaduce, 290
"breaking story," 84–85, 134–35
Brecher, Dan, 159–61, 177–80, 185–86, 188, 190, 221, 229, 234–35, 296
Bressler, Sandy, 46
Brian Benben Show, The, 293
Bridget Loves Bernie, 82
Bright Lights, Big City (McInerney), 21
Brillstein, Bernie, 259
Brillstein-Grey, 162, 186, 191, 233
Brimley, Wilford, 94–95
Broder, Bob, 46
Broder, Kurland, Webb, Uffner (BKWU), 46–47, 160
Broder-Webb-Chervin-Silbermann, 160–61, 285, 304
Brooklyn Bridge, 105
Brooks, James L., 102, 104, 127
Brother Bear, 154–55
Brush, Bob, 33, 121, 127, 257
Buffalo Bill, 105
Buffy, 18, 208, 213, 247, 304
Burnett, Carol, 99
Burnett, Mark, 285, 290
Burns, Allan, 102, 104–5, 127
buzz, 91, 138, 180–81, 246–47

C

C:16, 186–87, 191–95, 197, 199, 257–58
cable markets, 68, 71, 73, 106, 146–49, 156–57, 212
Cagney & Lacey, 24
Caesar, Sid, 56
Cain, James M., 97
Candid Camera, 281
Capital News, 93, 109
Captain Kangaroo, 121

Carnegie Mellon University (CMU), 8, 9, 14, 19, 22, 53, 126, 196
Carol Burnett Show, The, 18, 99
Caroline in the City, 119–20
Caron, Glenn Gordon, 46, 105, 255
Carter, Chris, 178
Carter, Judy, 150
CBS, 43, 109, 148, 156, 220, 233, 280–81, 295
CBS/MTM Studios, 93, 98–100
CBSP (CBS Productions), 156, 233
Chandler, Raymond, 97
Chaplin, Charlie, 37
character: arcs, 134–35; -driven story, 23–24; "spin-off" payments, 70
Charles, Glen and Les, 46, 104
Charles in Charge, 50, 66
Chase, Adam, 255
Chase, David, 63, 300
Chayefsky, Paddy, 57, 290
Cheers, 46, 66, 76, 104, 119, 158, 218
Cherry, Marc, 300–301, 304–6
Chervin, Ted, 160–61, 165
Chestnut, Morris, 191, 193
Chetwynd, Lionel, 66, 67
Chicago Hope, 105, 192
China Beach, 9, 22, 66, 123, 255, 306
CHiPs, 80
City of Angels, 220
CNN, xi
Coach, 105, 120
coexecutive producers, 69, 168
Cold Feet, 230, 234–35
Cole, Lester, 56
Cole, Paula, 245
colleges and universities, 19–22
Columbia TriStar Television (CTTV), 162, 174, 232–34, 249; shut down, 293–95, 304
Columbia TriStar Television Distribution (CTTD), 294–95
comedy, 110–11, 134

conglomerates and consolidation, ix, 184, 203–5, 216–20, 222–23, 292–93, 298, 305
Contender, The, 285
Conversations with My Agent (Long), 158
Cop Rock, 15
coproducer, 69
Cosby, Bill, 43
Cosby Show, The, 9, 41, 43, 104, 110, 119, 218, 306
Costner, Kevin, 41
Courtship of Eddie's Father, The, 16
Cowan, Ron, 134–35, 257
Craft of the Screenwriter, The (Brady), 57
Craig, Charlie, 167
Crash Bandicoot, 245
Crazy Like a Fox, 80
Creative Artists Agency (CAA), 5, 31, 40–41, 46, 132, 158–59
creative consultant, 164–65
Crime Story, 22
Cronkite, Walter, 99
Cruise, Tom, 40
Cupid, 233
Cuts, 212
CW network, 303
Cybill, 218
cycles, 148–49

D

Daily Racing Form, The, 94
Dalva (Harrison), 93
Daniel, Brittany, 250, 252
Daniels, Stan, 104
Daniels, Susanne, 162
Danson, Ted, 10
David, Hadley, 237–38, 256
David, Larry, 149, 258
David, Marjorie, 192
Davis, Hadley, 160–61
Dawson's Creek, x, 1–7, 78, 209, 230–76, 304; Columbia TriStar

Dawson's Creek (cont.)
shutdown and, 294–95; executives and, 206; favorite episodes of, 256–57, 276; final seasons of, 273–76; hired for staff job on, 230–35; Kiss and, 6–7, 252, 256, 306; path of, to Season Three, 240–48; pitch and pilot for, 174–76, 180; premier of, 195, 208; producing, in Wilmington, 263–76; product placement and, 244–47; race and, 213, 223; revamped, 253–59, 261–63; staffing meeting for, 186–88, 190–91; syndication of, 293, 295; writing staff at, 1–7, 248–53, 275–76, 279–80, 283, 286–87, 292, 303
Days and Nights of Molly Dodd, The, 22, 25, 34–35, 41–42, 46, 74, 76, 105, 127, 178
Deadwood, 97
Dead Zone, The, 151
Dear John, 119
Denny, Reginald, 140
deregulation, ix, 184, 204, 219–20. *See also* Financial Interest and Syndication rules
Designing Women, 232
Desilu, 100
Desperate Housewives, 300
development deals, 68, 71, 130–31, 164–69, 249, 255, 279, 286, 289–91, 294, 305
development season, 189
DeVito, Danny, 294
Dharma & Greg, 141, 147, 168, 193
Dick Van Dyke Show, The, 14, 18
Different World, A, 119, 218
Diff'rent Strokes, 218
DiFranco, Ani, 224
digital delivery, 302–3
Diller, Barry, 74, 259
Diller, Ralph, 13
Director, Roger, 33

Disney, Roy, 184
Disney-ABC, 164, 193. *See also* ABC
Disney Channel, 292
Disney Company (Walt), 156, 204, 232–33, 280
Disney Feature Animation (Walt), 153–55, 161, 169
domestic market, 147–48, 156–57
Donna Reed Show, The, 18
Dos Passos, John, 97
Dougherty, Joe, 85, 197–98, 200, 203–7, 222, 224, 252, 257–58, 261, 297, 305
Doyle, Tim, 168
"dramedy" genre, 127–29
DreamWorks, 230, 285
Dreiser, Theodore, 97
Drew Carey Show, The, 168
Driscoll, Mark, 167
Duggan, Michael, 187, 192
Dukes of Hazzard, The, 80
DVDs, 282–83, 303
Dytman, Jack, 159

E

Earth 2, 126
Earth: Final Conflict, 148
earthquakes of 1992 and 1994, 145
Ed, 296
Ehrin, Kerry, 105, 234
Eisner, Michael, 153, 170, 184
Electra, Carmen, 200–202, 229
Ellen, 167
Ellis, Bret Easton, 21
Emmy awards, 12, 14, 33, 73, 198
Empty Nest, 119
Entertainment Weekly, 3, 202, 238, 240, 243, 248
Entourage, 76, 302
Entous, Barry, 123
Equalizer, The, 80
ER, 4, 78, 120, 147, 157, 167
Eve, 212

Everwood, 276
Everybody Loves Raymond, 2, 148, 168
executive producers, 69, 134, 168
executive script consultants, 134
executive story consultant, 132–36
executive story editor, 67, 69

F

Fall Guy, The, 80
Falsey, John, 105
Family Law, 295
Family Matters, 64
Family Ties, 21, 105
Fante, John, 97
Fattore, Gina, 237, 239, 250, 256–57, 261, 263, 276, 305
FCC, 100–101, 155–56, 218–19
Fear Factor, 290
Felicity, 6, 168, 202, 208, 213, 229–31
Ferber, Bruce, 70
Ferrer, Heidi, 253, 254
films, 30–31, 36–38, 41, 55–57, 97
Financial Interest and Syndication ("Fin-Syn") rules, 101, 103–4, 106; repealed, 155–57, 183, 213–14, 218–19, 247
Fincannon, Lisa and Craig, 269–70
first-run syndication, 103, 148
Fitzgerald, F. Scott, 97
Flint, Carol, 124
Flintstones, The, 82
Fontana, Tom, 105, 255
Ford Motors, 244–45
foreign markets, 60, 71, 146–47, 156–57, 283
Forman, Chaka, 207
For Your Love, 213
48 Hours, 73
Fowler, Mark, 90
Fox, Michael J., 11
Fox, Rick, 196
Fox Broadcasting Company, 24, 136, 147, 174–75, 208, 221, 233, 289; Cable Networks, 147; local stations, 149
Fox Television, 165
Frank's Place, 22, 105, 127
Frasier, 120
Freaks and Geeks, 230
Freddy's Nightmares, 66
freelancers, 81, 83–84, 150–51, 169, 189, 253–54
Fresh Prince of Bel-Air, The, 19, 140
Friends, 4, 119, 148, 162–63, 165, 167, 198, 290, 306
Fries, Charles, 59
"fronts," 56
Frost, Mark, 105
Fuchs, Daniel, 97
Full White (Blue, Pink), 273
Funt, Allen, 281

G

Gansa, Alex, 3, 5–6, 248–50, 252–54, 257, 265
General Electric, 156, 204, 219–20, 280
Get Smart, 82
Gilligan's Island, 99
Gilliland, Eric, 126
Gilmore Girls, 78, 302, 305
Glen Campbell Goodtime Hour, The, 100
Glory Days, 248
Goldberg, Gary David, 105
golden age of television, 100; second, 24, 66, 204
Golden Girls, The, 18, 119
Goldman, Wendy, 198, 296–97
Goldman, William, 17, 75
Goldsmith, Josh, 167
Gomer Pyle U.S.M.C., 39, 100
Good Times, 218
Goodyear Television Playhouse, 56
Gordon, Jill, 127
Gosselaar, Mark-Paul, 198, 207

INDEX

Grace Under Fire, 120, 218
Green Acres, 99
Greenstein, Jeff, 107
Gretzky, Wayne, 63
Grey's Anatomy, 302
Grossi, Len, 294
Grounded for Life, 218
Growing Pains, 64, 119

H

Haggis, Paul, 255
Hair & Makeup trailer, 266–67
Hall, Barbara, 105
Hall, Brad, 167
Hamilton, Anne Lewis, 192, 197, 257–48, 261, 305
Hammett, Dashiell, 56, 97
Hanks, Tom, 54, 125
Happy Days, 16, 18
Harbinson, Patrick, 192
Hardcastle and McCormick, 80
Hardy Boys Mysteries, The, 66
Harmon, Angie, 191
Harris, Mel, 293
Harrison, Jim, 93, 109
Harry and the Hendersons, 45
Hart to Hart, 80
Harvard Lampoon, 18–19
Have Faith, 109
Hawaiian Heat, 80
HBO, 73, 147, 286
Head of the Class, 119
Hee Haw, 100
Helford, Bruce, 168
Hellman, Lillian, 56
Herskovitz, Marshall, 105, 197
Hertz, Tom, 167
Hervey, Winnie, 140
Hill Street Blues, 23, 92, 94, 102
Hispanic writers, 214
Hoffman, Dustin, 40
"Hollywood Ten," 56
Hollywood Writers Report, 211
Holmes, Katie, 3, 6–7, 240, 252

Home Front, 198
Home Improvement, 70, 120
Homicide: Life on the Street, 105
Hooperman, 22, 64, 127
House Un-American Activities Committee (HUAC), 55–56
Houston Knights, 80
Hsiao, Rita, 126, 153, 231
Huff, 304
Humanitas Awards, 33, 94, 198
Hunter, 80
Hunter, Holly, 10
Hunter, Ian McLellan, 56
Hyperion Bay, 197–207, 210, 223–24, 229, 242, 301

I

I'll Fly Away, 105
I Love Lucy, 57–58, 99, 100
independent production companies, 100–106, 164, 120, 204, 218–19, 218, 221
Infinity radio stations, 280
in-flight usage fees, 71
International Alliance of Theatrical Stage Employees Local 839 (Cartoonists' Union), 155
International Creative Management (ICM), 31, 46, 159, 304
Internet, 283
interracial kiss, 206–7, 222–23
It's Garry Shandling's Show, 77

J

Jack and Jill, 213
Jackson, Josh, 3, 6–7, 240, 242
Jake and the Fatman, 80–81
Jamie Foxx Show, The, 213
Janollari, David, 162
J. Crew, 244
Jeffersons, The, 218
J.J. Starbuck, Private Eye, 80

Jonas, Tony, 206
Josiah's Canon, 126
Judd, Ashley, 139
Judge, Mike, 168
Jung, Carl, 275
Junge, Alexa, 167
Justice League of America, 185
Just in Time, 9
Just Shoot Me!, 167, 168

K

Kapinos, Tom, 237, 239, 250,
    256–57, 261, 263, 265, 276,
    295, 305
Katz, Evan, 186
Katzenberg, Jeffrey, 285
Kazan, Elia, 56
Kelley, David E., 105
Kellner, Jamie, 207–9, 234
Kellner, Melissa, 234
Kelly, David, 136
Kemp, Barry, 46, 105
Keyser, Chris, 134–36, 167
King, Jeff, 126
King, Rodney, 140
King of Queens, The, 167, 232–33,
    293, 295
King of the Hill, 168
Klein, Paul, 100
Klugman, Jack, 10
Klum, Heidi, 259
Knight Rider, 80
Koch, Howard, 56
Kohan, Buz, 18
Kohan, David, 18
Kozoll, Michael, 23
Kraft Television Theatre, 56
Kurland, Norm, 46
Kurtz, Swoosie, 133, 139

L

labor unions, 38, 55–56, 61–62. *See
    also* Writers Guild of America

L.A. Doctors, 293
L.A. Law, 12, 24, 66, 76, 136, 306
Lardner, Ring, 56
Latham, Lynn, 296, 297
Laurents, Arthur, 56
Law and Harry McGraw, The, 80
L.A. Weekly, 86
Law & Order, 105, 167, 187
Law & Order: CI, 198
Law & Order: SVU, 192
Lawson, Bianca, 223
Lawson, John Howard, 56
Lear, Norman, 17, 59, 102–3
Leave It to Beaver, 18
Lechowick, Bernie, 198–99, 201,
    235, 296–97, 301
Legends of the Fall (Harrison), 93
Le Lay, Patrick, 144
Levin, Jordan, 162, 243
Levin, Mark, 126, 127
Levinson, Richard, 59
Levitan, Steven, 168
license fees, 39, 157–58, 233, 289
Lifetime network, 147, 212, 221
Lipman, Dan, 134–35
Lippman, Amy, 134–36, 167
literary boutiques, 46–48, 157,
    160, 285, 304
Litvack, John, 201–6, 224, 234, 253
Long, Rob, 158
LOP (Least Objectionable
    Programming), 100–102
Lorre, Chuck, 168
Los Angeles Times, 13, 168, 236
Lost, 18, 302
Lou Grant, 102, 104–5
Lowe, Chad, 152
Lowry, Brian, 294

M

MacGruder and Loud, 80
MacGyver, 80
Mad About You, 232, 294
Maggie Winters, 293

Magnum, P.I., 80
MAGR (modified adjusted gross revenues), 72
Mahern, Michael, 283
Major Dad, 109–20, 127, 242
Make Room for Daddy, 39
Malcolm in the Middle, 300
Manimal, 80
Manning, Paul, 167
Mark, Bonnie, 192
Marlens, Neal, 64
Married . . . with Children, 24
Martial Law, 293
Marty, 57
Mary Hartman, Mary Hartman, 103
Mary Tyler Moore, 16, 98, 104, 127
M*A*S*H*, 16, 127, 148
Masius, John, 105
Matlock, 80
Matt Houston, 80
Maude, 16
Mayberry R.F.D., 100
Mazza, Tom, 294
McCoy, Horace, 97
McHale's Navy, 82
McInerey, Jay, 21
McKee, Robert, xi, 115
McLuhan, Marshall, 196
McRaney, Gerald "Mackie," 110, 112, 116, 242
Medium, 105
"meet 'n' greet," 79, 121–22, 140, 181–85
Melrose Place, 200, 202, 208
Melvoin, Jeff, 105
merchandising, 72, 290. *See also* product placement
Meyer, Marlene, 198
MGM, 104
Miami Vice, 105
Midnight Caller, 66
Mike Hammer, 80
Milch, David, 66, 92–98, 105, 107, 109–11, 131, 143, 167, 216, 255, 257

Millennium, 178
Miller, Arthur, 56
minority writers, 211–14, 218, 220, 302
Minow, Newton N., 27, 100
MIPCOM, 146
Mirkin, David, 105
Mittleman, Rick, 82
momentum, 91, 138
Moonlighting, 24, 46, 105, 127, 255
Moore, Mary Tyler, 98, 102
Mosko, Steve, 294
MTM Enterprises, 93–100, 102–6, 108–9, 131, 159, 203, 210
MTV, 280
Munsters Today, The, 66
Murder, She Wrote, 80
Murdoch, Rupert, 147
Murphy Brown, 76, 120
Muscle, 207
Music Corporation of America (MCA), 38
Mutchnick, Max, 18
My Name Is Earl, 302
My So-Called Life, 105, 176
My Three Sons, 99

N

Nanny, The, 120
Nanny and the Professor, 82
narrowcasting, 211, 216
National Labor Relations Board, 66
NATPE (National Association of Television Program Executives), 146
NBC, 23, 43, 45, 62, 66, 100, 157, 162, 209, 219, 233, 290, 296
NBCP (NBC Productions), 156
Network, 290
networking, 25–26, 53–54, 197
Newhart, 46, 104, 105
News Corp., 204, 280
NewsRadio, 19, 233
New Yorker, 96, 97

New York Observer, 259
New York Times, 41, 129–30
Nichols, Nichelle, 223
Nicholson, Jack, 46
Nickelodeon, 147
Nielsen ratings, 256, 278–81
Night Court, 119
nonunion productions and writers
  (nonscripted shows), 73, 105,
  278–82, 292, 302–3
nonwriting executive producer
  (EPs), 137–38, 187
Northern Exposure, 105, 153,
  177–78, 229
Noticiero Univision, 214
Noveck, Lanny, 41–44
NYPD Blue, 66, 76, 97, 167,
  191–93

O

Oakley, Bill, 19
Odd Couple, The, 18
Odets, Clifford, 56, 97
off first–run syndication, 148
Office, The, 76, 302
off-network syndication, 148–49
Ogilvy & Mather, 21–22, 65,
  243–44, 257
Ohara, 80, 131
Okie, Rick, 74, 84, 86–87, 110
one-hour dramas, 60, 78, 133–40
One on One, 212
One Tree Hill, 126, 303
On the Waterfront, 56
Oprah, 148
Overmyer, Eric, 25
Ovitz, Mike, 40–41, 255, 259, 289
Oz, 105

P

packaging, 38–41, 43, 46–48,
  109–10, 157–59; dropped,
  289–90

Palone, Gavin, 159, 294
Paltrow, Bruce, 105
Paramount, 18, 109, 148, 151,
  156, 186, 255
Paramount Digital Entertainment,
  150
Parent 'Hood, The, 207
Parents Television Council, 241
Parker, Dorothy, 56, 97
Partners in Crime, 80
Party of Five, 3, 136, 147, 167, 249
Pasadena, 293
Paul Sand in Friends and Lovers,
  102
Peil, Mary Beth, 275–76
Perry, Mark, 126
Pet Rock Productions, 123
Petticoat Junction, 99
Philco Playhouse, 56
Phyllis, 102, 104
Picket Fences, 105
Pickett, Cindy, 198
Pickford, Mary, 37
pickup season, 171, 184
Piller, Michael, 151–52
pilot(s): development season,
  171–76; downturn of 2001–2002
  and, 291; presentation tapes,
  175–76, 289; production season,
  171, 175, 179–81; staffing sea-
  son and, 180, 185–186; writing,
  in 2001–2002 season, 286–87
pitching, 79–84, 141, 171–74
Pittsburgh Press, 88
Playhouse 90, 56, 111
POD (producer overall deal), 137
Pollack, Sydney, 41
Pollack, Tom, 104
Pomerantz, Earl, 46, 105, 110,
  112, 115, 118–20, 257
Popular, 213
Practice, The, 105
Prange, Greg, 264–66, 270
Prey, 167
producer, 69. *See also* nonwriting

producer *(cont.)*
  executive producer; writer-
  producers
production schedule, 111–17
product placement and integration,
  244–47, 290
Profiler, 178–79, 191, 229
program fees, 70–71
Providence, 105

R

race issue, 210–23
Rae, Cassidy, 202, 207
Rain Man, 41
Reagan, Ronald, 20, 61, 90
reality TV, ix–x, 66, 279–95, 302
Real World, The, 282
recession of 1994, 145
recurring-character payments, 70–71
Redstone, Sumner, 1
Reilly, Kevin, 45, 162
Remington Steele, 80
Rescue Me, 304
residuals, 58, 60, 68, 70–71, 168,
  283
Rhimes, Shonda, 302
Rhoda, 102, 104–5
Ricki Lake Show, The, 294
Riordan, Richard, 284
Ripley's Believe It or Not!, 294
Riptide, 80
Risky Business, 21, 237–38, 252
Robbins, Michael, 191
Robbins, Tom, 17
Roberts, Eric, 191
Rockford Files, The, 16
Roman Holiday, 56
Romano, John, 105
Ronn, David, 167
Room 222, 102, 127
Room for Two, 198
Rose, Reginald, 57
Roseanne, 64, 119, 120, 126, 193,
  218

Rosenthal, David, 165, 259, 305
Rosenthal, Phil, 2, 168
Roswell, 213
Rothman, Robb, 160
Rothman-Brecher, 160–61, 304

S

Sackheim, William, 59
Sarnoff, Mr., xi
satellite networks, 146–49
satellite TV, 146–48
Savalas, Telly, 30
Scarecrow and Mrs. King, 80
Scherick, Jay, 167
Schneider, Bonnie, 237–38, 256
Schulberg, Budd, 56
Screen Actors Guild, 20
Screen Gems, 269, 273
screenwriters, 153
Screen Writers Guild (SWG),
  54–56, 58
Scrubs, 302
Second Time Around, 212
Secret of My Success, The, 11
Seinfeld, 4, 76, 119, 147, 306;
  earnings of, 149, 157
September 11, 2001 attacks, 289
Serling, Rod, 57
7th Heaven, 6, 208
Sex and the City, 76
Shatner, William, 223
Sheinberg, Bill, 108–9
Sheinberg, Sid, 54
Shell Game, 8
Shepard, Scott, 185
Sherman-Palladino, Amy, 302
She's Having a Baby, 225
Shield, The, 76
showrunner, 99, 136, 175, 177,
  179–82, 184, 264–65, 291, 295;
  actors and, 268; *Dawson's* and,
  243, 248–49, 255–56; defined,
  25; demographics of, 211–12;
  importance of, 25, 40; specs and,

76–77; staffing season and, 182; story room and, 111–12, 119; training of, 47–48, 305
Showtime, 292
Sikowitz, Mike, 165
Silbermann, Chris, 160–61
Silverman, Fred, 23
Simms, Paul, 19
Simon & Simon, 74–76, 78–80, 84–89, 92, 102, 110, 178
Simpson, Nicole Brown, 125
Simpson, O.J., 145
Simpsons, The, 8, 19, 24, 104, 160
Singer, Robert, 66
Single Guy, The, 120, 167
Sisters, 132–42, 249
sitcom: demise of, 119–20; invention of, 57–58; production schedule and writing of, 110–19; writers of, and dramedy, 127–28
60 Minutes, 209
Slap Maxwell Story, The, 22, 105, 127
Sledge Hammer!, 43
Smirnoff, Yakov, 150, 190
Songs of Dawson's Creek (CDs), 245
Sons and Daughters, 109
Sony, ix–x, 3–4, 6–7, 72, 174, 190, 232, 244–46, 249, 252, 254–56, 284; returns to TV business, 304; shuts down Columbia TriStar, 293–95, 304
Sony Consumer Products, 245
Sony Pictures Entertainment, 293
Sony Pictures Television, 149
Sopranos, The, 76, 300
South, Frank, 200–202, 224
Soviet Union, collapse of, 146
spec scripts, 15, 25–26, 34–35, 64, 108, 229–30; market for, 74–78; staffing season and, 177–78
Spelling, Aaron, 59, 63, 296
Spenser: for Hire, 80
Spielberg, Steven, 30, 41, 175

Spike TV, 292
Spin City, 105, 167
Sports Night, 168
staffing season, 171, 176–89, 229, 292, 295–97
staff writers: compensation for, 69, 69; getting job as, 109–10, 121–22, 161, 169, 197, 221; race, sex, and age biases and, 212, 221–22; record seasons for, in 1990s, 170–71, 183–95; reduction of, 291, 295–97; sitcom schedule and script development by, 112–17
Standards and Practices, 114, 271–72
Starr, Darren, 174, 255
Starsky & Hutch, 16, 66
star system, 37–39, 204
Star Trek, 148, 223
Star Trek: Deep Space Nine, 151
Star Trek: The Next Generation, 72, 141
Star Trek: Voyager, 151, 167
Steinberg, Doug, 105, 263, 297
St. Elsewhere, 24, 102, 105
Stepakoff, Charlotte, 276
Stepakoff, Elizabeth, 150–51, 224–27, 231–32, 276, 287–88
Stepakoff, Sophie, 251
Stern, Daniel, 128
Stern, Leonard, 59
Steve Harvey Show, The, 213
Stewart, Jimmy, 38
Stingray, 80
stock market drop of 2000, 280, 284
storyboard artists, 154
story editor, 69, 110–11, 212
story room (Room), 110–15, 118, 134, 238, 264
Streets of San Francisco, The, 16
"strips" or stripping, 148, 279
Strong Medicine, 212, 252, 294
Studio 60, 302

studios: consolidation of, 163; demise of, 183–84, 203–4; development deals and, 130–31, 164–66; executives, and writers, 30–31; film and, 37–38; Fin-Syn and, 103–4; packaging fees and, 39, 157–58; rise of, 204; SWG and, 55–56; WGA strike of 1988 and, 61–68; writers and, 9, 25, 30. *See also* independent production companies

Stupin, Paul, 2, 5, 174–75, 186–88, 190, 230–31, 237–38, 250, 270, 271, 295

superstations, 147

supervising producer, 69

Survivor, 280–82, 285, 290

Swartzlander, Ric, 168

S.W.A.T., 16

Sweeney, D.B., 191

syndication, ix, 39, 47, 71–72, 102–3, 146–49, 157–58, 168, 282, 295

T

Taken, 230

T. and T., 80

Tannenbaum, Eric, 162

Tarses, Jamie, 45–46, 48, 162, 193, 194

Tarses, Jay, 105

Tartikoff, Brandon, 62, 65–66

Tarzan, 154

Taxi, 104

TBS, 147–48, 156, 295

Teaching Mrs. Tingle, 248

Telecommunications Act (1996), 156

Television Critics Association (TCA) tour, 199

Tenspeed and Brown Shoe, 80

Texaco Star Theater, 56

That '70s Show, 218

That Was Then, 296

3rd Rock from the Sun, 218

thirtysomething, 14, 22, 65–66, 93, 105, 192, 197–98, 200, 306

Thompson, Robert J., 66, 24

Three, 185–86

Tick, The, 293

Tilden, Peter, 115–16

Time magazine, 13

TimeWarner, 156, 200, 204, 246, 280

Tinker, Grant, 98–99, 102, 104

Tinker, Mark, 105

T. J. Hooker, 80

TNT, 147

To Have & to Hold, 196, 293

To Heal a Nation, 66

Total Security, 194

Touchstone, 202, 296

Tour of Duty, 43

Toy Story 2, 126

"tracking," 108

Tracey Ullman Show, The, 104

Truman Show, The, 244

Trumbo, Dalton, 56

Tucci, Christine, 191

Turner, Ted, 147

TV executives: control of shows by, 203–4, 206; current vs. development, 181–84; new breed of, 161–64; pickup season and, 184–85; pilots bought by, 171–74; staffing season and, 181–85

TV Guide, 240

TV industry: changes in, of 2004–6, 301–5; consolidation and decline of, 155–57, 203–5, 219–23; cycles of, 298–99; earnings rise of 1990s and, 146–49; finances and, 4, 7, 58, 103; Fin-Sin repeal and, 155–57; Fin-Syn rules of 1970s and, 101–2; history of, to 1970s, 16–17, 56–58, 100–101; new breed and youth programming in 1990s, 161–63; new series and ratings, 234–35; quality of, and writers and, 31; renaissance of, in 1980s, 22–25, 106; seasons of, 171–77; segregation of writers and audiences in, 211–23; sitcoms and, 119–20; staffing season of 1997–98 and, 183–95; strike of 1988 and, 72–73; strike threat of 2001 and rise of reality shows, 278–95; success in, and timing, 128; upheaval of 2001–2002 in, 287–99; writer-producers vs. actors and crew in, 264–65. *See also* agents; studios; syndication; TV executives; TV networks; TV script writing; *and other specific issues and roles*

"TV is Good" slogan, 193

TV networks: advertising revenues of, 255–56; affiliates, 147; consolidation of, 163; damaged by 1988 strike, 72–73; *Dawson's* and, 242–43; executives, 30; Fin-Syn repeal and, 106, 156–57; independent producers and, 103; packaging fees and, 289–90; pilots and writers bought by, 174; PODs and control over shows, 137; prime-time payments 69, 71; takeover by, 203–6, 210. *See also* specific networks

TV scripts: acts and, 78, 81, 84–85, 114, 135; buzz words and, 178, 238; colors of, and rewrites, 273; deadline anxiety and, 1–2; jumping and fleshing and, 81; narration and, 128; punching-up and developing sitcom, 111–19, 195; recycling, 58, 61, 66, 283; rehearsals and, 116; scenes and, 85, 114, 135–36;

script fees and, 69, *69*, 168, 291; selling pitch vs. selling script and, 172–73; sets and, 114–15; setup/punch-line rhythm, 127; story development process, 30–31, 84–85; story engine and, 6–7; story lines, for one hour and, 135–36; structure of, 78; table read and, 113; teaser and, 78, 135, 177–78; timing and hit, 128; tone and, 5–6, 136, 270. *See also* pilots; spec scripts

TV writers and writing: agents and, 25–26, 31–36, 39–41, 43, 46–47, 158–62; animated films and, 152–55; awards and, 33; balancing life and work and, 143, 274, 306; breaking into, 8–11, 15, 18–21, 25–30; career span of, 142; Columbia TriStar shutdown and, 294–95; control of series by, 30–31; deadline anxiety and, 1–4; development deals and, 130–31, 164–67; development of, as showrunner, 47; dramedies and, 127–28; earnings of, 9–10, 14–15, 25, 67–73, 69, 123–24, 143, 205–6; earnings of, after 2001, 288–93, 296–98; earnings of, and emotional problems, 259–61; earnings of, in 1990s, 4–5, 7, 129–32, 165–69, 255; entertaining and, 124–25; fired, 205–6; first job offer and, 50–51; first script sold and, 74–75, 78–91; five-year plan and, 130–31; freelance, 81, 149–51; getting jobs after first, 107–10; lack of security and, 177; lifestyle of, in 1990s, 123–26; long-term contracts and, 293; luck and, 26; momentum and, 91, 138; MTM and grooming of, 93–106; networking and, 53–54; new, and

TV writers and writing *(cont.)*
agencies, 40, 43–45; new, and
lack of training, 247–48; new
breed of, in 1993–98, 109, 130,
145–46, 163–67; of 1950s,
56–58; *NY Times* interview on
being, 129–30; pitches and,
82–84, 172–73; punch-up doctors and, 115; reality TV and,
279–82; recommendations and,
197, 221; renaissance in, of
1980s, 22–25; seasons of
1997–99 and, 170–97; segregation of, and dominance of young
white males, 202, 211–23; sitcom production and script development and, 112–19; specs and
guesswork and, 74–78; staffing
season and, 176–91; staff writing and, 126–30, 133, 143,
170–205; story process and
pitching paradigms and, 5–6;
strike of 1953 and, 58; strike of
1988 and, 62–68; strike threat of
2000–2001, 283–85; as structured craft, 78; tone and, 128;
what makes good, 261–62; why
people make career of, 97–98;
writer-producers of 1960s and
1970s and, 58–59; writing teams
and, 134
20th Century, 104, 109, 168–69,
233, 259, 286
21st Century Project, 294
24, 186, 302
Two and a Half Men, 120

U

Uffner, Beth, 32–36, 46–48, 77, 86,
90–92, 94, 120–21, 132,
138–40, 142, 158–61, 177, 231
Unhappily Ever After, 207
United Talent Agency (UTA), 160,
202

Universal, 29–30, 45, 49–51, 54,
65, 74–76, 78–89, 91, 104,
109–11, 126, 242, 280
Univision network, 214
upfronts, 184–85, 193, 209
UPN, 156, 212, 247, 303

V

Van Der Beek, James, 3, 239, 242,
250, 267–68
Variety, 233, 293
Varsity Blues, 239
vaudeville, 36, 39, 56
Veronica Mars, 302
vertical integration, 100–101, 204,
280–81
Viacom, 156, 204, 280
Vidal, Gore, 57
video-on-demand, 283, 302–3
V.I.P., 294

W

Wall Street, 21
Ward, Sela, 133
Warner Brothers, 15, 58, 132,
156–57, 162, 165, 197, 200,
205–6, 233, 295. *See also*
TimeWarner; WB
Warren, Robert Penn, 94
Washington Post, 216
Wasserman, Lew, 30, 38, 50, 81
Wasteland, 248
Waters, Joanne, 196
Wayans Bros., The, 207
WB, 4, 156, 162, 175–76, 190,
197, 200–213, 220, 222–23,
233–34, 243–46, 249, 271, 282;
shut down, 303–4
WEA/Warner Brothers, 245
Webb, Elliot, 46
Weinberger, Ed, 104
Weinstein, Josh, 19
Weithorn, Michael, 33

INDEX

Welch, Jack, 123
Wells, Belinda, 53
Wells, John, 8–10, 15, 19, 22,
25–26, 67, 126, 131, 197, 278,
283, 285
West, Nathanael, 94
Westinghouse, 156
Weston, Riley, 202
What About Joan, 293
What a Country?, 150
What Makes Sammy Run
(Schulberg), 56
Whedon, Joss, 18, 247
White, E.B., xi
White Shadow, The, 105
Who's the Boss?, 119, 192, 232
Who Wants to Be a Millionaire?,
279, 281, 282, 285
Wife Swap, ix, 290
Wild Card, 297
Will & Grace, 18
William Morris Agency (WMA),
25, 31–32, 35–37, 39, 41–46,
48, 141, 159, 285, 289–90
Williams, Michelle, 3, 240, 250,
253
Williamson, Kevin, 3, 174–75, 239,
241, 247–48, 265
Wilson, Hugh, 105
Winchester '73, 38
Witter, Pacey, 196
Witt/Thomas, 109
WKRP in Cincinnati, 105
Wolf, Dick, 105, 285
women writers, 211–14, 217, 302
Wonderful World of Disney, The,
279
Wonder Years, The, 22, 66,
120–21, 126–29, 133, 142, 147,
153, 176, 295

Woodward, Lydia, 33, 105, 120
Woody, Russ, 33, 105
"writer-based" drama, defined, 24
writer-producers, 58–59, 72,
66–67, 99, 137–38
Writers Coalition (Union Blues), 66
Writers Guild Awards, 33
Writers Guild of America (WGA),
14, 45, 138, 142, 155; formation
of, and early strikes, 58–59, 102;
membership of, 50–51, 145–46,
170; Pension and Health Fund,
72; reality TV writers and,
302–3; Showrunner Training
Program, 305; strike of 1988,
26, 29, 32–33, 34, 48–51,
59–69, 72–73, 105–6, 284, 285;
strike threat of 2001 and, 278,
281–86
WTAA International, 245

X

X Files, The, 3, 178

Y

Year in the Life, A, 22, 105
Yerkovich, Anthony, 105
Young, John Sacret, 255
Young Americans, 213
Your Show of Shows, 56
youth audience, 161–62, 201–2,
208–9, 280–82
Yuspa, Cathy, 167

Z

Zoe, Duncan, Jack & Jane, 213
Zwick, Ed, 197